IMAGES
of America

SCHUYLKILL COUNTY
VOLUME II

I0806420

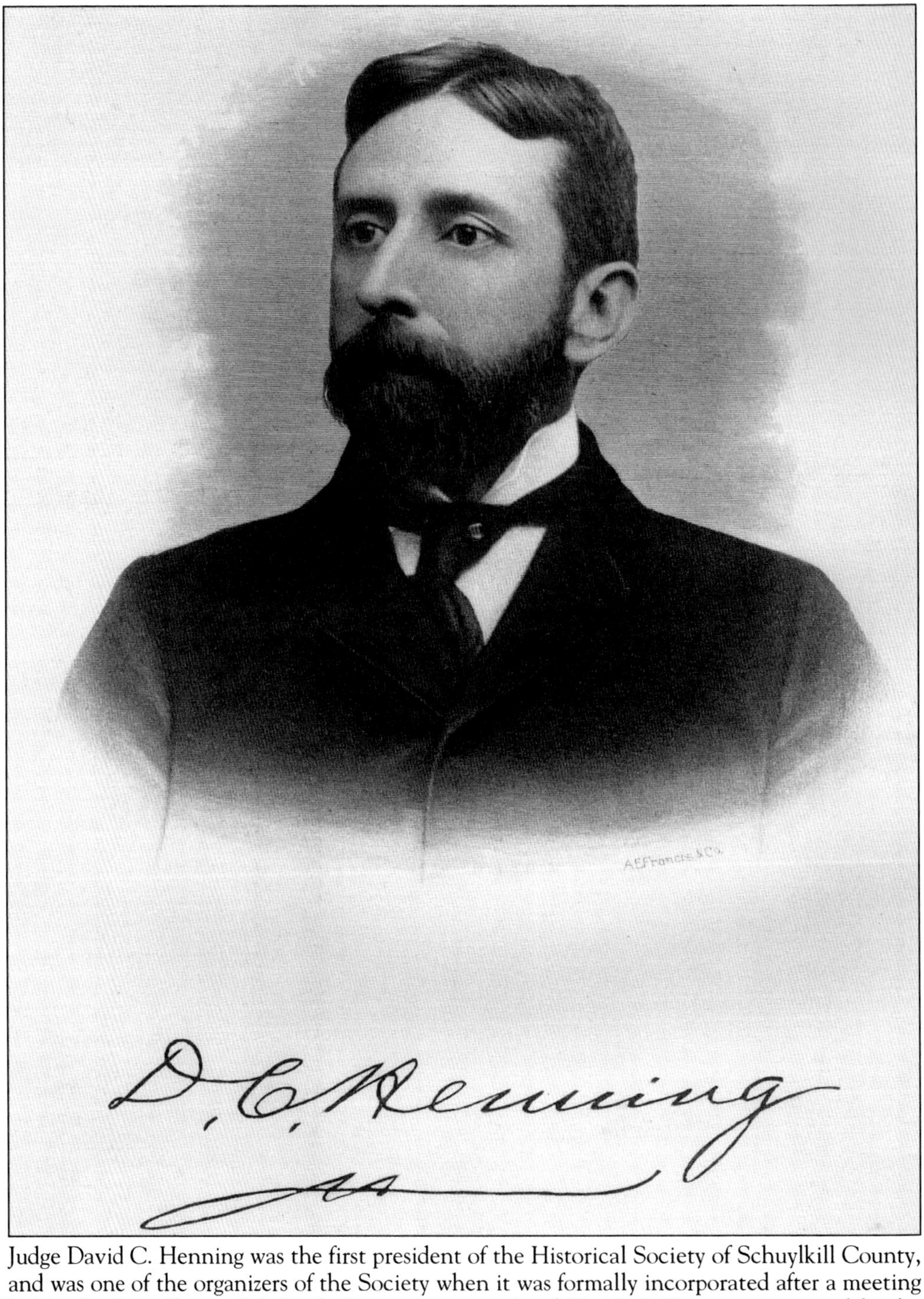

Judge David C. Henning was the first president of the Historical Society of Schuylkill County, and was one of the organizers of the Society when it was formally incorporated after a meeting held in his law office at 208 South Centre Street on April 27, 1903. Henning was noted for the stories that he wrote about the early history of Schuylkill County that were published in the Pottsville *Miners' Journal* during the years 1896–1897. Judge Henning gave a copy of all of the published "Tales of the Blue Mountains" to the Society, with the understanding that they would not be published during his lifetime. The Society published them in 1911 after his death.

IMAGES
of America

SCHUYLKILL COUNTY
VOLUME II

Leo L. Ward and Mark T. Major

ARCADIA
PUBLISHING

ISBN 978-07385-8712-7

Published by Arcadia Publishing
Charleston, South Carolina

Printed in the United States of America

Library of Congress Catalog Card Number: 96-231025

For all general information contact Arcadia Publishing at:
Telephone 843-853-2070
Fax 843-853-0044
E-Mail sales@arcadiapublishing.com
For customer service and orders:
Toll-Free 1-888-313-2665

Visit us on the Internet at www.arcadiapublishing.com

Contents

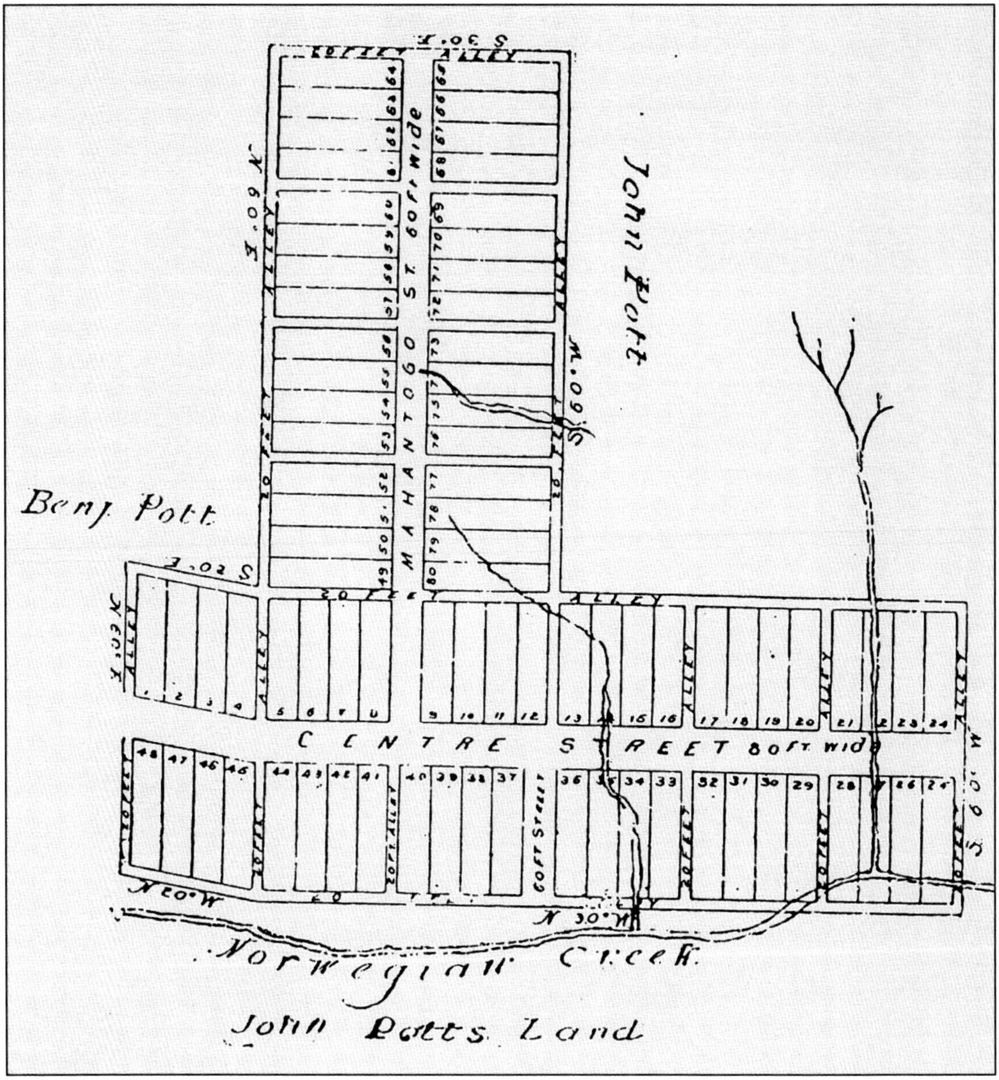

In 1808 John Pott purchased the land that would become the heart of the small village of Pottsville, named for him. The original town plot laid out by Pott in 1816 included only the lots on each side of Centre Street, between Union and Race Streets, and the lots on Mahantongo Street as far as Sixth, or Courtland Street as it was once called. Pott had a log cabin on "lot number 4," which he donated to the Trinity Episcopal Church in 1827. The Benj Pott seen on this map was a son of John Pott.

INTRODUCTION

The images in this book have been selected to tell a visual story of a small part of the history of Schuylkill County, Pennsylvania. From 1860 to 1941, there were 21 photographers in Pottsville and other towns in the county, including Tamaqua, Mahanoy City, Shenandoah, Ashland, and Minersville.

Much of the work of these men has not survived. For example, George M. Bretz, the brilliant photographer who specialized in mining scenes, had some 30,000 negatives destroyed in a disastrous fire in 1892 when his studio burned down. Fires claimed a great amount of important work of other photographers in the 19th century, and much of their work has been lost, or discarded, over the years

The story we are telling in this popular format includes photographs made by George M. Bretz, the "Photographer in the Mines," and images that were made many years ago, including postcards of Pottsville that were printed in a booklet shortly before World War I, images of churches, construction of Route 122/61 in the 1940s and 1950s, railroad stations and crossings, and scenes throughout the county.

George M. Bretz, the Pottsville photographer who became famous for taking the first pictures in a coal mine using electric lights, came to Pottsville from Carlisle around 1870 after serving in the Civil War. He studied photography in the studio of A.M. Allen, who was probably the first photographer to have a studio in Pottsville. Soon Bretz had his own studio that he operated for about 20 years across the street from Allen's studio.

In 1884 Bretz went into the mines to make photographs at the request of James Templeman Brown, collector for the Smithsonian Institute. Brown wanted photographs made of the Mammoth Vein, the thickest vein of anthracite coal, at the Kohinoor Colliery in Shenandoah. Bretz made the exposures using electricity generated by five steam engines. These were the first pictures ever made in a mine using electricity for illumination. Unfortunately, the famous negatives of these pictures were destroyed by the 1892 fire suffered by Bretz.

The Historical Society of Schuylkill County has the ledger books that Bretz used to record his work and how much he charged for each photograph that he made. The ledger books tell the story of coal mines, wealthy people, families, and just common people who went to Bretz to have their picture taken.

A "Souvenir of Pottsville, Pennsylvania" is the title of a collection of postcard scenes of Pottsville that was published about 1914. The first page of the collection gives a brief history of Pottsville telling the story of how John Pott, founder of the town, purchased the old Reese

& Thomas furnace and then began to slowly build homes in the small village. Pott laid out the town in 1816.

Examples of military history, industries in the town, Pottsville as the business center of the county, paved streets, the fire department and its equipment, the magnificent courthouse, and the trolley system are described in the introductory history.

In these images are found school buildings, hotels, the business district on Centre Street, railroad stations, quiet street scenes, Tumbling Run, industry, and mansions on Mahantongo Street. Enjoy the images of how Pottsville looked during this placid time before the great catastrophe in Europe that erupted into WW I.

Since the 1750s, settlers and residents of Schuylkill County have erected their houses of worship in every section of the county. These images depict but a few of the churches and one of the synagogues situated in the towns and valleys of Schuylkill County, Pennsylvania.

In the 1940s and 1950s, the age of the automobile changed the commerce, travel, and the landscape across the countryside. Route 122 through Schuylkill County experienced major development as a new freeway cut its path through the county. The building of this major highway through Schuylkill County followed the path of the early King's Highway and Centre Turnpike that were built in the early 1800s. This collection of images traces that path from Port Clinton north to Pottsville and beyond.

Passenger railroad service began to disappear from Schuylkill County during WW II. Today it is all gone. However, Schuylkill County's railroad heritage remains vivid through the images captured many years ago, from Delano to Pine Grove and from Auburn to Shenandoah. This collection of popular and rare railroad stations and crossings brings back memories of the old passenger stations and railroad crossings that no longer exist.

The landscape of Schuylkill County changes with every generation. The sampling of images from every corner of Schuylkill County recalls what has disappeared from view, but has not been forgotten. Readers will take a trip down memory lane as they view images of businesses, historic buildings, and sites that are no longer on the Schuylkill County scene.

One

Photographer in the Mines

George M. Bretz came to Pottsville from Carlisle, Pennsylvania, as a student of A.M. Allen about 1870. In 1873 he set up his own studio at the northeast corner of North Centre and East Market Streets as seen in this image. Even though they were competitors, Bretz and Allen collaborated to make stereos and views of Pottsville. Bretz was famous for making photographic images in a coal mine by using electricity for illumination. The studio shown in this image burned in a disastrous fire in 1892 resulting in the loss of 30,000 negatives.

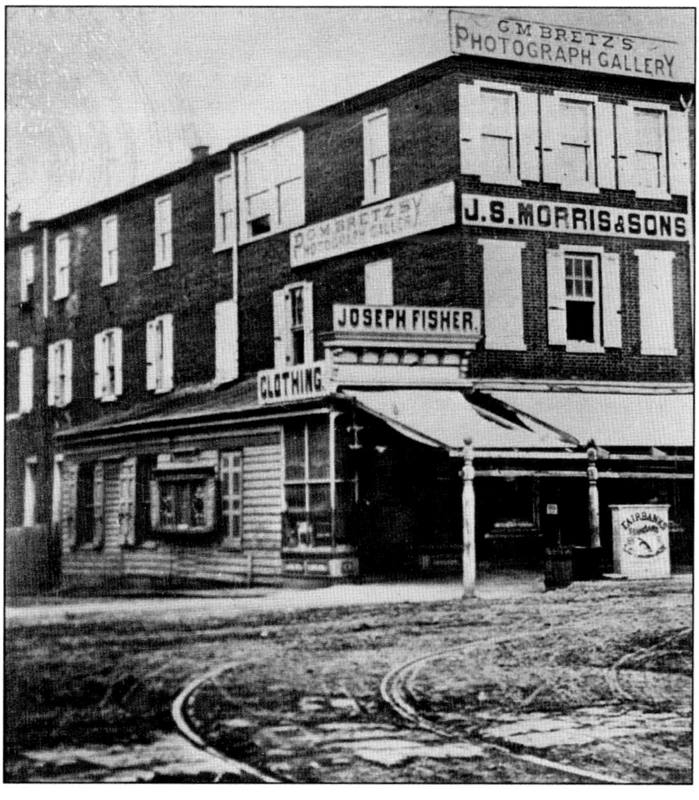

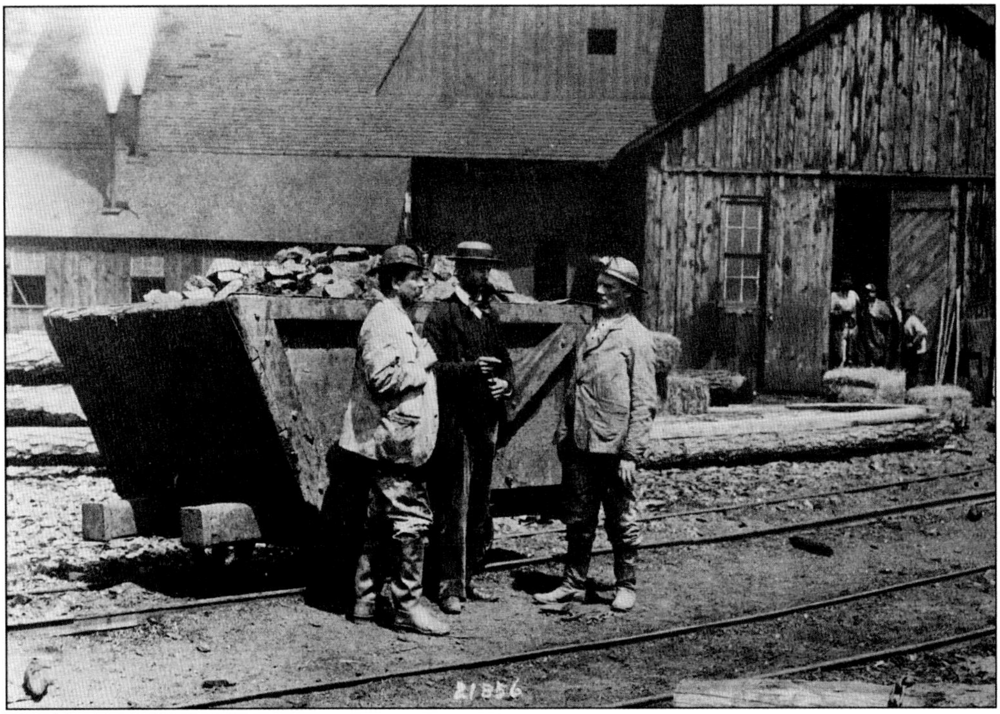

A typical scene at a colliery was composed by Bretz when he photographed these three bosses at the Kohinoor Colliery in Shenandoah in 1884. The photographer was famous for his images of anthracite coal mining that he made from 1873 to 1895.

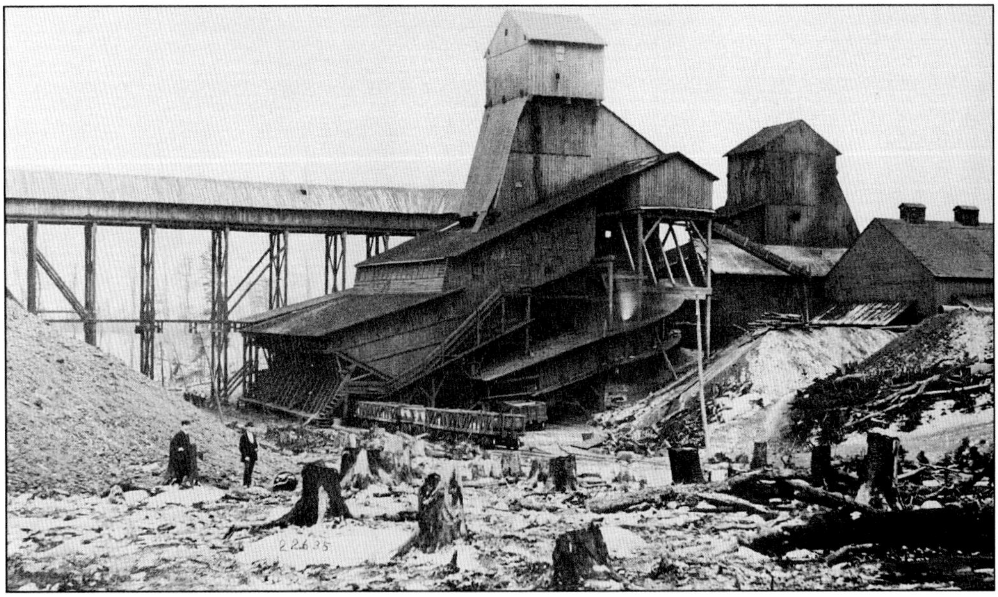

Kohinoor Colliery, Shenandoah, Pennsylvania, was opened in 1868 by Heckscher & Co. The Mammoth Vein was 140 yards under the surface and was 40 feet thick. In 1884 James Templeman Brown, collector for the Smithsonian Institute, came to Schuylkill County and employed Bretz to make photographs of scenes in an anthracite coal mine using electric lights for illumination.

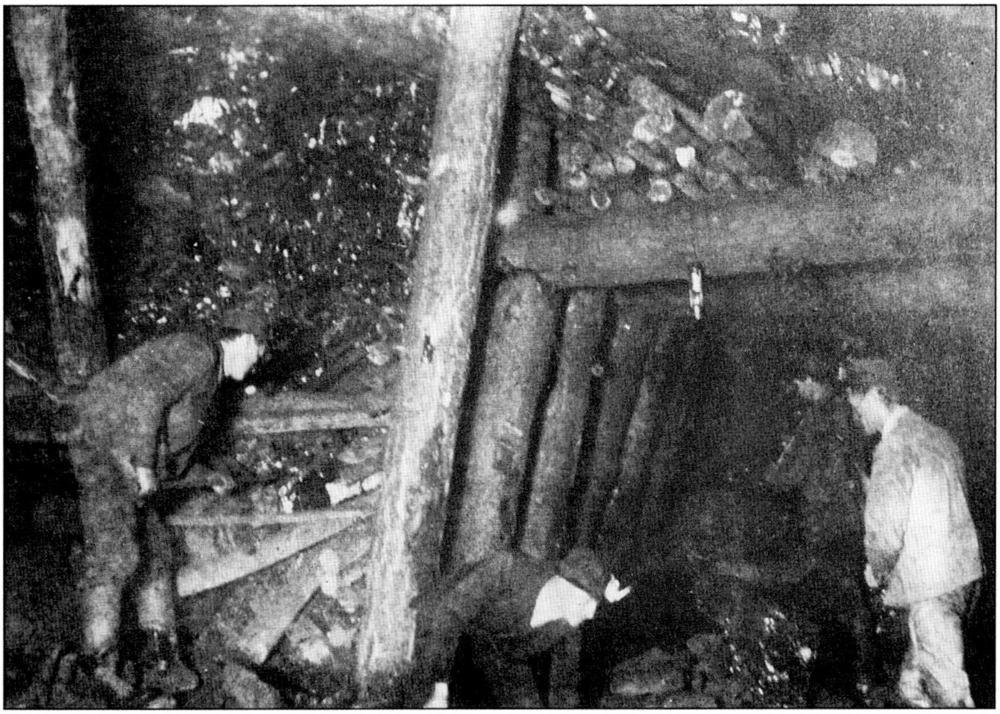

Miners working at a breast in a mine were captured by Bretz in this image. The negatives of the first photographs made by Bretz in a coal mine were destroyed in the disastrous fire that occurred at his studio in 1892. His original photographs, made in 1884, probably looked like this image.

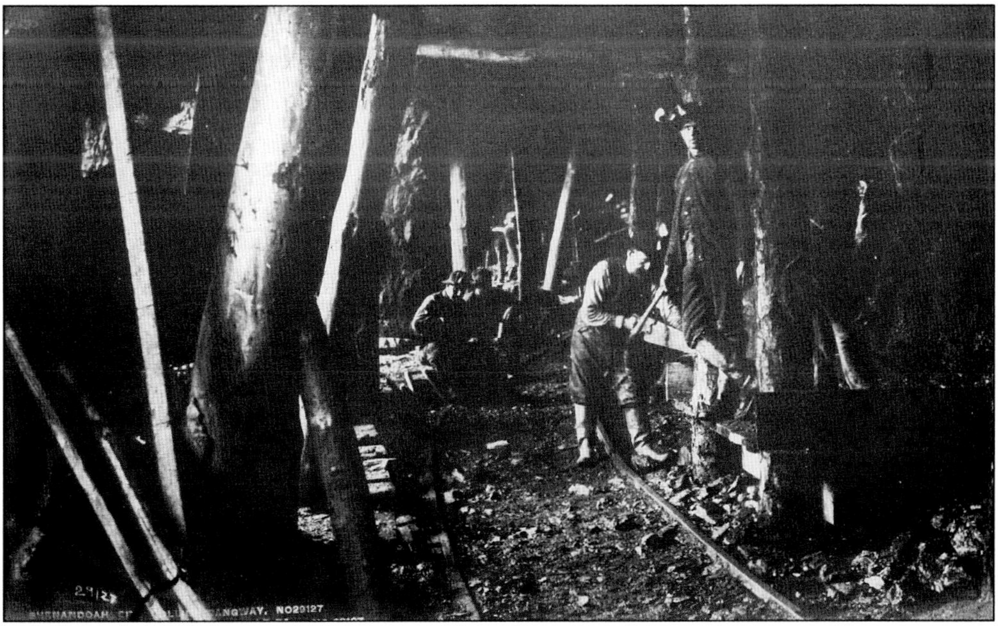

This is the Shenandoah City Colliery, negative no. 29127 by Bretz. He had to set his camera for a ten-minute exposure to make the negatives, so the miners in the picture had to pose for that much time.

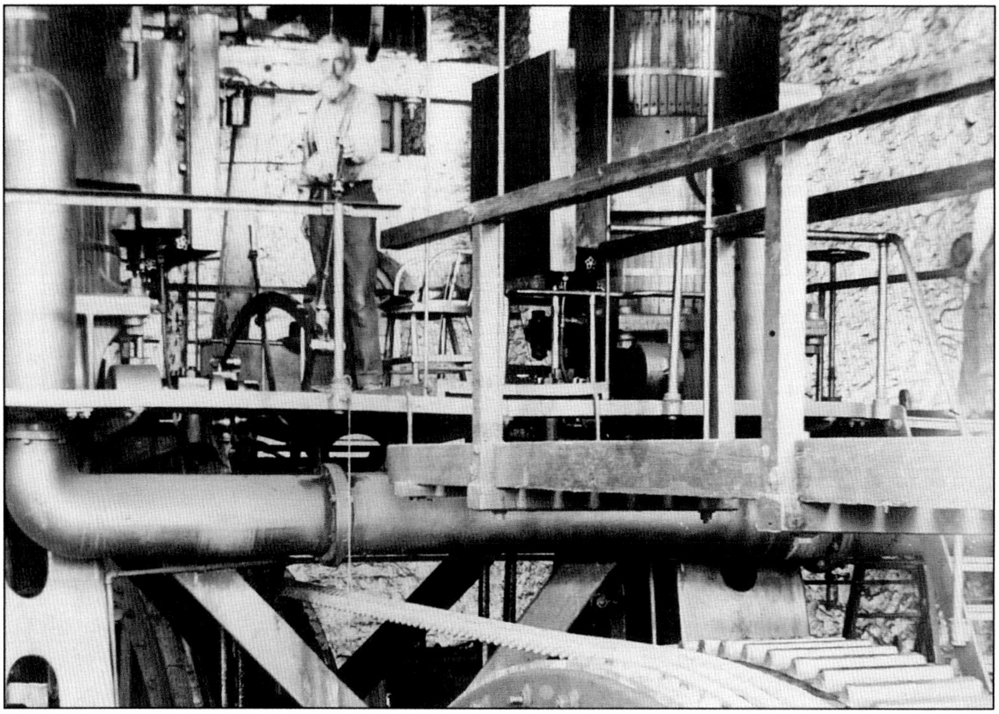

The engine room of the Mahanoy Plane stood at the top of Broad Mountain near Frackville. The huge drums, shown in this image, hoisted three coal-filled cars up the mountainside every three minutes at a rate of 35 feet per second. Empty cars acted as a counterbalance.

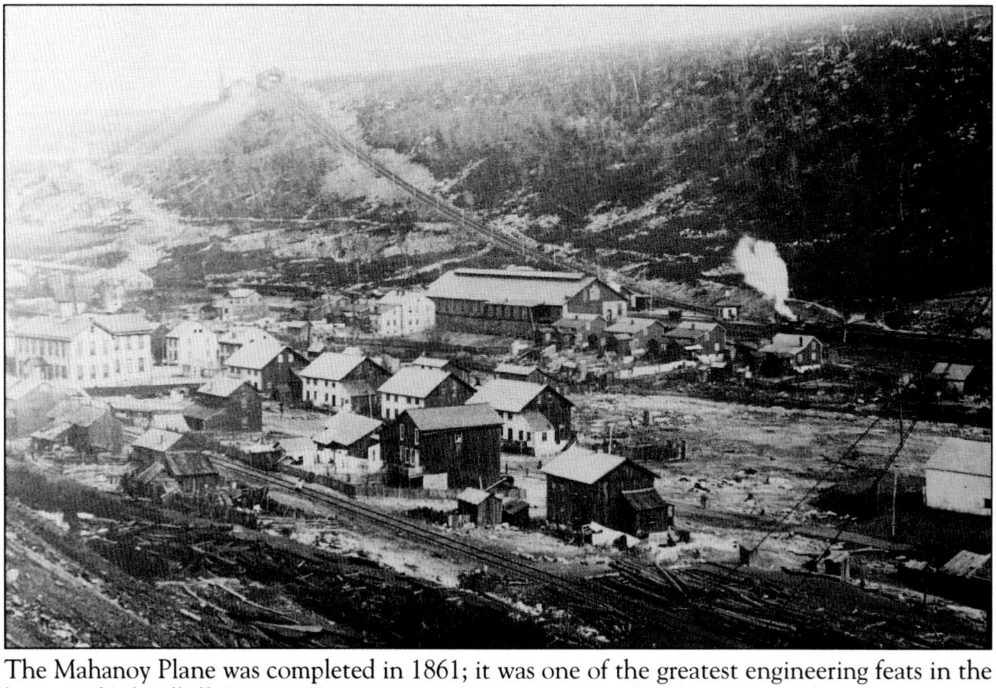

The Mahanoy Plane was completed in 1861; it was one of the greatest engineering feats in the history of Schuylkill County. For 71 years, starting in 1861, the plane was used to hoist coal out of the Mahanoy Valley. The plane finally closed during the 1930s.

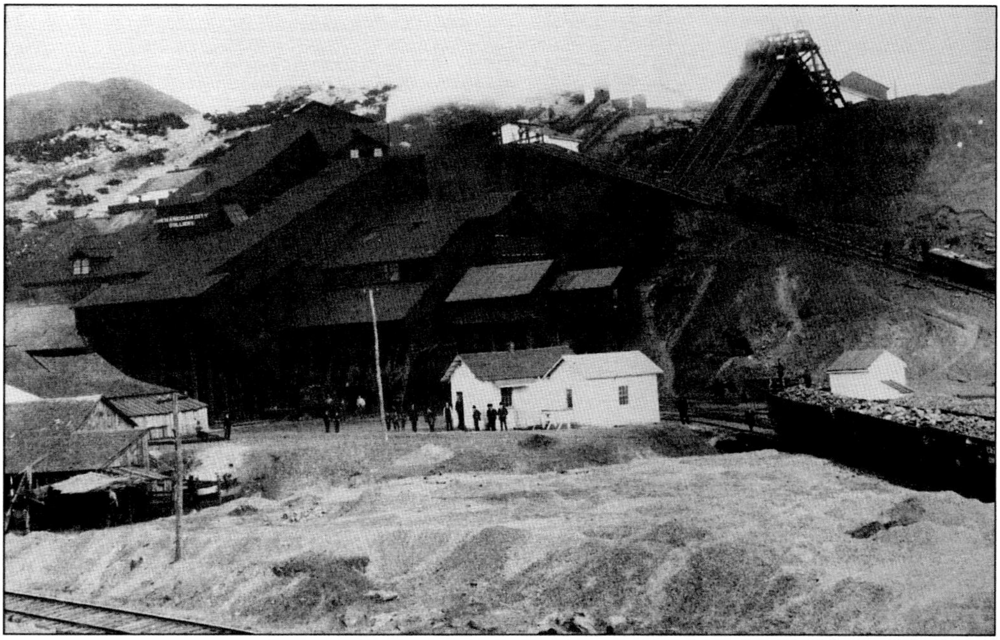

The Shenandoah City Colliery was the first colliery opened in the vicinity of Shenandoah; it was located on the southern edge of the borough. The breakers and buildings, including 47 tenant houses and a large boardinghouse, were completed in 1863. In 1878 it was purchased by the Philadelphia & Reading Coal & Iron Company.

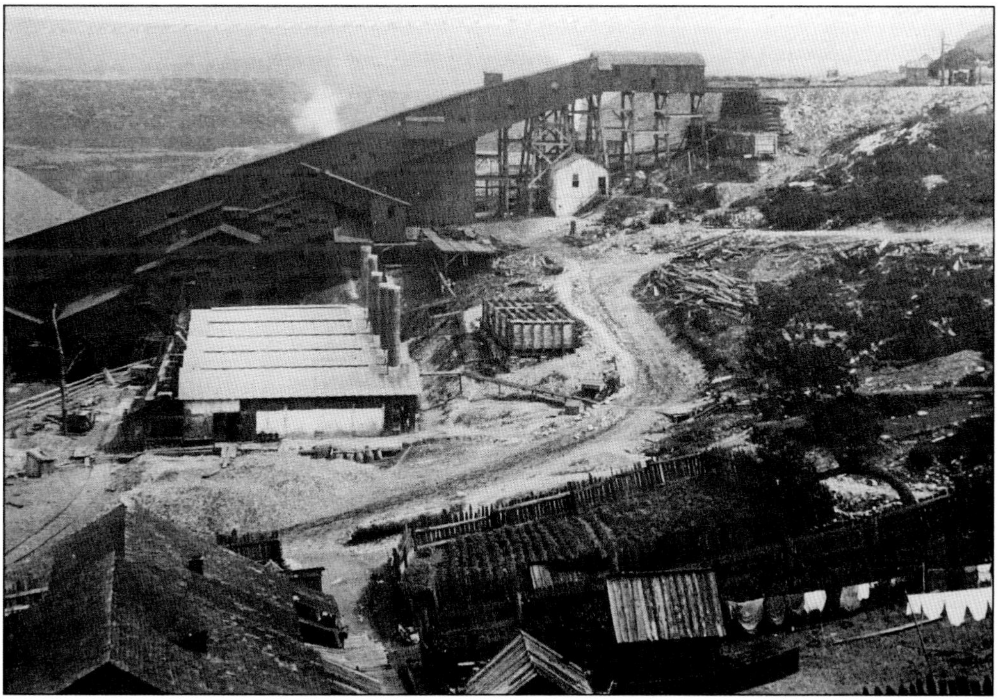

The name of this colliery is not known, but Broad Mountain can be seen in the background. The homes in the foreground were owned by the company and leased to the miners who worked for the company. Notice the laundry drying on the clothesline in the foreground.

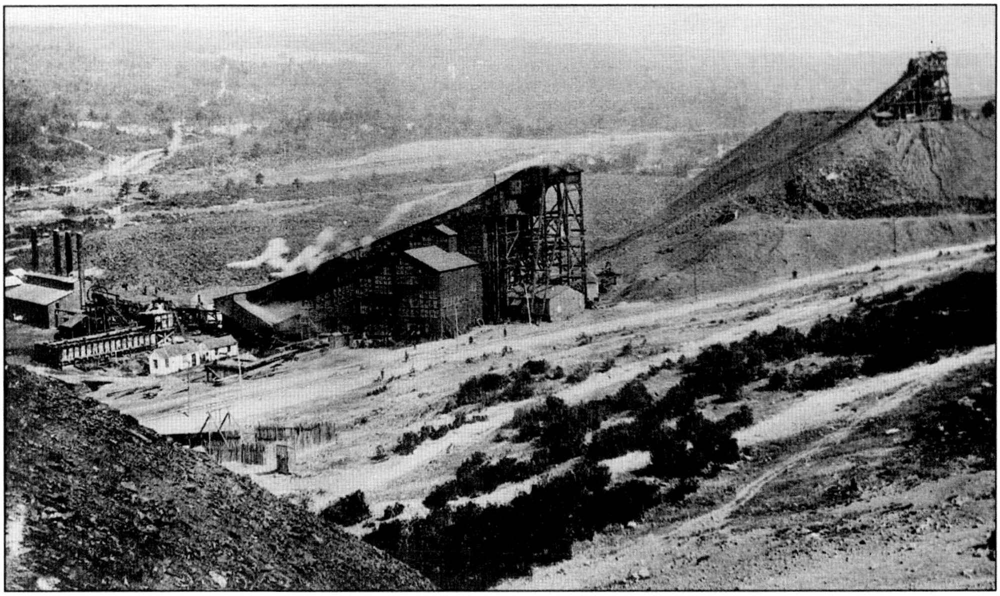

The Indian Ridge Colliery in Shenandoah was opened in 1870 by William Kendrick & Co. The P&R C&I Co. bought it in 1873. The shaft was sunk on the Mammoth Vein, and the colliery employed three hundred men and boys. James McParlan, the Pinkerton detective who infiltrated the Molly Maguires, worked here for a short time.

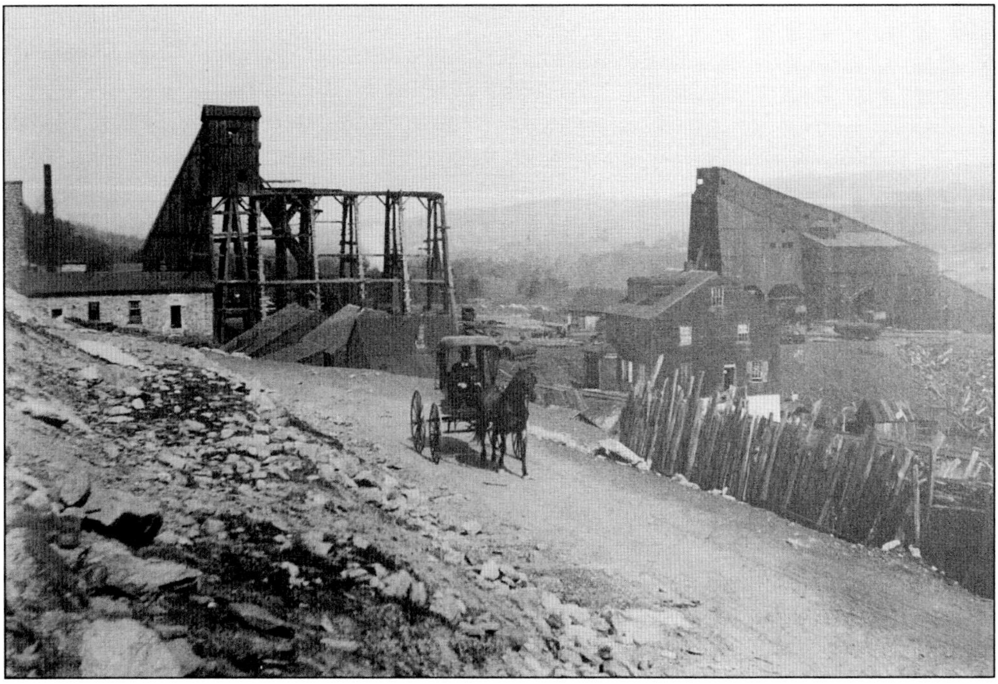

A solitary, unknown man drives his horse and buggy by a colliery. Bretz centered his camera on this scene and left this unidentified image as another record of life in the coal region as it appeared many years ago. Notice the wooden fence in the foreground on the right of the image.

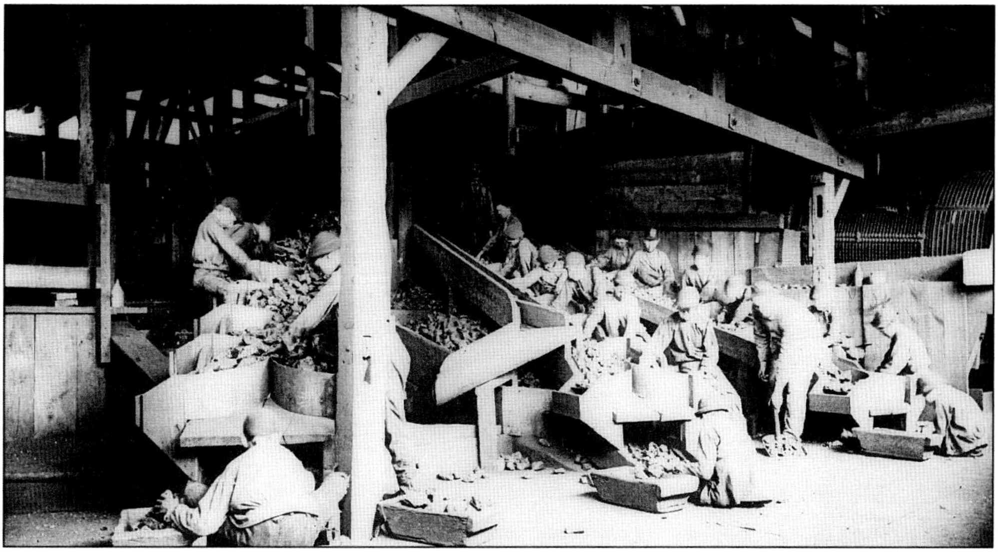

These are some breaker boys in Packer no. 2, Shenandoah, Pennsylvania, 1894. The breaker boys were stationed at wooden chutes running from the screening stage. They were required to remove all foreign materials from the cleaned and sized coal before it was directed into the loading pockets. Bretz scratched the number 143 into the lower right hand corner of the negative.

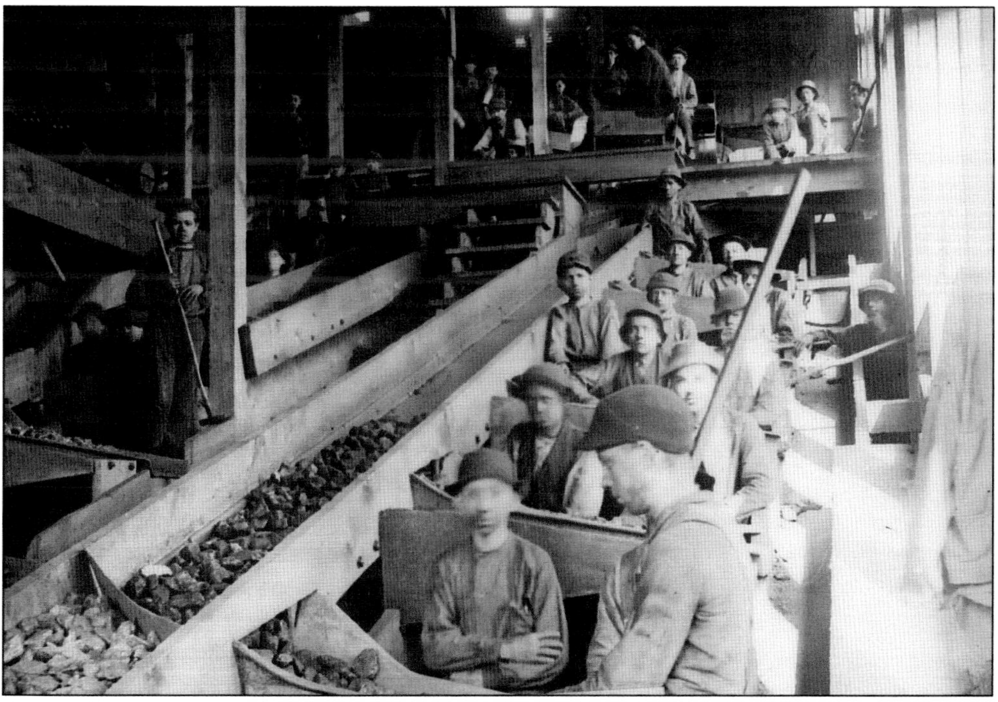

Breaker boys were photographed at the North Ashland Colliery, Ashland, Pennsylvania. The age of breaker boys ranged from eight to 16 years. The first law in Pennsylvania setting the minimum age for boys working around the mines was passed in 1885. The only proof required was a certificate signed by a parent or guardian claiming the boy was of age. Bretz scratched the number 144 into the lower right hand corner of the negative.

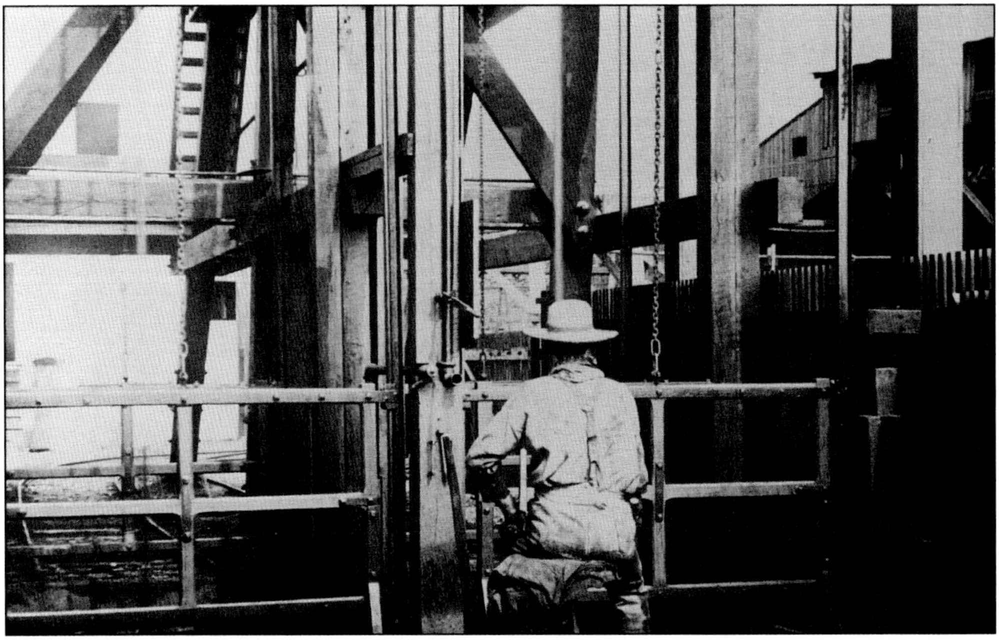

This image of a man operating an elevator in a shaft is a classic work of art created by the magic of Bretz's camera. The massive part of the shaft that is above ground, towers over the seated man, as he sits with his back to the camera. The identity of the operator is unknown, but Bretz left us this image of a man working on the surface of the earth high above the depths of the mine.

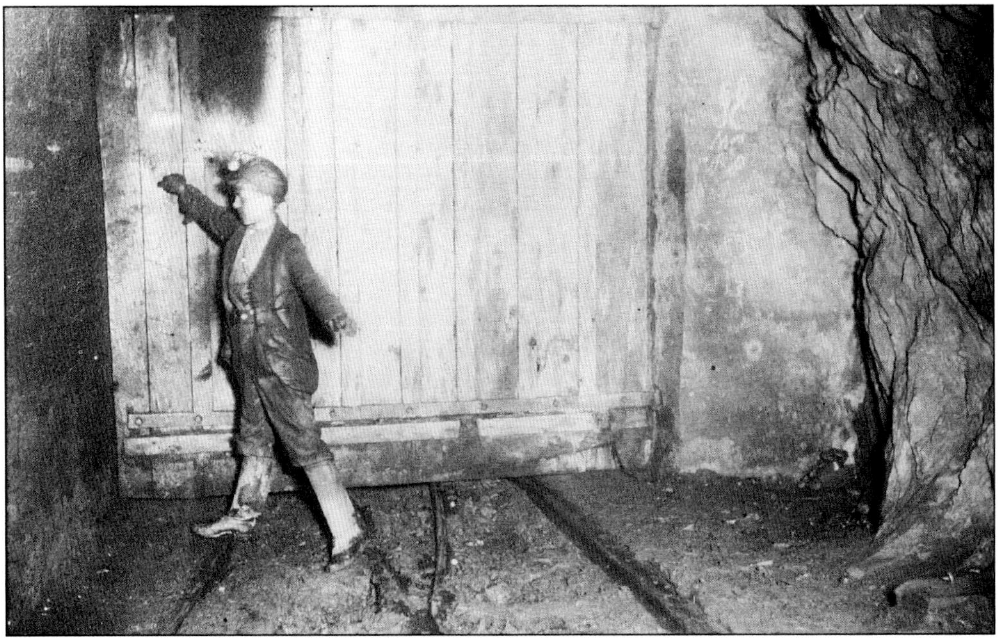

Boys worked inside the mines as this image shows a "door" boy at work. In order to keep air from blowing through the mine, thereby reducing the air temperature, a door in the mine was opened and closed by an attendant, usually a young boy as seen here. These boys were only paid $1 to $3 per week.

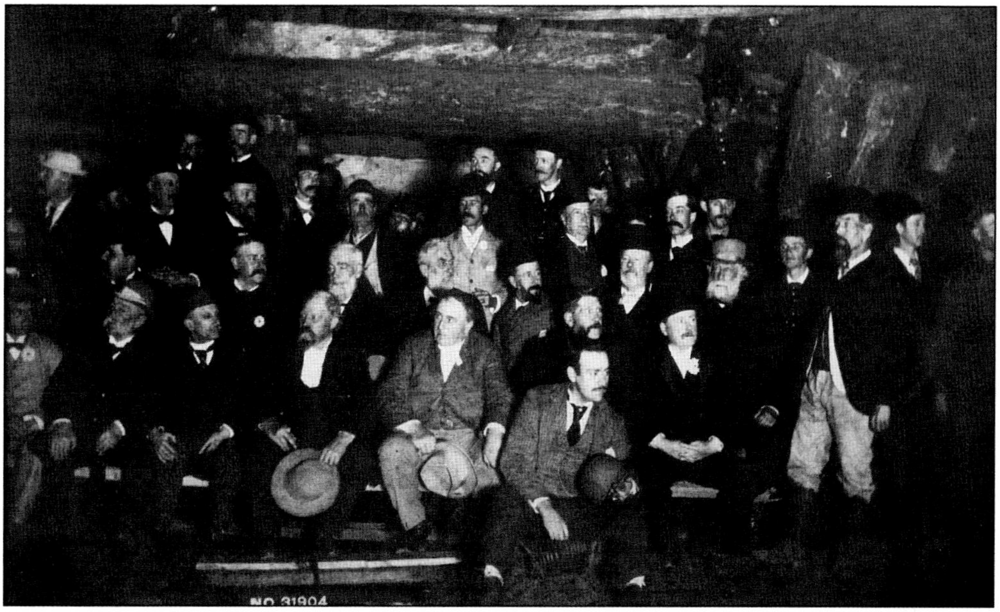

This is Bretz's negative no. 31904. The Directors of the City Trusts of Philadelphia are inside a mine leased by P&R C&I. Co. from the Girard Estate. The group was photographed by Bretz using electric lights. The directors of the Girard Estate made annual inspection trips to Schuylkill County.

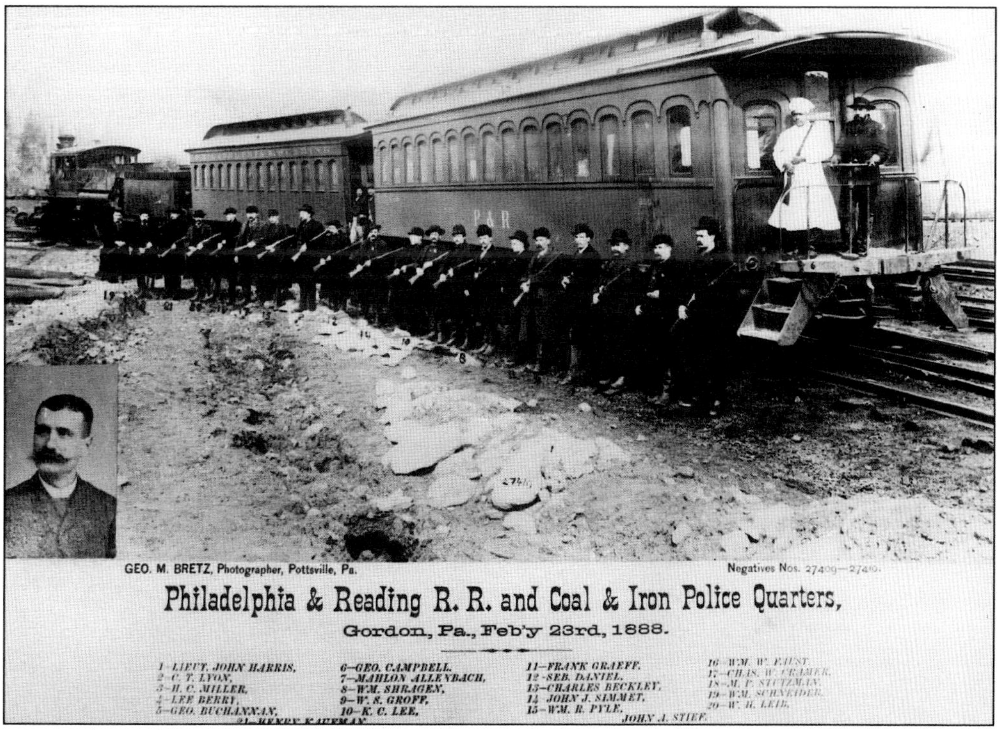

This is the Philadelphia & Reading RR Coal & Iron Police Quarters in Gordon, Pennsylvania, February 23, 1888. All of the men are holding a gun as they pose for this picture, even the cook. The man standing behind the cook does not have a gun in his hands.

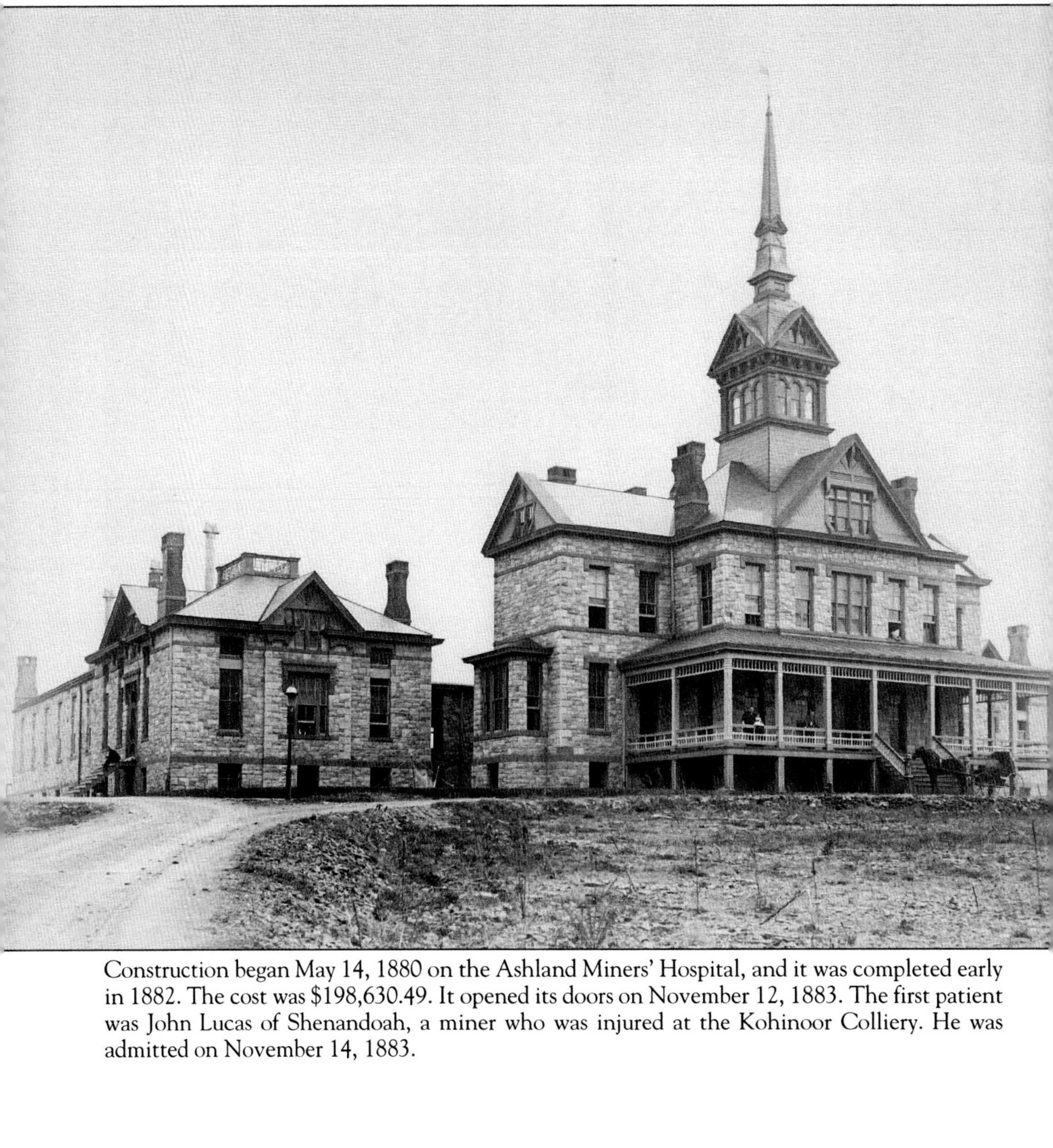

Construction began May 14, 1880 on the Ashland Miners' Hospital, and it was completed early in 1882. The cost was $198,630.49. It opened its doors on November 12, 1883. The first patient was John Lucas of Shenandoah, a miner who was injured at the Kohinoor Colliery. He was admitted on November 14, 1883.

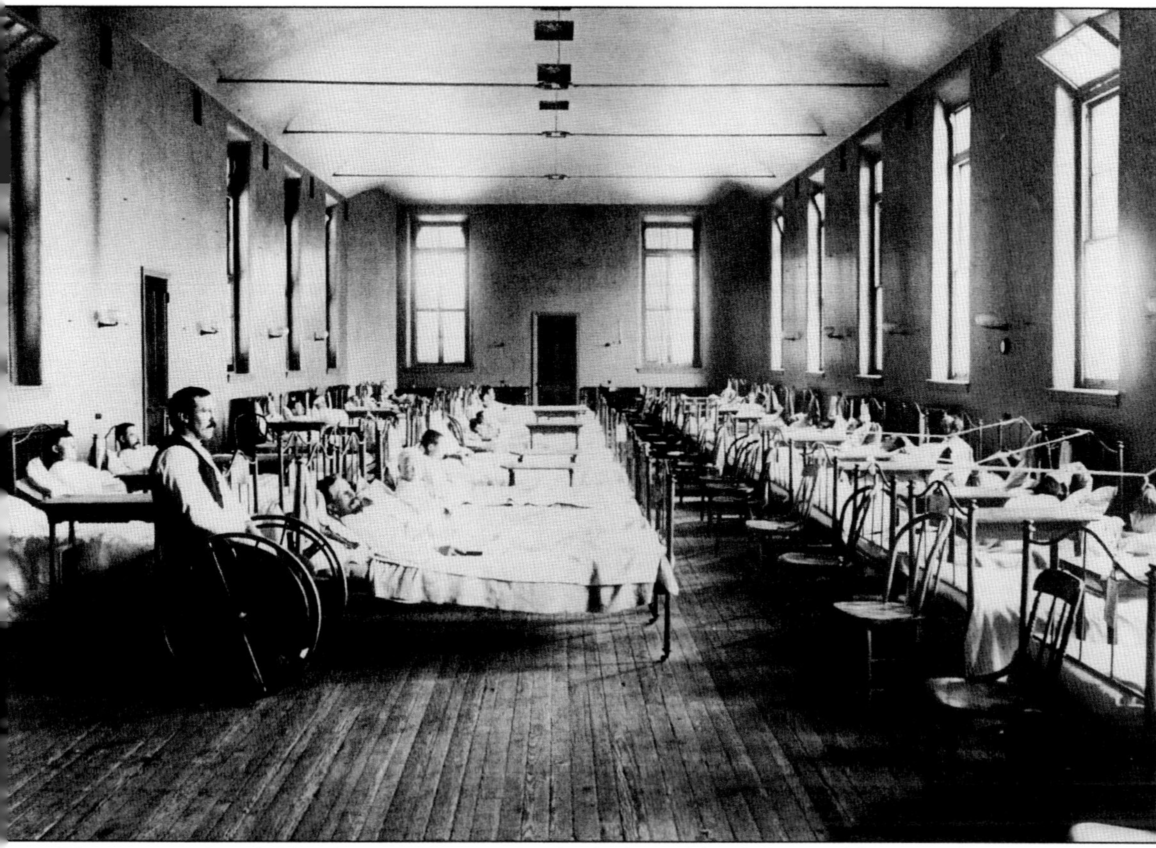

This is a ward in Ashland Miners' Hospital. The beds could only be used by injured miners, railroad workers, and textile workers, in that order. Within a year after it opened, 313 miners were treated—the daily average being 75 patients.

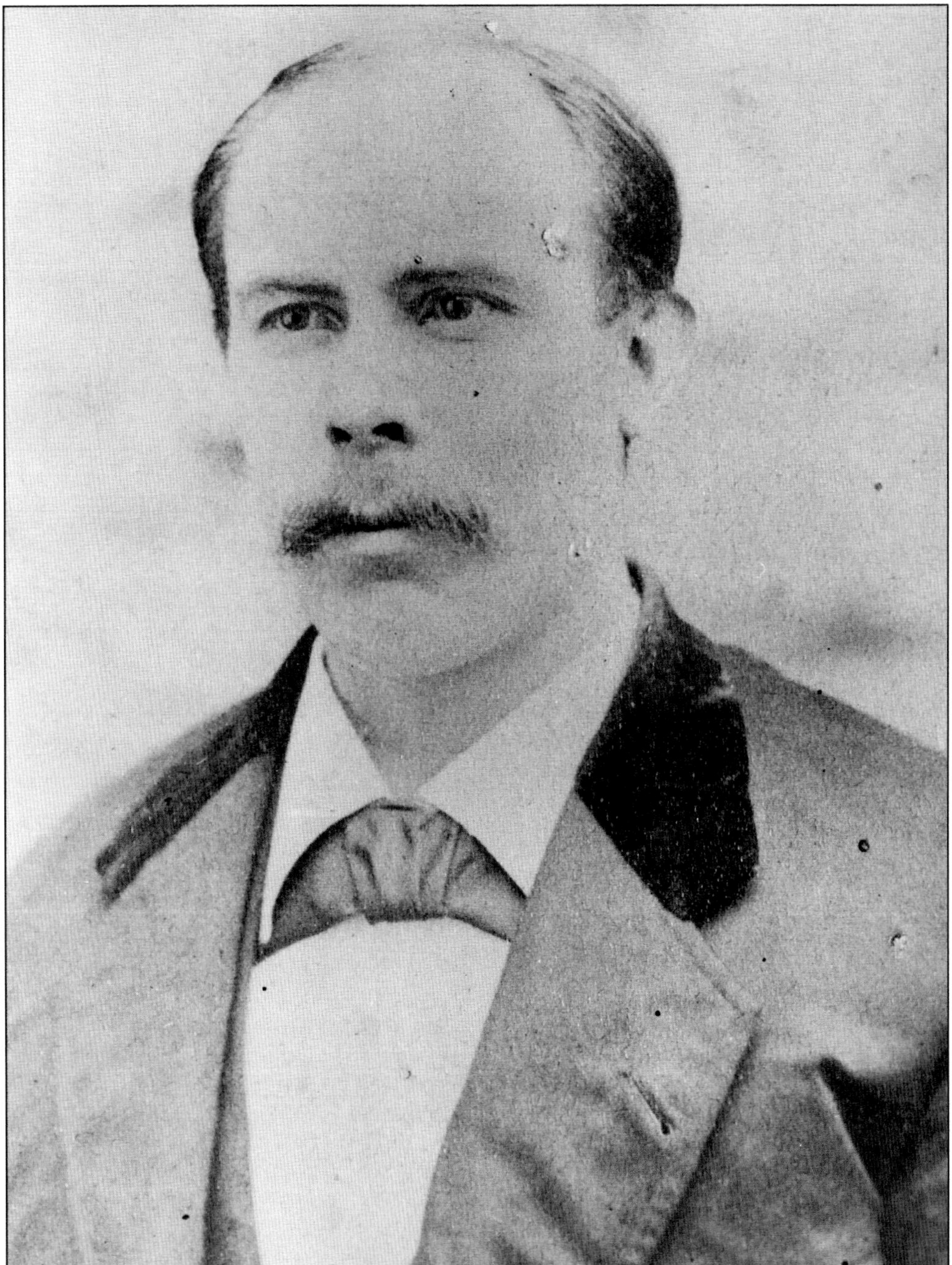

Thomas Munley, a member of the Molly Maguires, was hanged June 21, 1877, for the murder of Thomas Sanger and William Uren at Raven Run in 1875. All of the Mollies stood before Bretz's camera the day before they went to meet their maker. The Historical Society of Schuylkill County has two of these images in its collections; this one is of Munley.

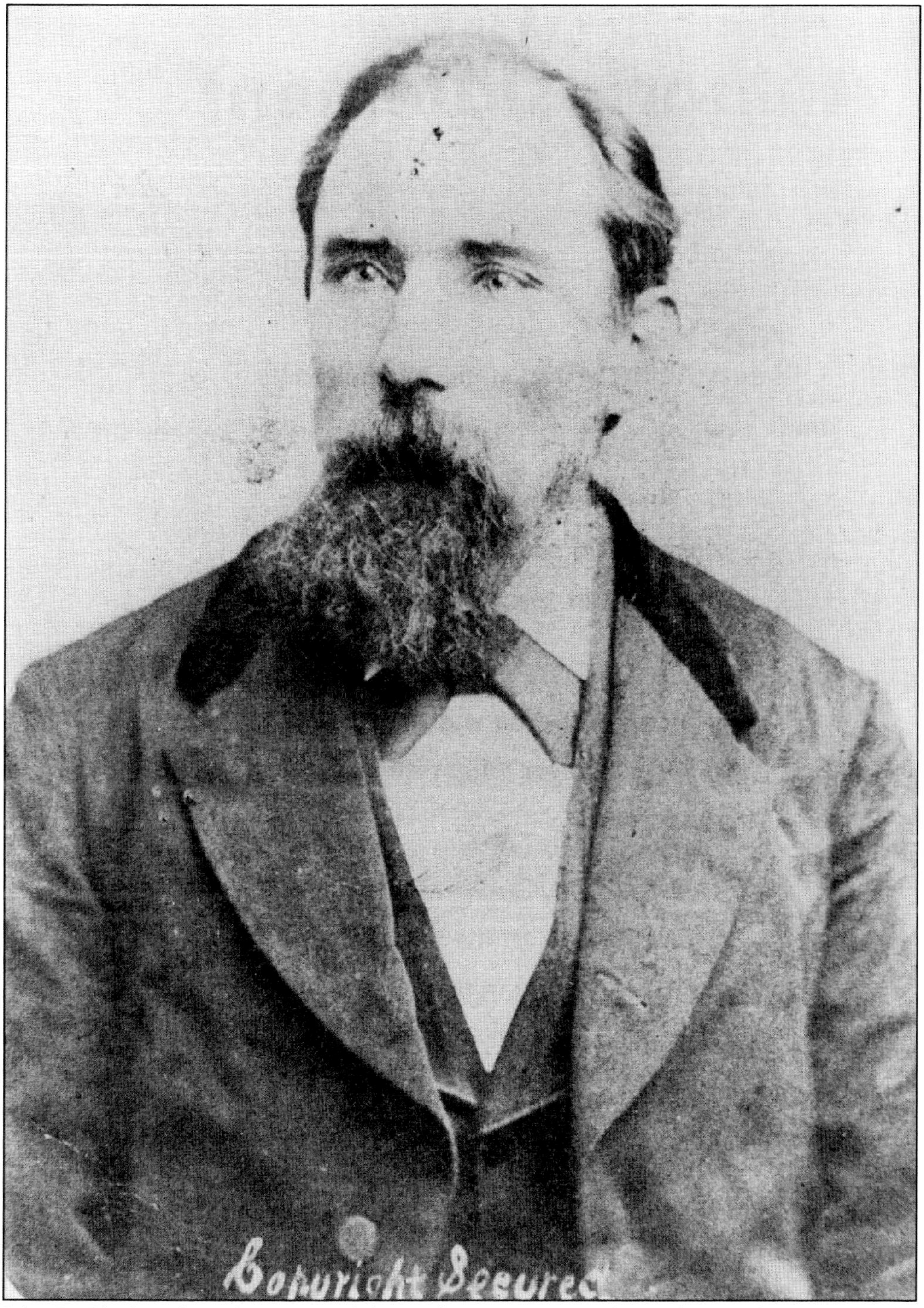

John J. "Black Jack" Kehoe, King of the Molly Maguires, was hanged December 18, 1878, for the murder of Frank W.S. Langdon at Audenreid on June 14, 1862. Notice that Bretz has put "Copyright Secured" on the bottom of the image. He made carte de vistas of these pictures and sold them to an eager public.

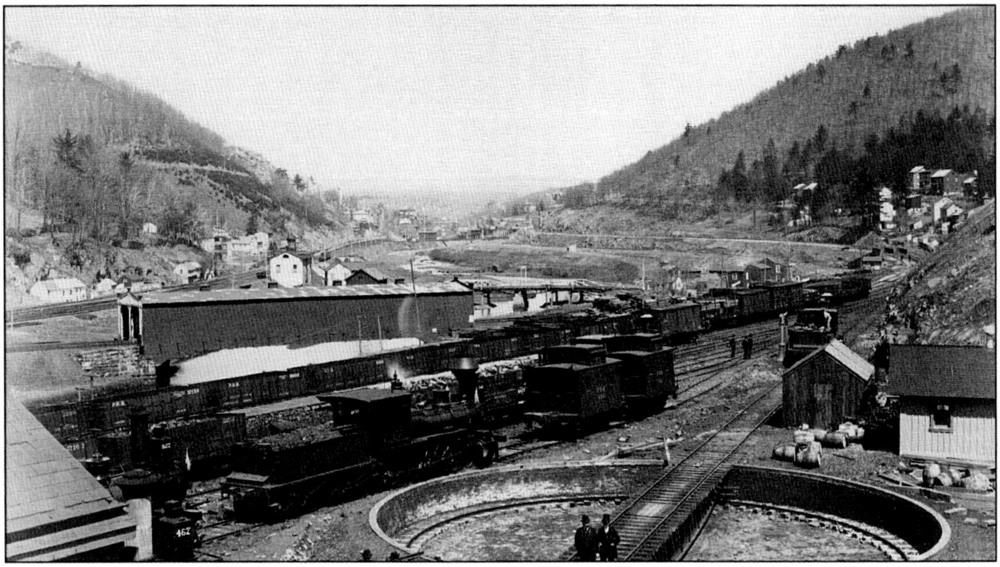

This rare image shows railroad officials inspecting the Pennsylvania Railroad roundtable at Mount Carbon. The "Pennsy" first came to Pottsville on November 15, 1886, 44 years after its rival, the Philadelphia & Reading Railroad, had arrived at Mount Carbon. Notice the "Pottsville Gap" in the background.

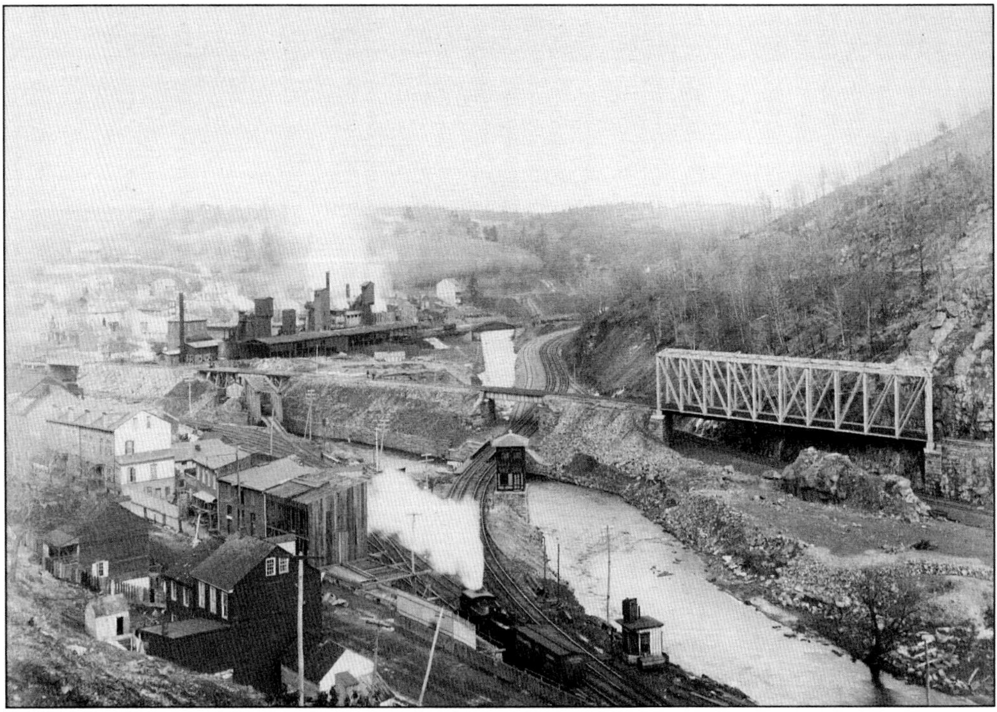

This is a view from Sharp Mountain overlooking Pioneer Island at the southern entrance to Pottsville. The bridge at the right carries the Pennsylvania Railroad over the remains of the Schuylkill Canal as it crosses Pioneer Island on its way into Pottsville. The Reading Railroad snakes across the Schuylkill River in the middle as it moves off to the east toward Port Carbon. Smoke is rising from the Atkins Iron Works in the background.

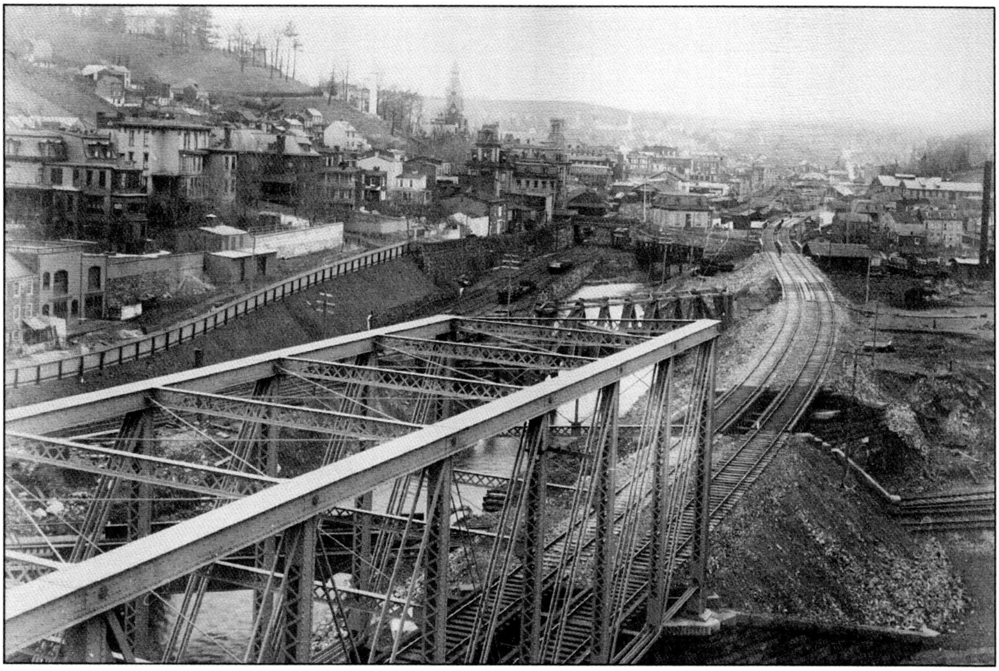

Bretz has moved across the river to make this view of the Pennsylvania Railroad bridge at the southern entrance to Pottsville. The Atkins Iron Works can barely be seen on the right, while the homes on the left are on South Centre Street.

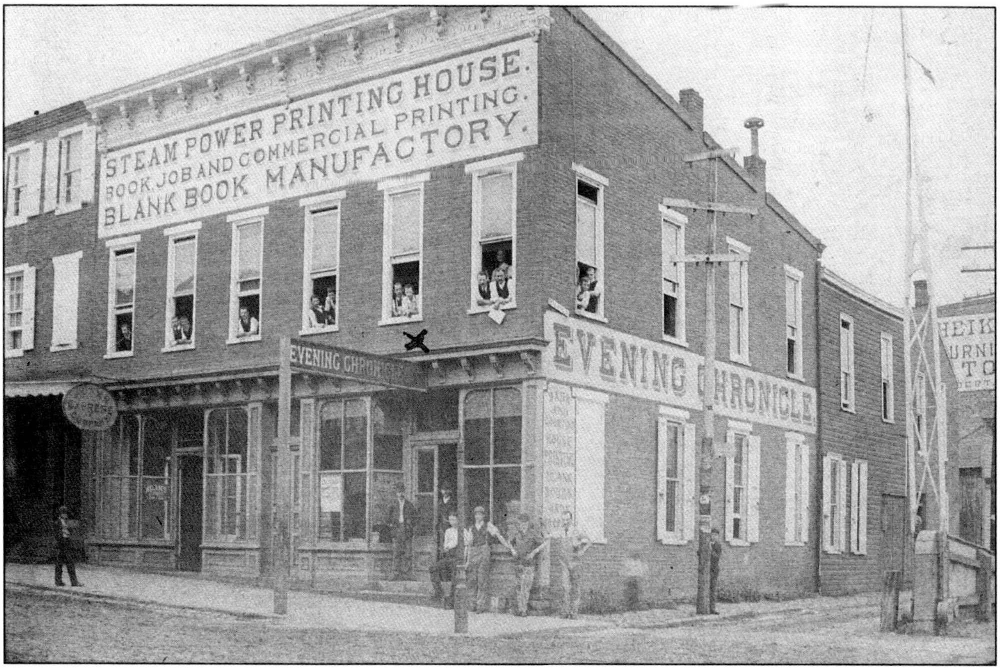

The *Evening Chronicle* newspaper was located at the northwest corner of East Norwegian and Railroad Streets only one block west of the Pennsylvania Railroad passenger station. Notice how Bretz has posed the employees leaning out of the second floor windows and how he has posed people on the sidewalk in front of the building.

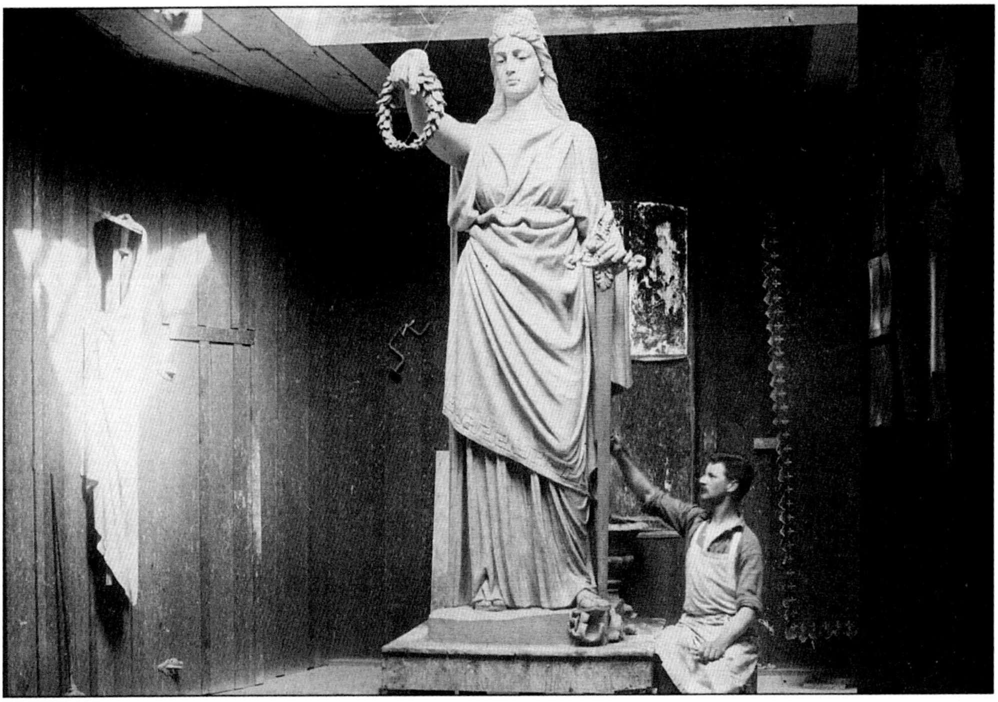

The camera of Bretz has captured artist August Zeller as he works on the statue of the Genius of Liberty in his studio on Mauch Chunk Street. In January 1889, the wax monument froze while it was in the studio. Zeller and his assistant, George L. Schreader, had to thaw Liberty out so they could continue to work on it.

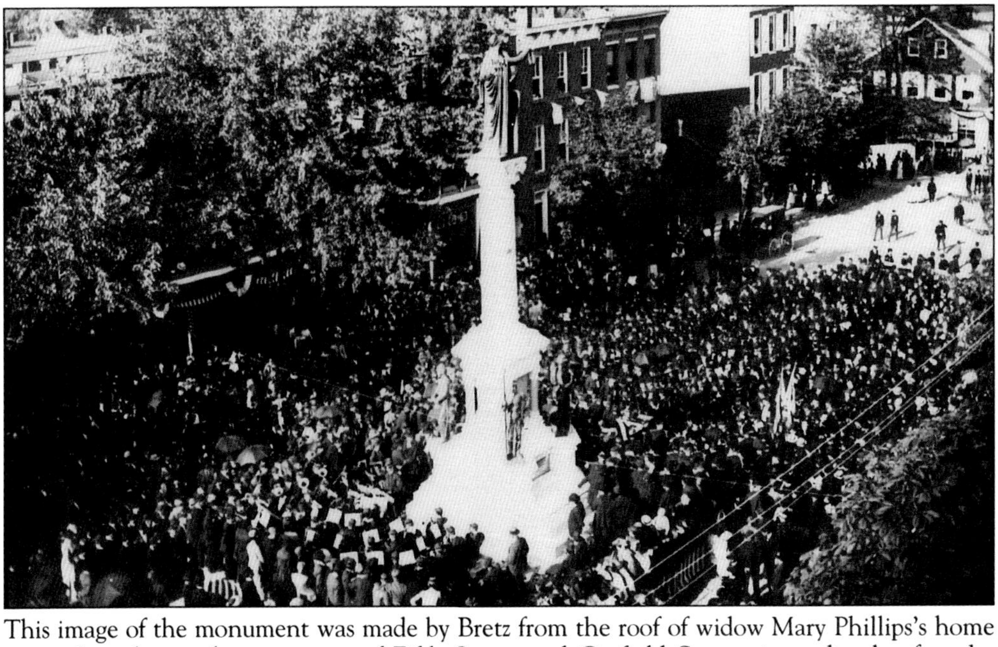

This image of the monument was made by Bretz from the roof of widow Mary Phillips's home situated at the southwest corner of Fifth Street and Garfield Square immediately after the monument was unveiled. Notice the music sheets of the Third Brigade band to the left of the foot of the monument. The new courthouse is visible in the upper left-hand corner.

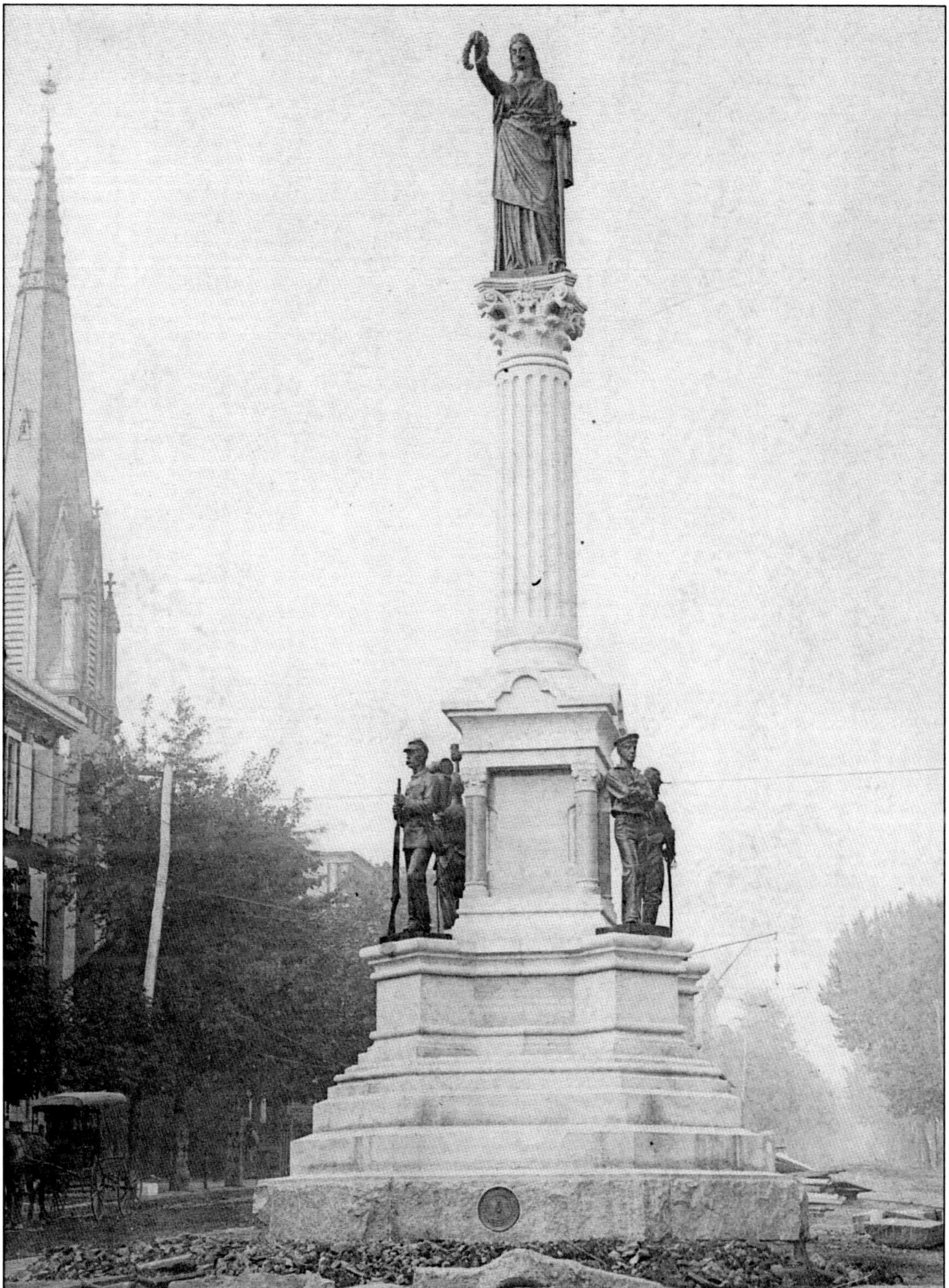

Bretz made this image of the finished Soldier and Sailors Monument after it was unveiled on Monument Day, October 1, 1891. More than six thousand people marched in the parade on one of Pottsville's proudest days. Thousands of people arrived in Pottsville on trains for the great day.

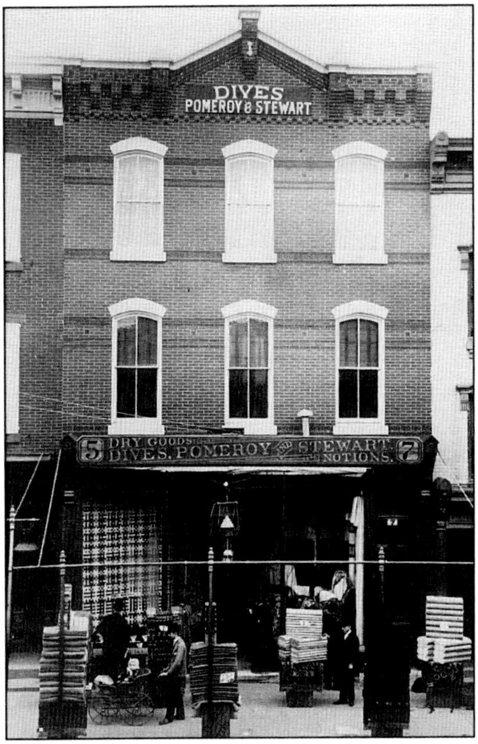

Bretz made this souvenir image, compliments of Dives, Pomeroy, & Stewart, Pottsville, Pennsylvania, when the store was located on North Centre Street. It is now at the southwest corner of Mahantongo and South Centre Streets. On the back of the photograph the store advertised the type of merchandise that it carried.

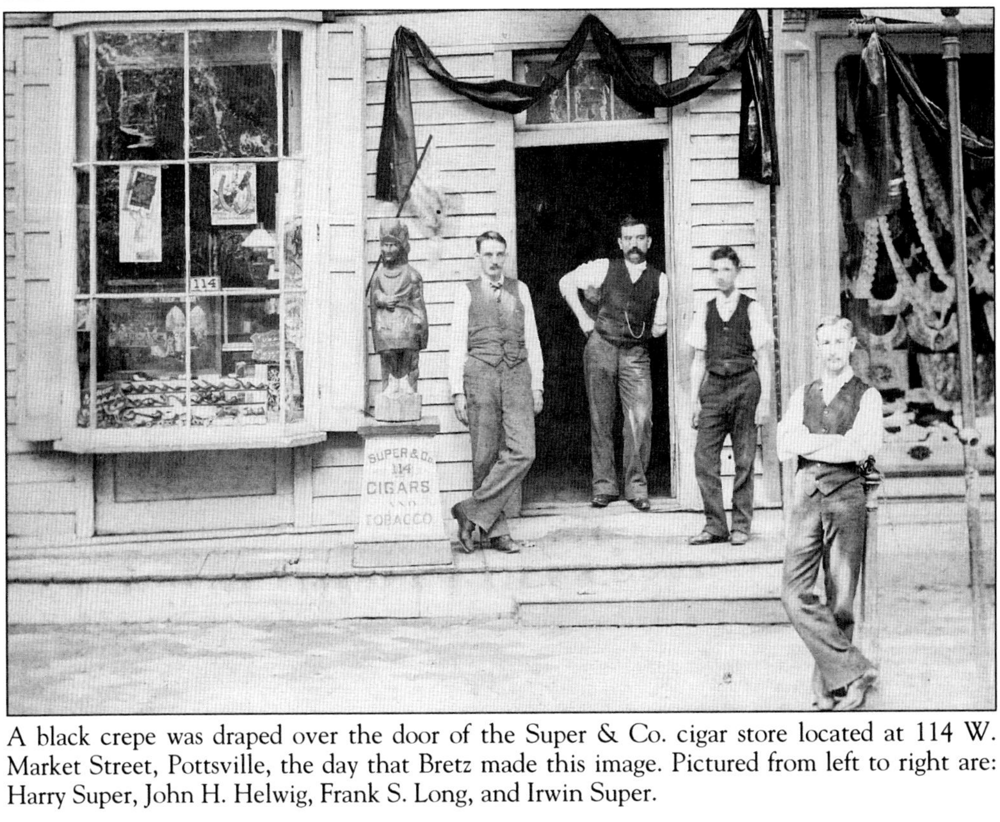

A black crepe was draped over the door of the Super & Co. cigar store located at 114 W. Market Street, Pottsville, the day that Bretz made this image. Pictured from left to right are: Harry Super, John H. Helwig, Frank S. Long, and Irwin Super.

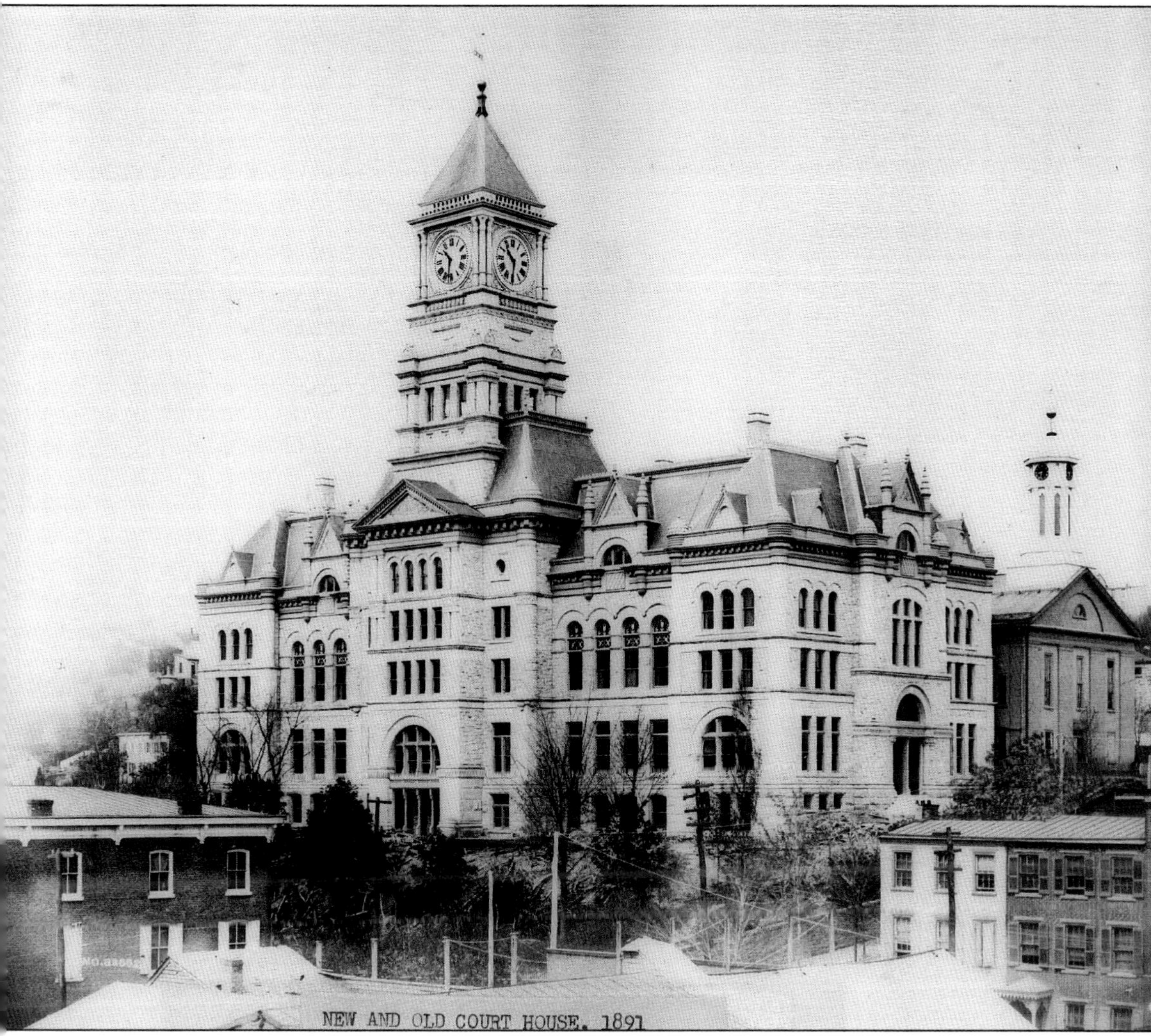

This remarkable image by Bretz shows the old and the new courthouses in Pottsville. The legislature passed an act to move the courthouse from Orwigsburg to Pottsville, and an election followed confirming that the citizens approved the moving of the courthouse. The construction of the first courthouse was begun at Second and Sanderson Streets, in October 1849. The cornerstone for the courthouse that replaced the original was laid in 1891.

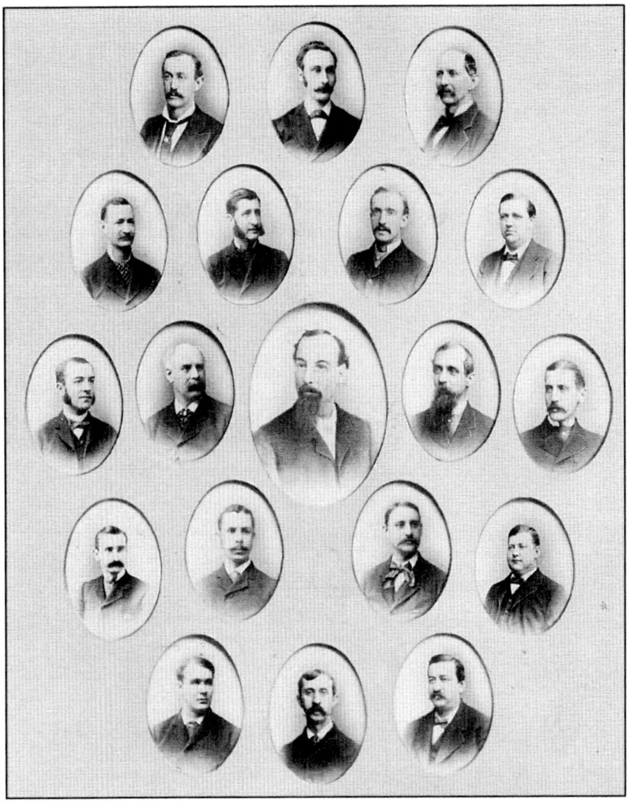

All of the members of this unidentified social club were framed in this 1882 image by Bretz. His studio was at 3 W. Norwegian Street.

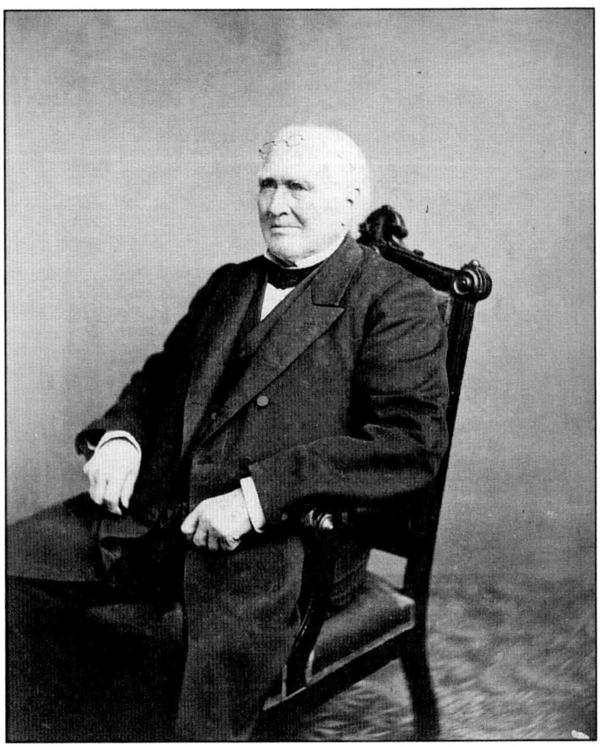

William Donaldson became the owner of a large tract of land in western Schuylkill County. He proceeded to develop the land and built the Swatara railroad, which connected his coal lands with the Mine Hill Railroad and Union Canal. He was born at Danville, July 28, 1799, and while there was appointed an associate judge by Gov. David R. Porter. The town of Donaldson was named after him.

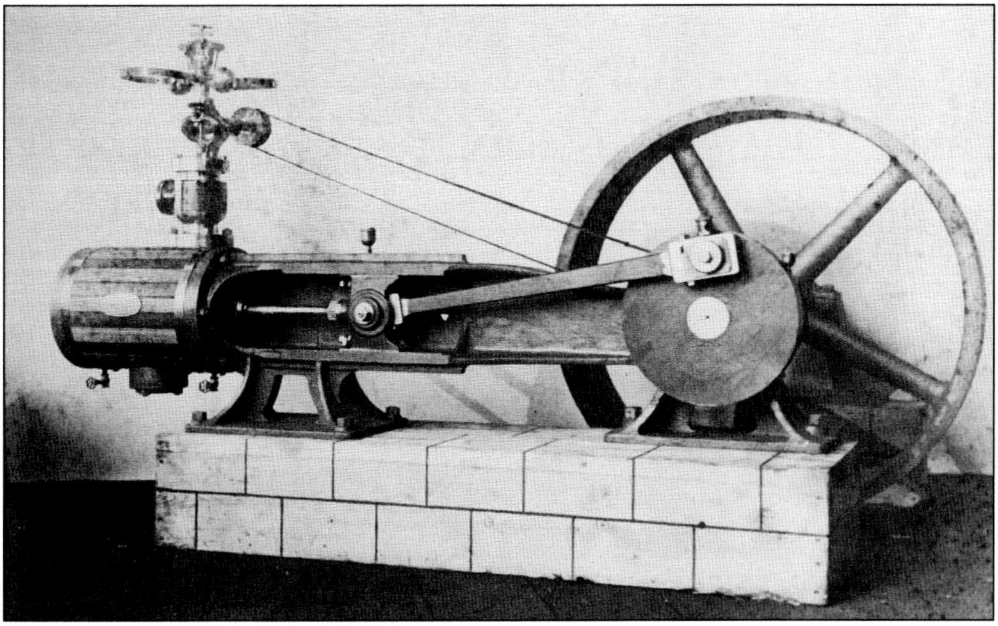

The Pennsylvania Diamond Drill Company was organized on October 20, 1869, and was first located at Reading, Pennsylvania. Samuel Griscom, then operating the William Penn Colliery, moved it to Pottsville. His nephew, Lewis Griscom, was the superintendent when Bretz made this image of one of the firm's products.

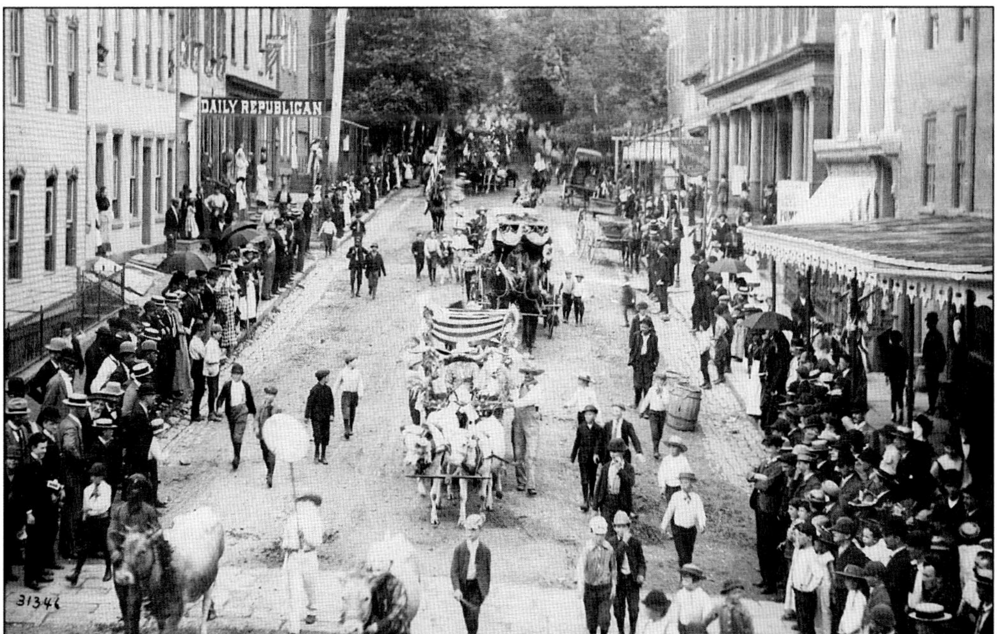

The milkmen's parade comes down Mahantongo Street where it meets South Centre Street in June 1890. The *Daily Republican* sign can be seen on the left, while the Academy of Music, which was destroyed by the great Pottsville fire of 1914, can be seen on the right with its columns at street level. The roof at the right was Rosengarten's food store. Bretz marked this negative no. 31346.

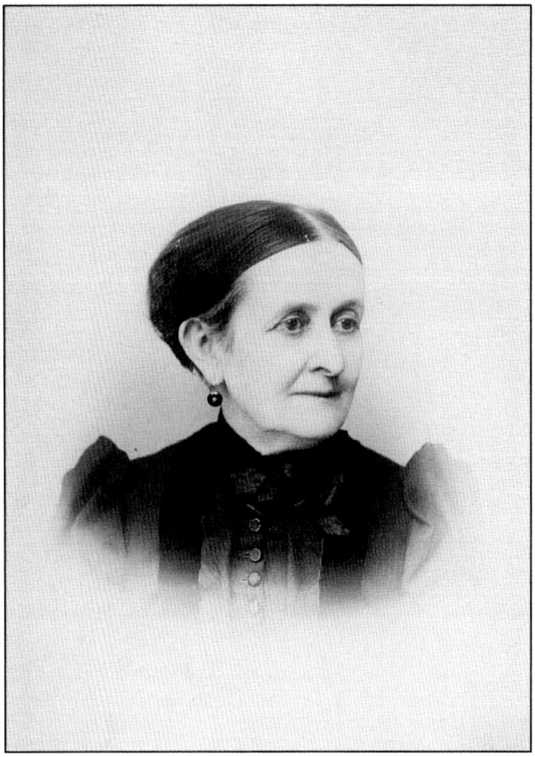

Bretz made hundreds of images of people during his career. This photograph of an unidentified woman was made in his studio at 9 South Centre Street, Pottsville, Pennsylvania. She was a married woman and can be seen with her husband in the next image. This is negative no. 31496.

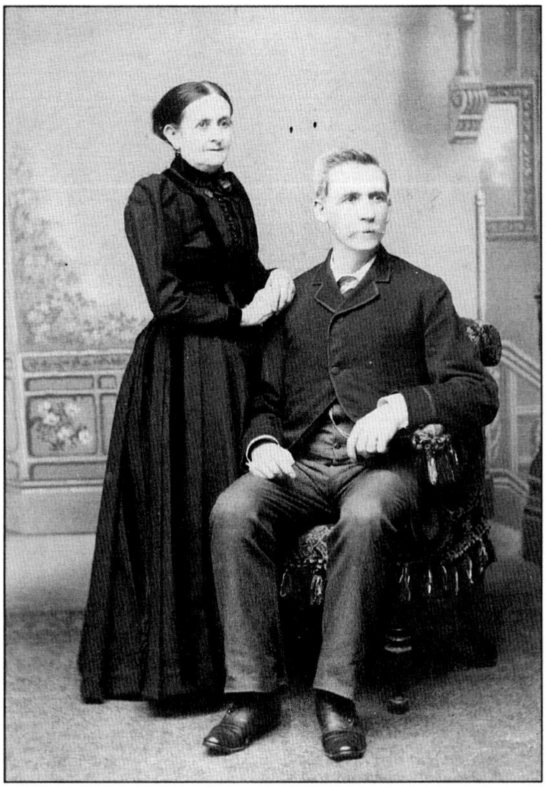

This image of a husband and wife was made by Bretz in his new galley in the Shissler Building at 9 South Centre Street. The names of the couple are not written on the back of the photograph. This is negative no. 31497.

George A. Schalk, master gunsmith, had his shop at 115 E. Norwegian Street, Pottsville. The rifles that Schalk made had a national reputation. He also made violins that were highly acclaimed by musicians. Schalk submitted samples of his guns to the War Department during the Civil War, and the Historical Society of Schuylkill County has drawings of these unusual guns. The guns were not accepted by the War Department at that time.

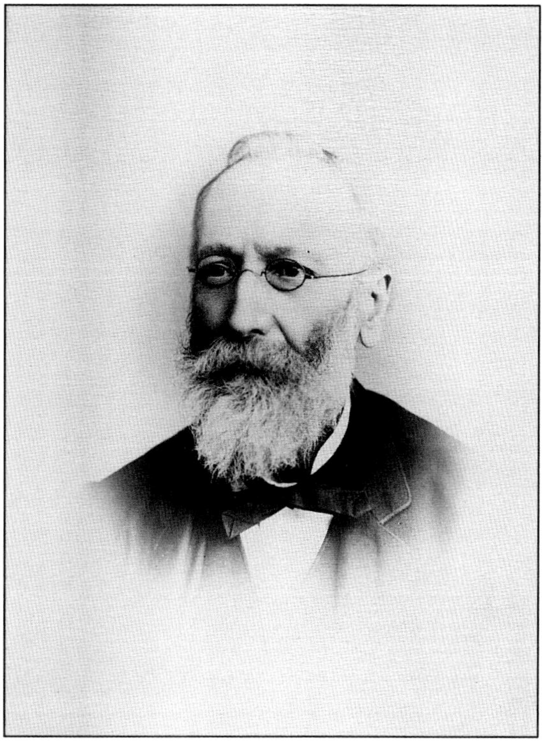

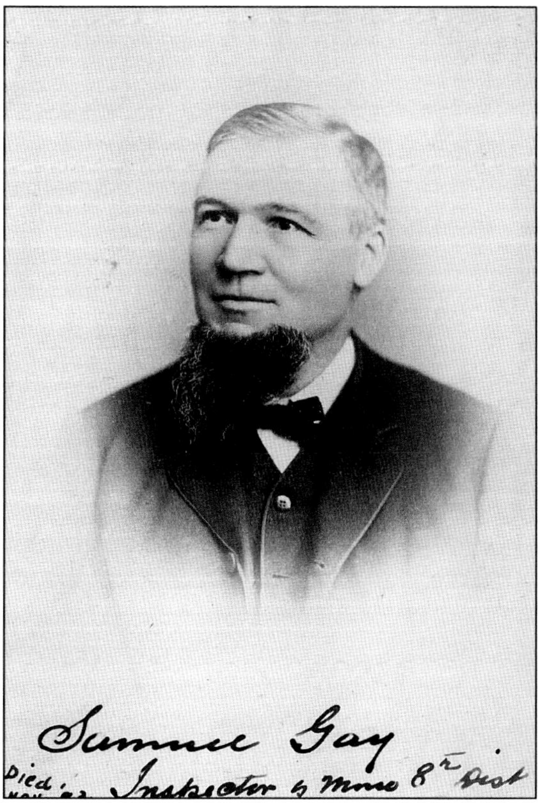

"Sir: I have the honor herewith of presenting my sixteenth annual report as inspector of coal mines for the Seventh Anthracite district for the year 1890," wrote Samuel Gay, in his report submitted to the secretary of Internal Affairs dated Pottsville, March 3, 1891. The popular Gay, shown in this image, died in November of 1893. On the back of this image someone wrote, "For he was a man. Taking him all in all, we shall never see his like again."

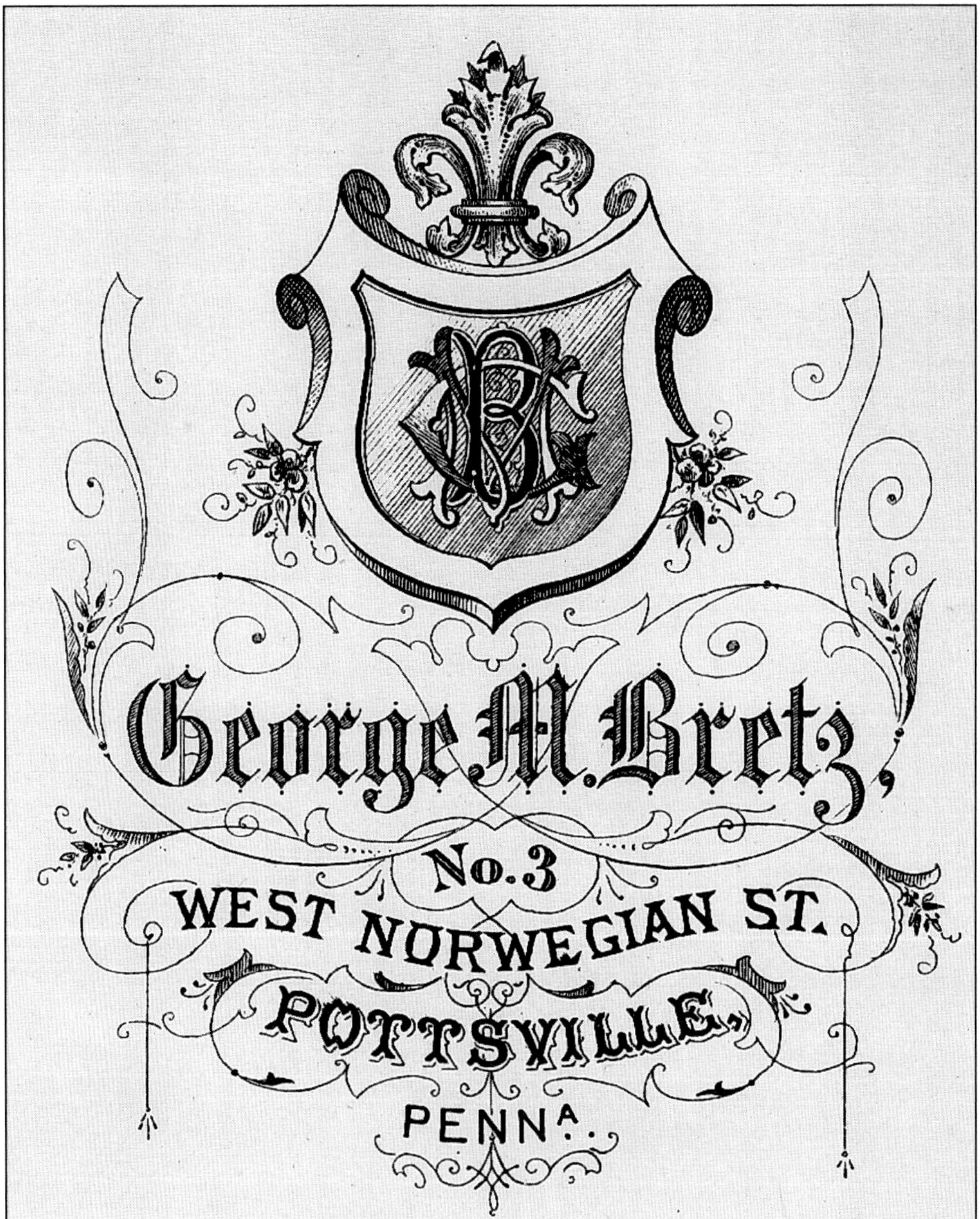

This is the Bretz logo.

Two

Souvenirs of Pottsville

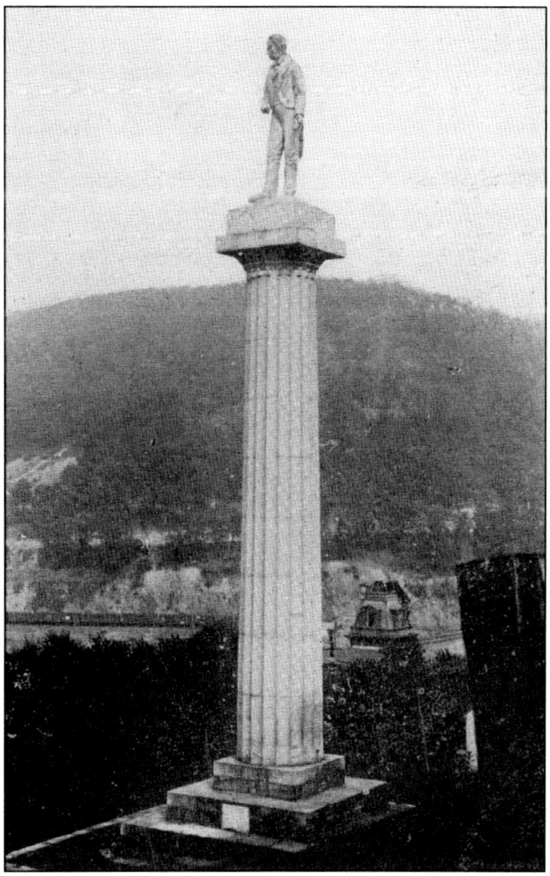

Immediately upon the death of the great statesman Henry Clay, the citizens of Schuylkill County decided to honor his memory by erecting a monument to him. Clay proposed a tariff that would protect American industries from imports from Great Britain. This tariff created an impetus to the iron industry in the United States, which created a demand for anthracite coal produced in Schuylkill County. The foundation of the monument was laid in 1853, and it was dedicated on July 4, 1855.

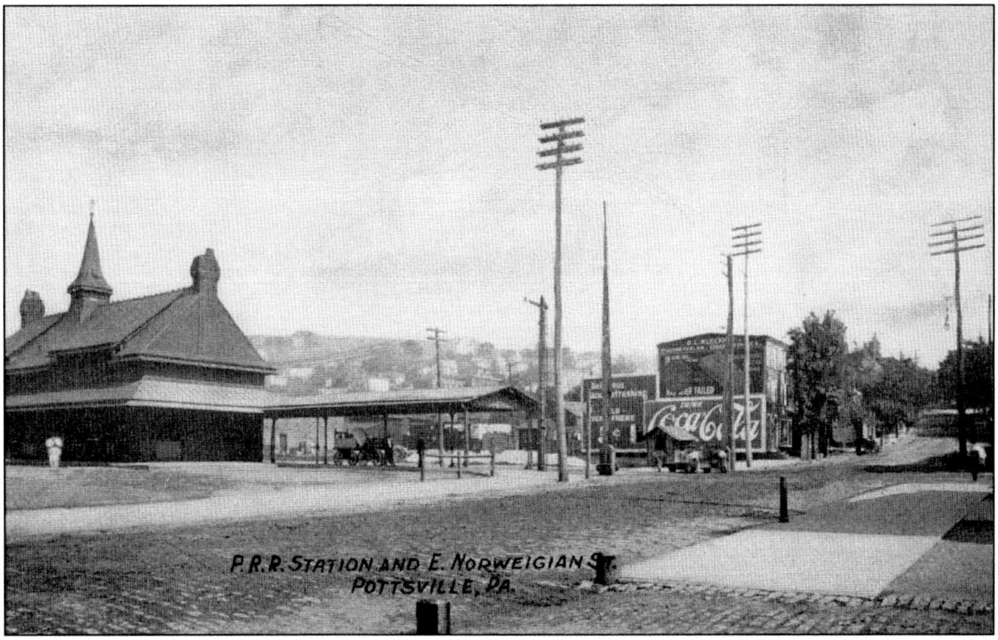

The Pennsylvania Railroad arrived in Pottsville on November 15, 1866. The Pennsylvania Railroad passenger station was located at Coal and E. Norwegian Streets, Pottsville, Pennsylvania, now the intersection of Route 61 and E. Norwegian Street and the location of the Richard B. Ryon insurance agency. By 1943 passenger traffic had dwindled so much that it was used as a bus terminal. Later, in 1950, the building was razed and a modern bus terminal built.

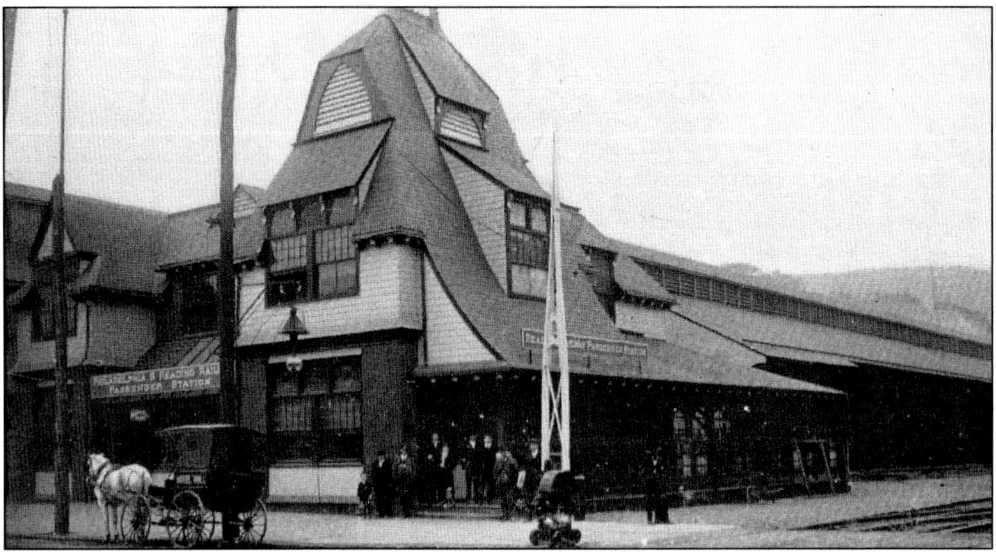

The Philadelphia & Reading Railroad arrived in Mount Carbon in 1842 where a passenger station was built. In 1851 the station was moved to Railroad and Union Streets, until it was necessary for the railroad to move into the heart of Pottsville. On June 21, 1887, the Philadelphia & Reading Railroad station, seen in this image, was formally opened for business. In the 1960s, passenger service was closed at this station and it was razed to make way for a downtown parking lot for shoppers.

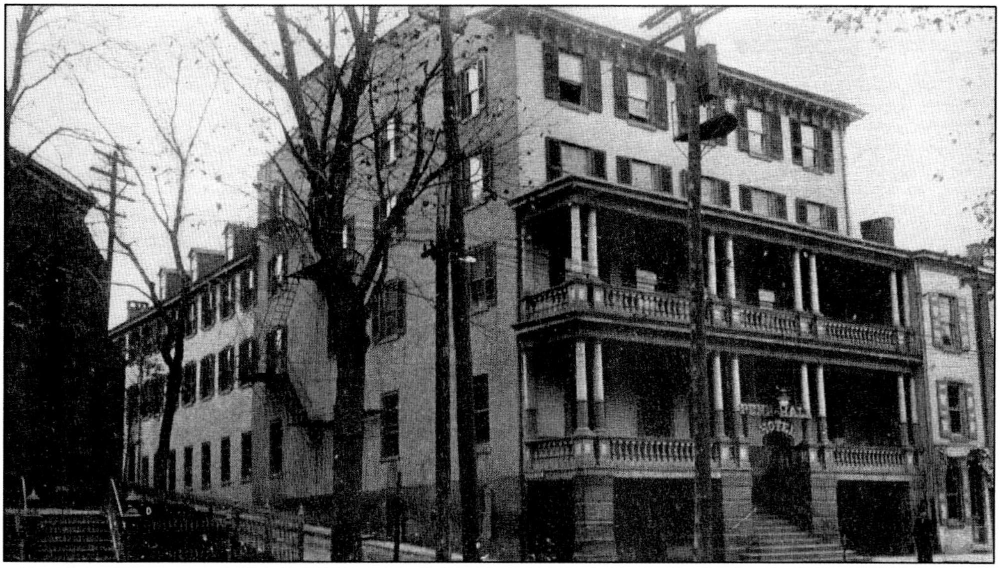

The Pennsylvania Hall Hotel was built at the corner of South Centre Street and Church Alley, now known as Howard Avenue, in 1830. It was opened to the public by Col. George Shoemaker on July 11, 1831. A large number of men, who came to the coal regions and later became prominent in the coal trade, made their home in it. Over the years, the business of the hotel declined and, finally, in 1956 it was razed.

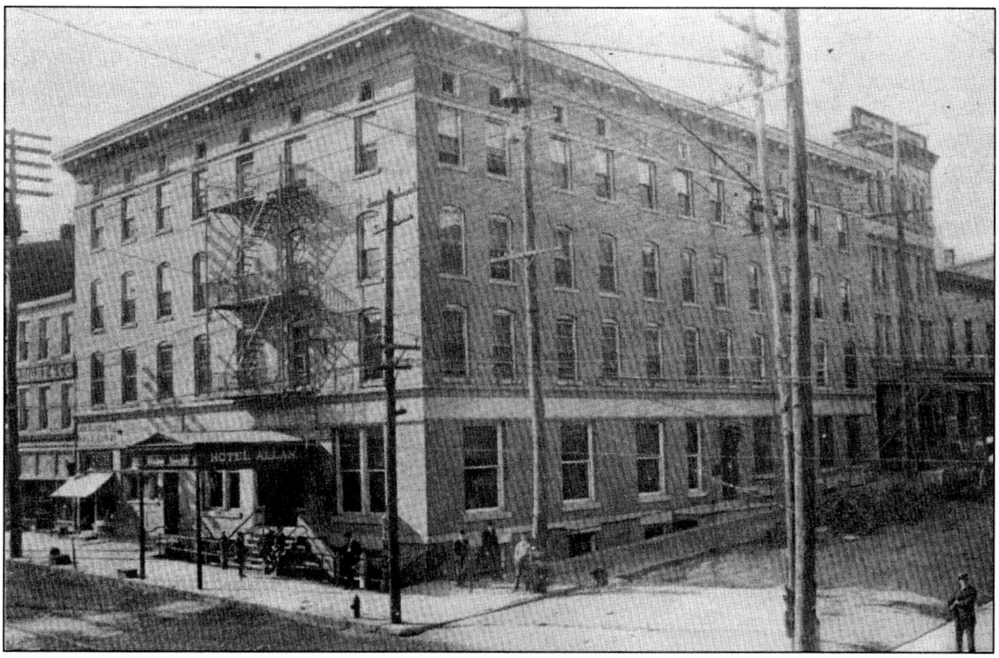

The earliest hotel in Pottsville was the White Horse Tavern, or hotel, located at the southwest corner of South Centre and Mahantongo Streets. Over the years the property was enlarged and it finally came into the possession of Thomas G. Allan on February 14, 1898. Allan replaced the structure with a brick building and called it the Hotel Allan. The hotel existed until 1926 when it was razed and became the location of the popular Necho Allen Hotel.

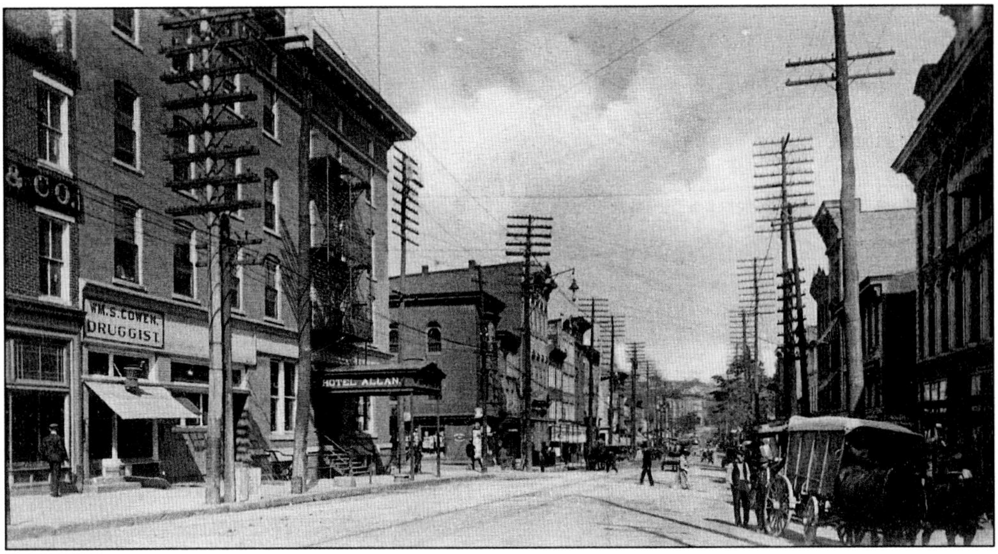

Centre Street was lined with electric-light poles as seen in this view looking north from the Hotel Allan near the corner of South Centre and Mahantongo Streets. Notice that the Union Bank and Trust Company, designed by Pottsville architect Francis X. Reilley, has not yet been built. William S. Cowen, druggist on the left, later moved to the middle of the block between Mahantongo and West Norwegian Street after the great Pottsville fire of 1914.

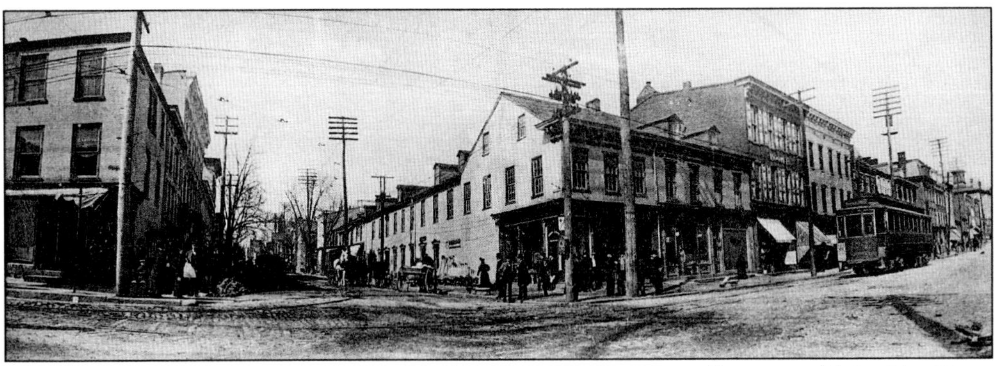

This postcard, no. 163, Corner Centre and Market Streets, Pottsville, was published by Dives Pomeroy & Stewart department store as a promotional item. That is the L.C. Thompson hardware store on the right and the familiar Thompson Building has not yet been built on the left corner. The space at the bottom of the card is for the message to be written by the sender. The back of the card read, "This side is for the address." The post office did not allow messages to be written on the back of postcards.

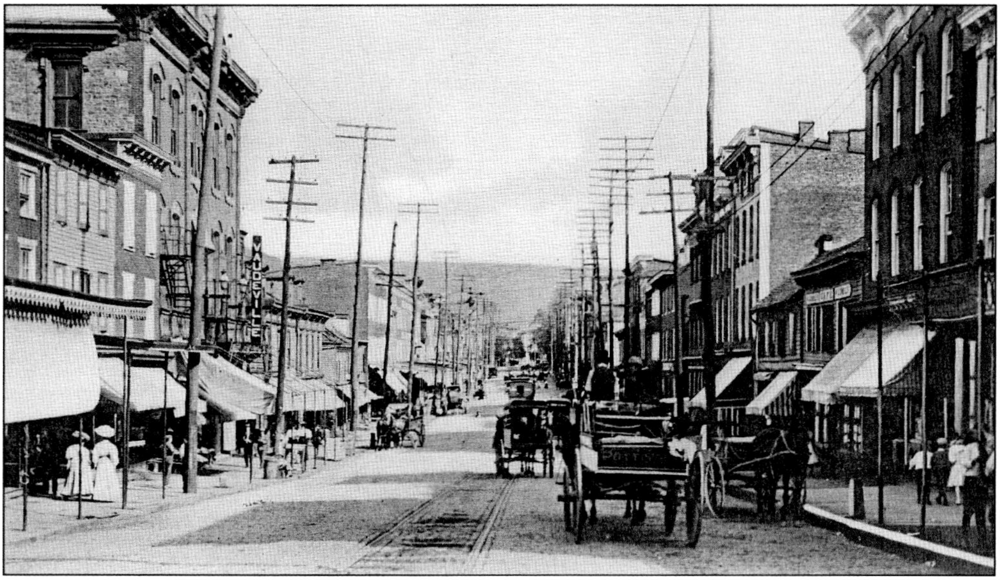

This is Centre Street looking south from Race Street. The large building on the left bearing the vaudeville sign is Centennial Hall. The first vaudeville in Pottsville was presented in Centennial Hall in 1905 as "polite vaudeville," because vaudeville was not yet considered proper family entertainment. The theater burned down and was later the site of the Capital Bowling Center.

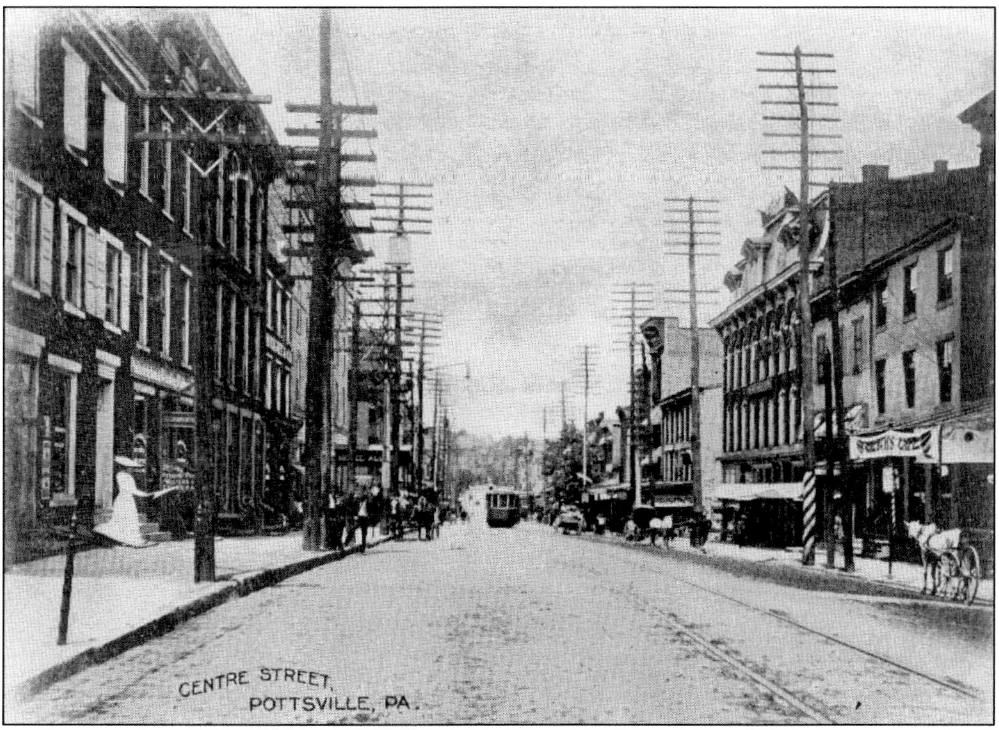

The blank space on the left of this penny postcard is for the sender to write the message. A trolley can be seen in the distance making its way up North Centre Street. The lady in the white dress on the left is doing her shopping in this view made about 1900.

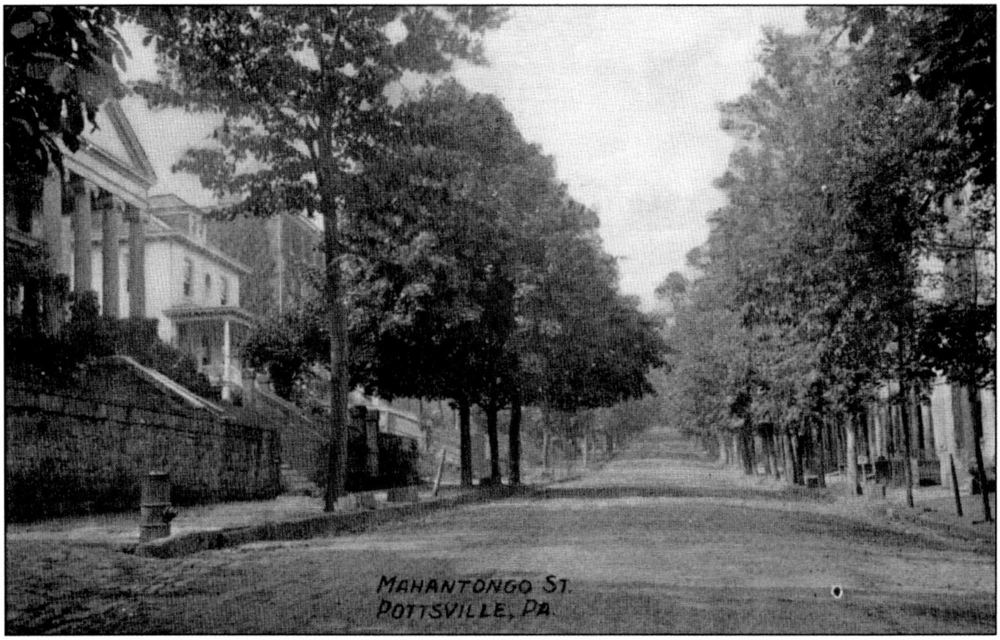

Trees lined Mahantongo Street in this scene looking west from Sixth Street. John Pinkerton, a coal operator who came to Schuylkill County in the 1830s, built the mansion with the columns that is seen on the left. In 1934 the mansion became the Braun School of Music. Pinkerton also built two other mansions not seen here, and the three homes were known as the "Pinkerton Cottages."

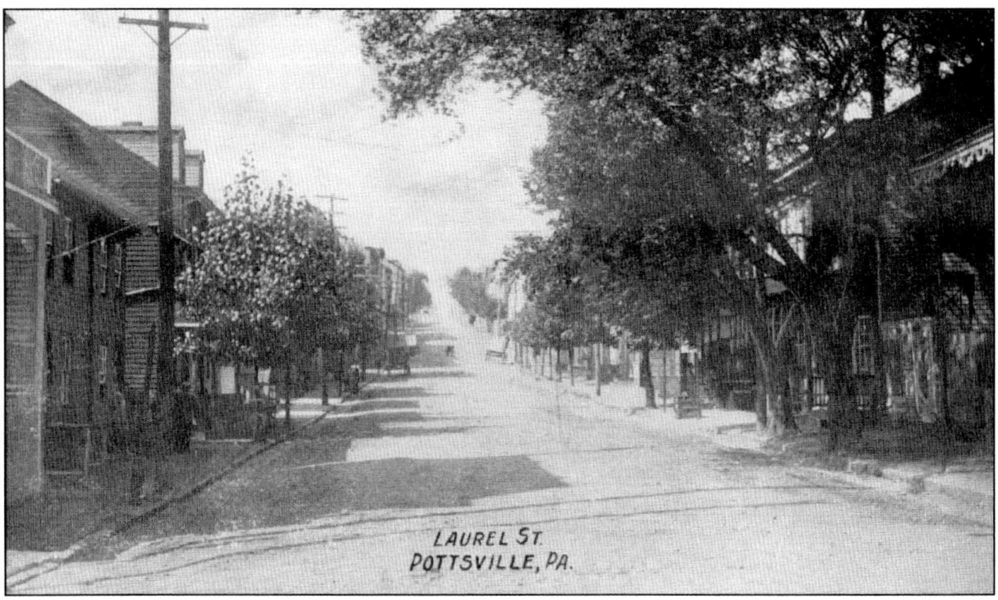

Laurel Street looking west is seen in this view. There was not much traffic the day that the photographer made this image. Only a lonely horse and buggy can be seen on the left.

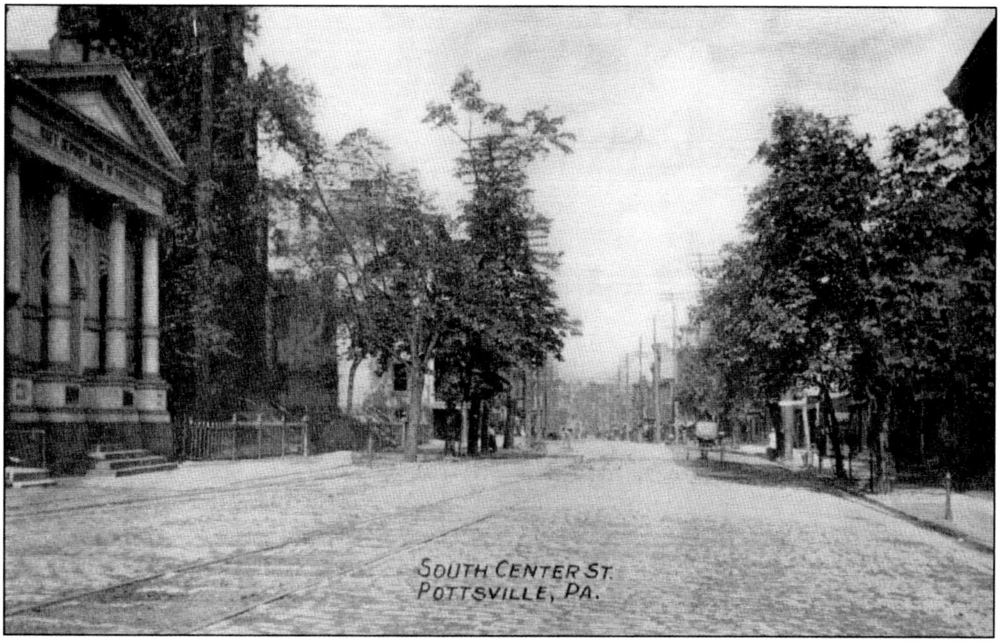

The Safe Deposit Bank, with its pillars in front, can be seen on the left in this view on South Centre Street. The bank disappeared from the Pottsville scene many years ago. Beside the bank is the Trinity Episcopal Church and next to it, hidden by the trees, is the Penn Hall Hotel. A horse and buggy are seen on the right.

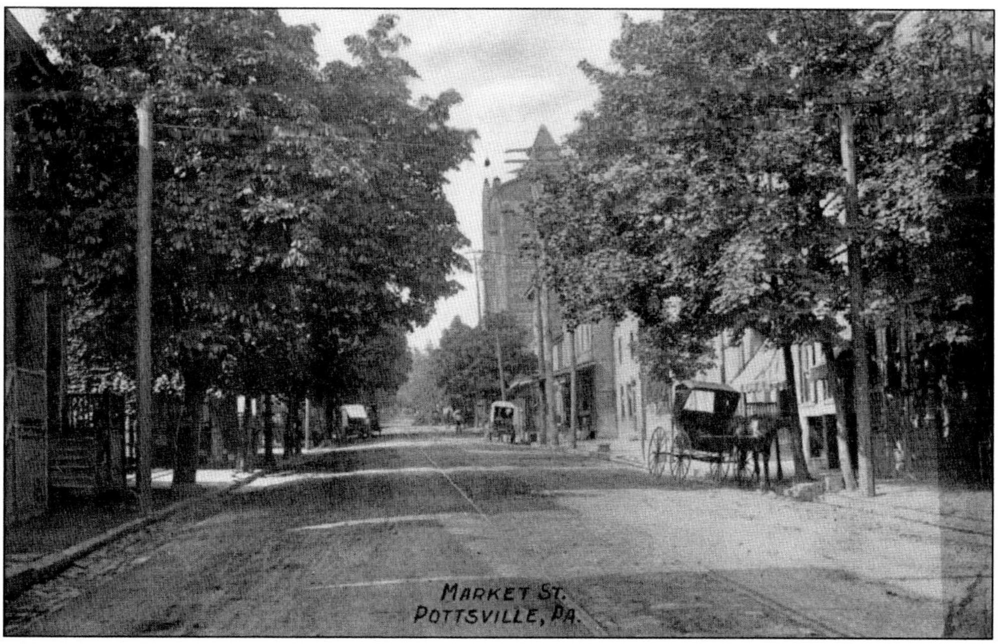

This view is looking west on Market Street about the turn of the century. The scene is very placid in those bucolic days as only a few horses and buggies can be seen. A single trolley track can be seen in the middle of the street. The invention of the automobile was a few years in the future.

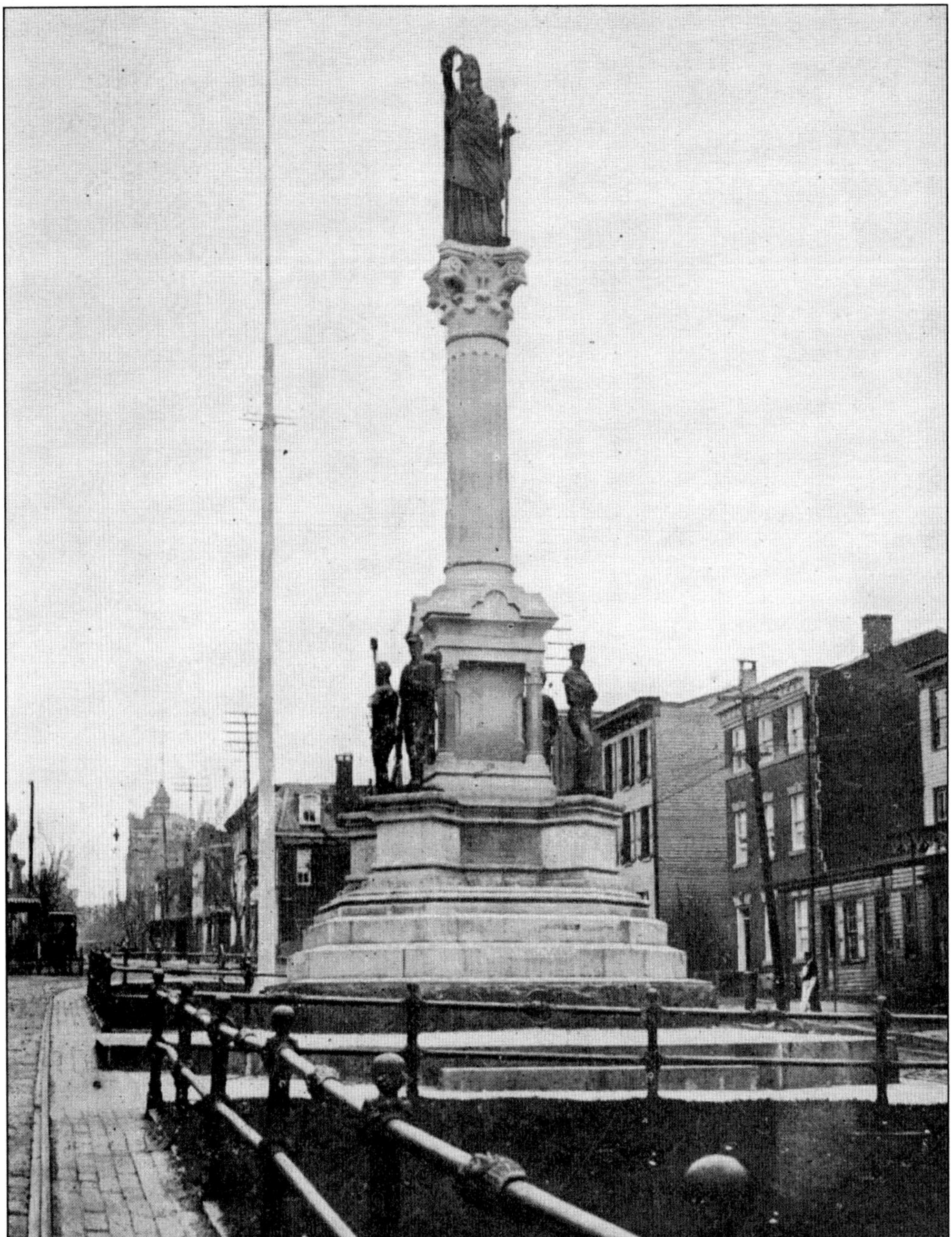

The Soldiers and Sailors Monument in Garfield Square was designed and sculpted by August Zeller. It was unveiled on October 1, 1891, on Monument Day in Pottsville when six thousand people marched in the largest parade in the history of Pottsville. Thousands of people crowded the street to watch it. The iron railing was a favorite place for boys to sit to watch parades as they went through the square.

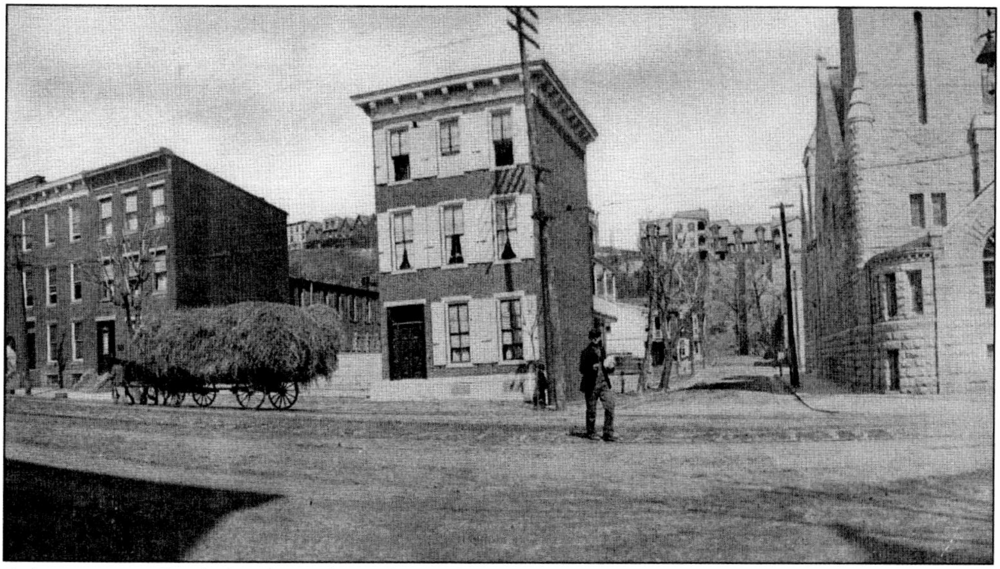

A hay wagon slowly lumbers through Garfield Square near the corner of Fourth and Market Streets. The First United Methodist Church is seen on the right. The home in the middle was razed a few years ago and the space is used as a parking lot for the Garfield Diner, which is located today in the space between the two houses.

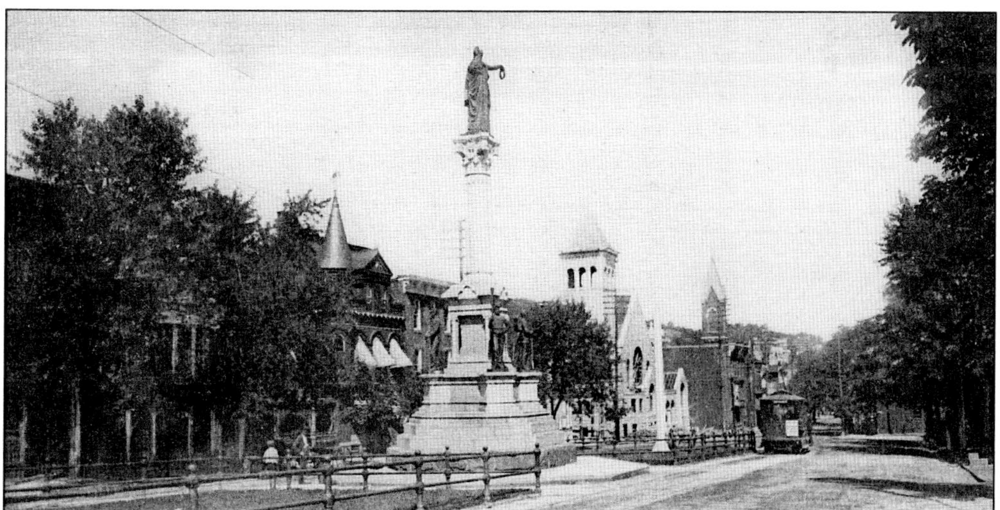

This view of the Soldiers and Sailors Monument in Garfield Square is looking west. The familiar First United Methodist Church just to the right of the monument was built in 1904. The spire of the Trinity United Church at 316 W. Market Street can be seen; later the spire was removed.

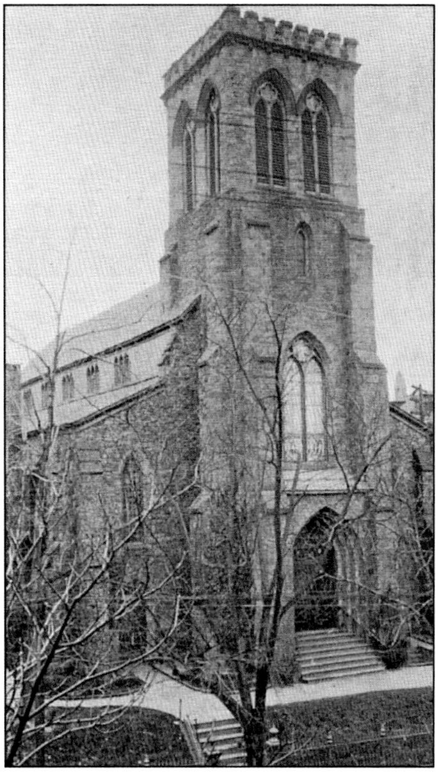

The Trinity Episcopal Church was organized in 1827 and a building site, known as "lot number 4," was given to the church by John Pott when he laid out Pottsville in 1816. The present church was built in 1847, and never got the spire that was planned for it.

The spire of St. Patrick's Church, located at Fourth and Mahantongo Streets, soars high in the air over the church. This church was built and dedicated in 1891, the same year that the Soldiers and Sailors Monument was dedicated in Garfield Square only two blocks north of the church.

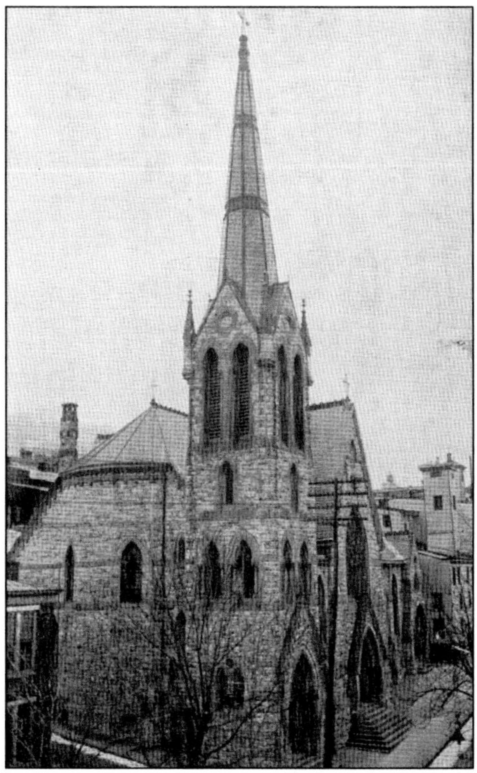

The First Presbyterian Church, founded in 1817, is just a block down the street from St. Patrick's Church, standing at the corner of Third and Mahantongo Streets. The present church was erected in 1874.

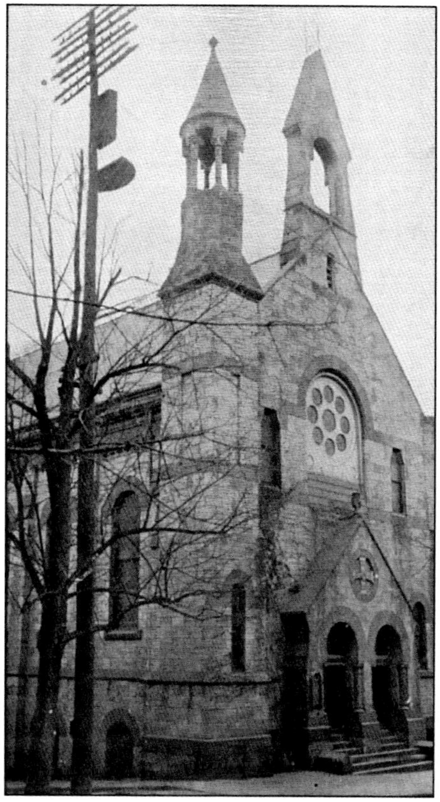

The First United Methodist Church stands prominently at the corner of Market and Fourth Streets. Ground for the new church was broken in August of 1902 with Miss Ann Hill, the oldest member, being allowed to drive the first pick. The church was built in 1904 and officially dedicated on September 17, 1905.

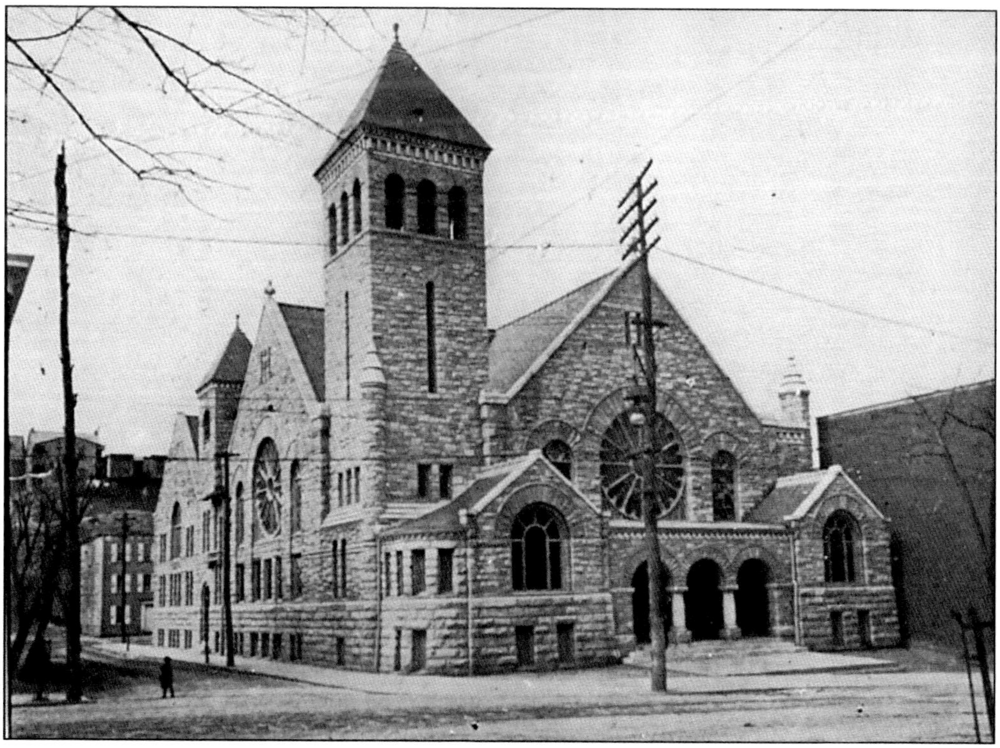

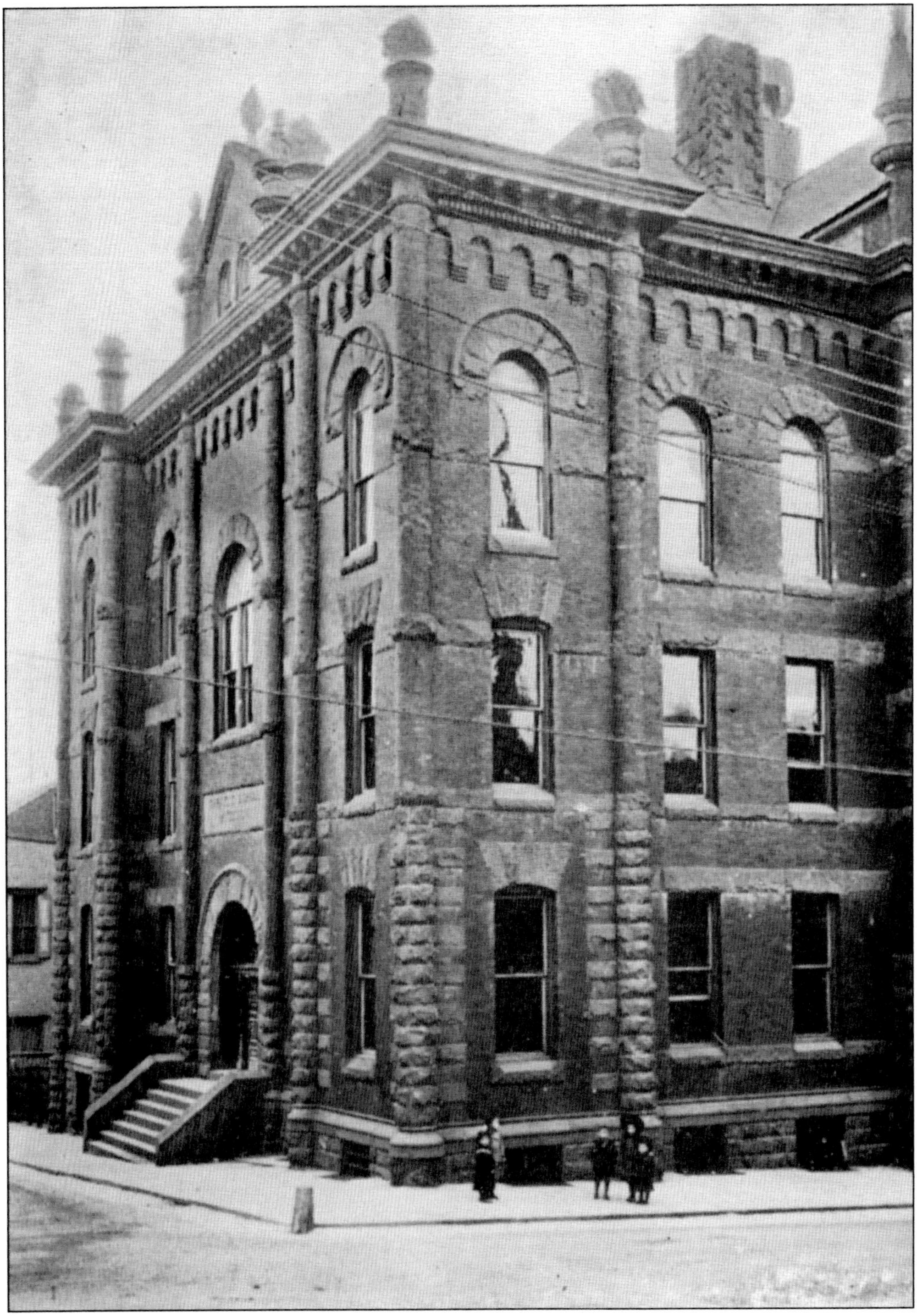

The land, on which the Garfield School stands, at fifth and West Norwegian Streets was purchased by the school board on June 5, 1844. The school building was built in 1893 and was opened on March 2, 1894. The entire third floor was used for the high school and the southeast corner of the second floor was used for the Commercial School.

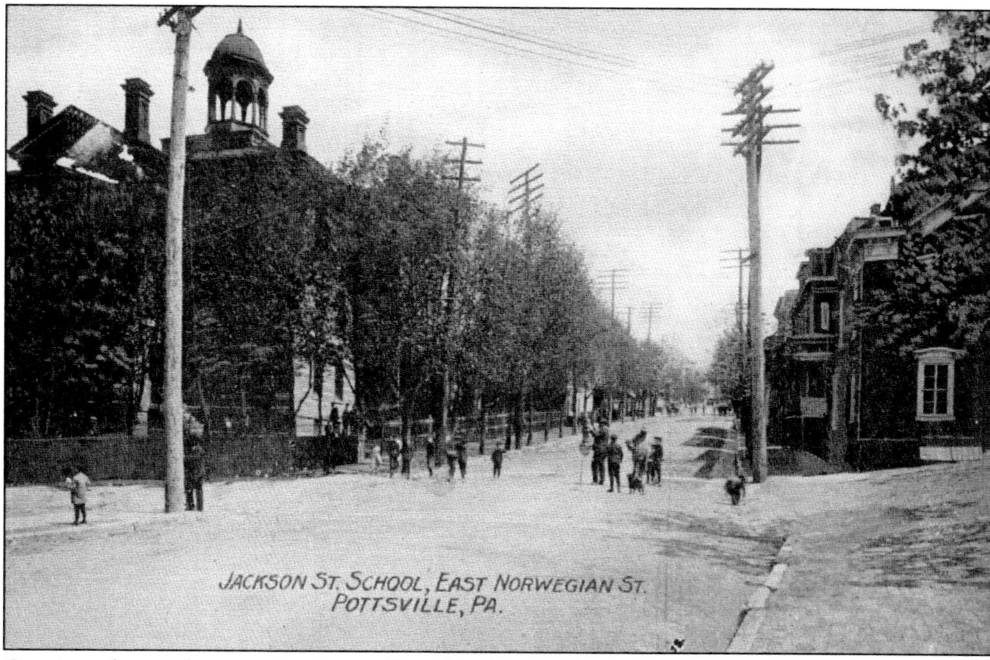

Continued crowding in the Pottsville schools was the impetus for the construction of the Jackson Street School on East Norwegian Street in 1876. The high school, which had been moved from the Bunker Hill Building to the Academy Building at Fifth and West Norwegian Streets in 1868, was re-located to the new Jackson Street building

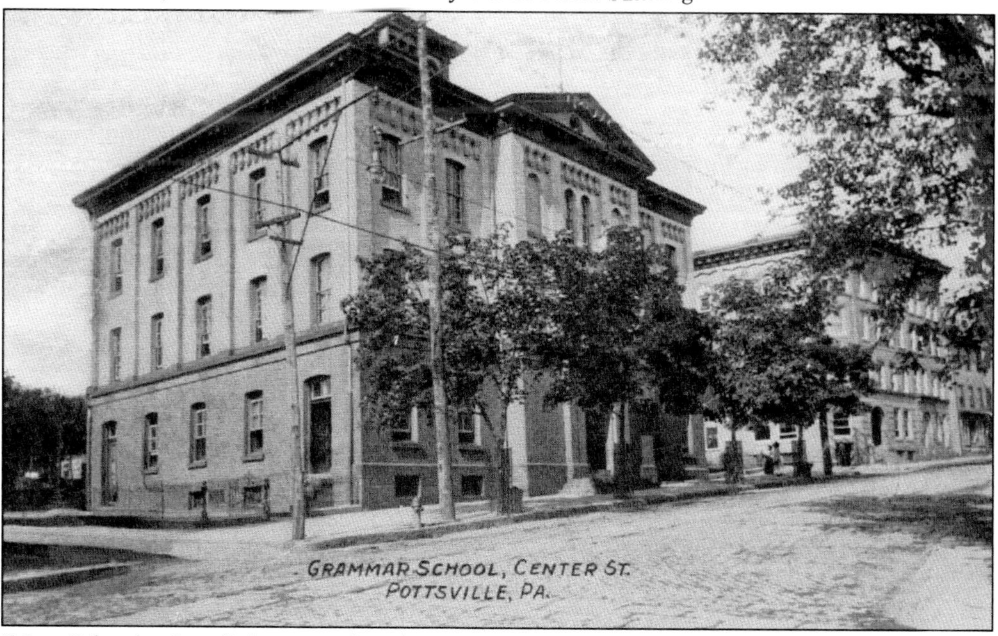

"New School at Last," that was what the *Miners' Journal* said in its April 25, 1863 edition. The newspaper proclaimed that "work will begin immediately, and the building is to be occupied by the first of April, 1864." The building was not occupied until September 25, 1865. The school has been purchased by the Historical Society of Schuylkill County and will become the future headquarters of the Society.

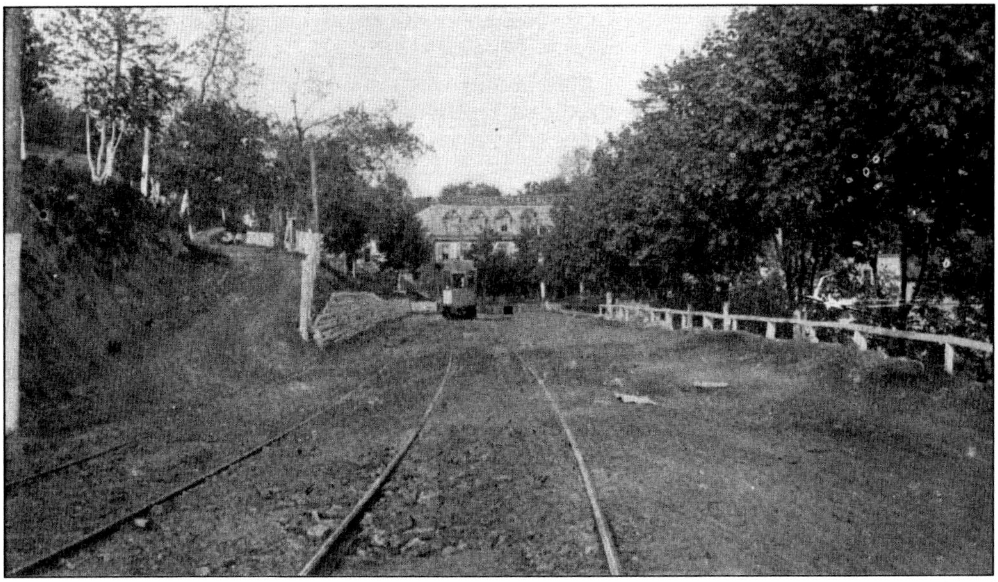

Tumbling Run was a popular playground for eastern Pennsylvanians for 35 years until it closed in 1913. A trolley is arriving at the entrance to Tumbling Run Park in this view. The famous Tumbling Run Hotel was situated at the main entrance. The trees on the right are still there. People sat in the shade under them as they waited for the trolley to take them home.

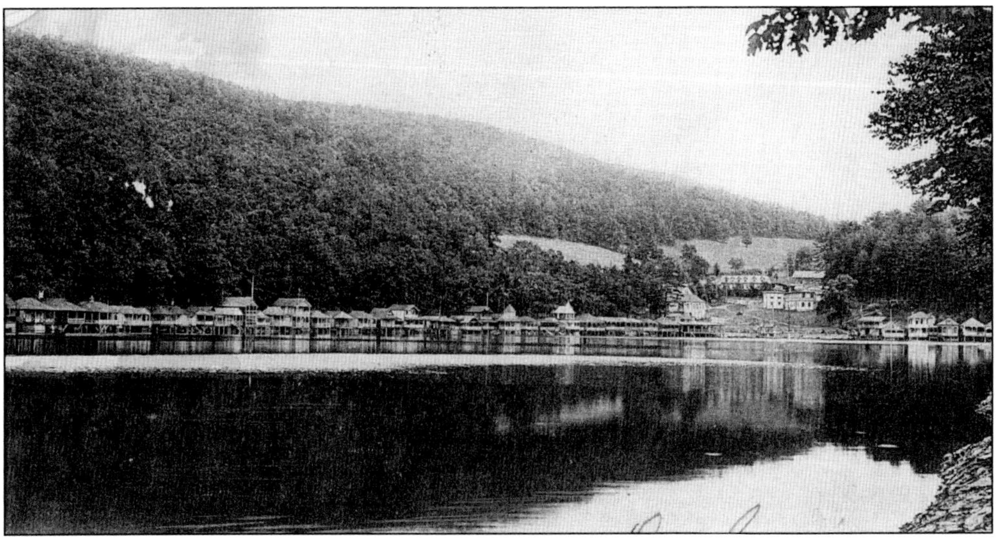

"Dear Cousin Minnie, I will be up on Sat. train leaves at 12:45 o'clock. Louise." That is the message written on this card showing a view of Tumbling Run Lake from the South Side. The card is postmarked Mahanoy City, December 8, 1905, and was sent to Mrs. William Eckhardt, 412 East Centre Street, Mahanoy City, Pennsylvania. There were no zip codes in those days.

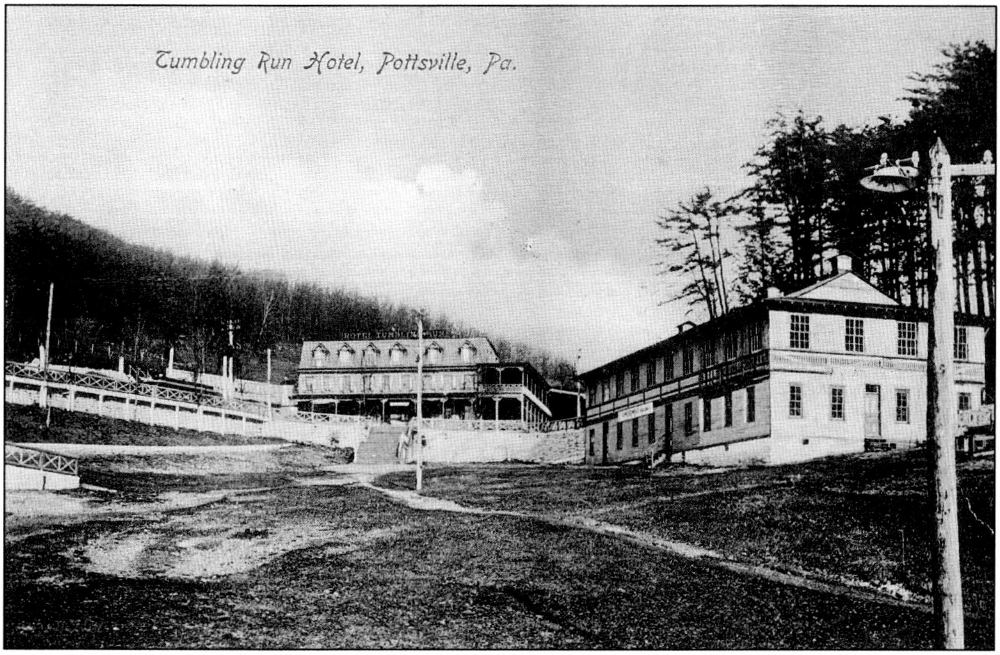

The Tumbling Run Hotel is seen in the middle of this card. The dance hall was on the top floor of the building on the right. The penny arcade was on the ground floor level. This view must have been taken early in the morning before any pleasure seekers had arrived.

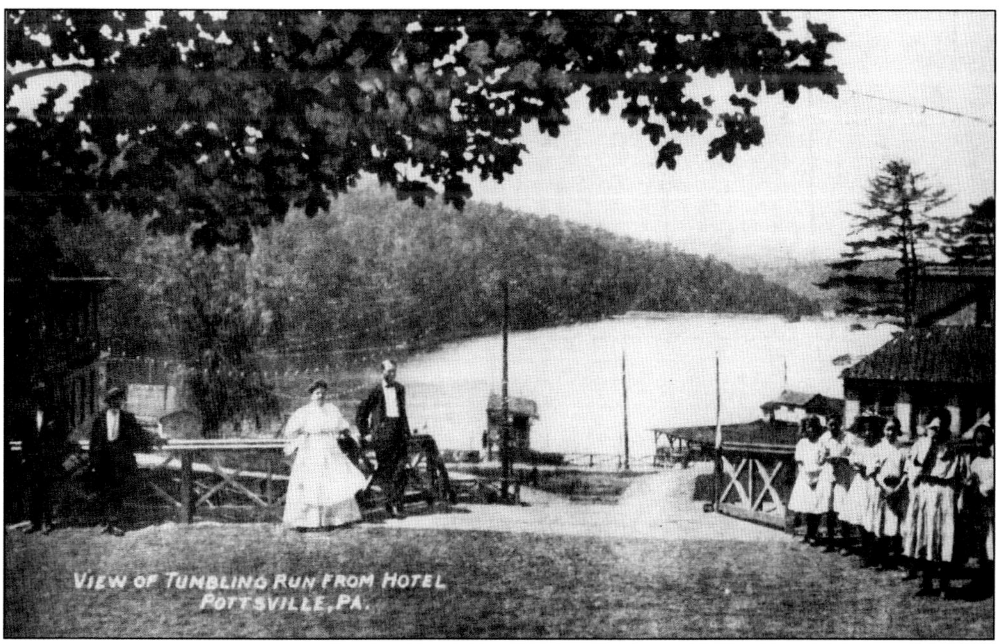

Postcards of Tumbling Run were very popular. The lake can be seen in this view of Tumbling Run from the hotel. Notice the long dress on the woman, and the man wearing a suit in the middle of the image. Young girls on the right are wearing their best dresses as they pose for the photographer.

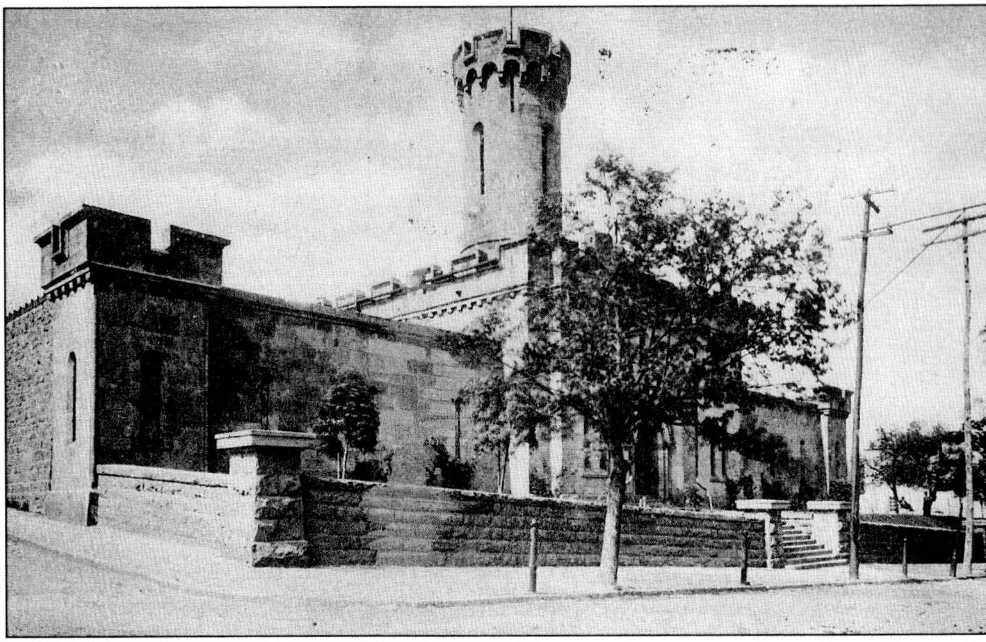

The Schuylkill County jail was built in 1853, and among the inmates that it housed were the Molly Maguires. The message on the right was dated February 27, 1906, and reads, "When will you be at home? C.E.H." It was addressed to Mr. Andrew Malick, Shamokin, Pennsylvania, c/o C.C. Leader's Store, so we know that it was not sent to a prisoner in the jail.

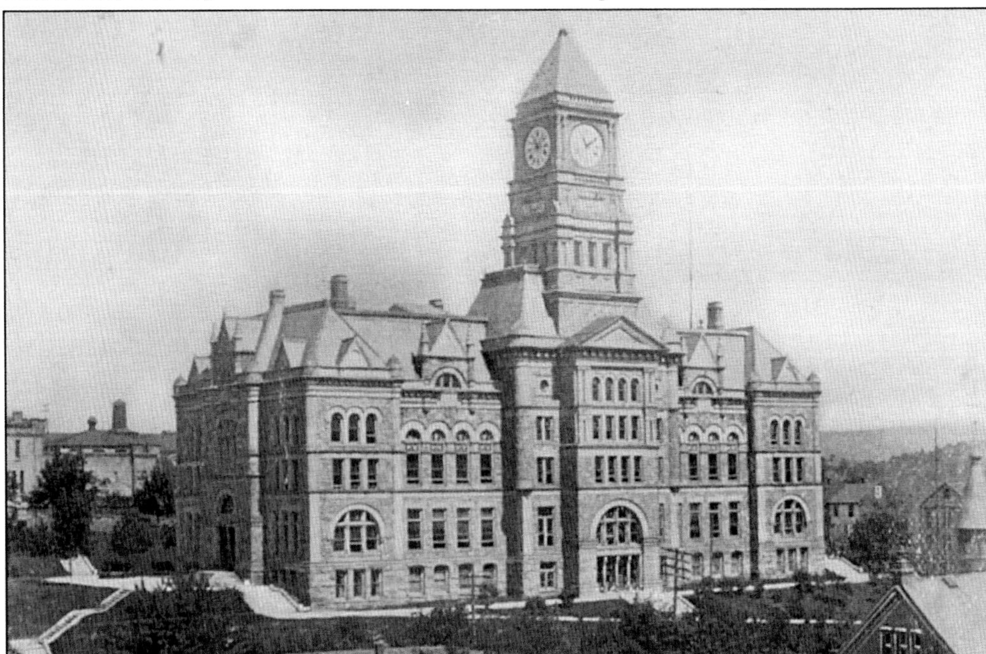

When Schuylkill County was formed on March 11, 1811, the first court was held in the tavern of Abraham Reiffsnyder in Brunswick Township. The county seat was moved from Orwigsburg to Pottsville in 1851. The first courthouse in Pottsville was replaced by the present ornate and elegant courthouse that was built in 1891.

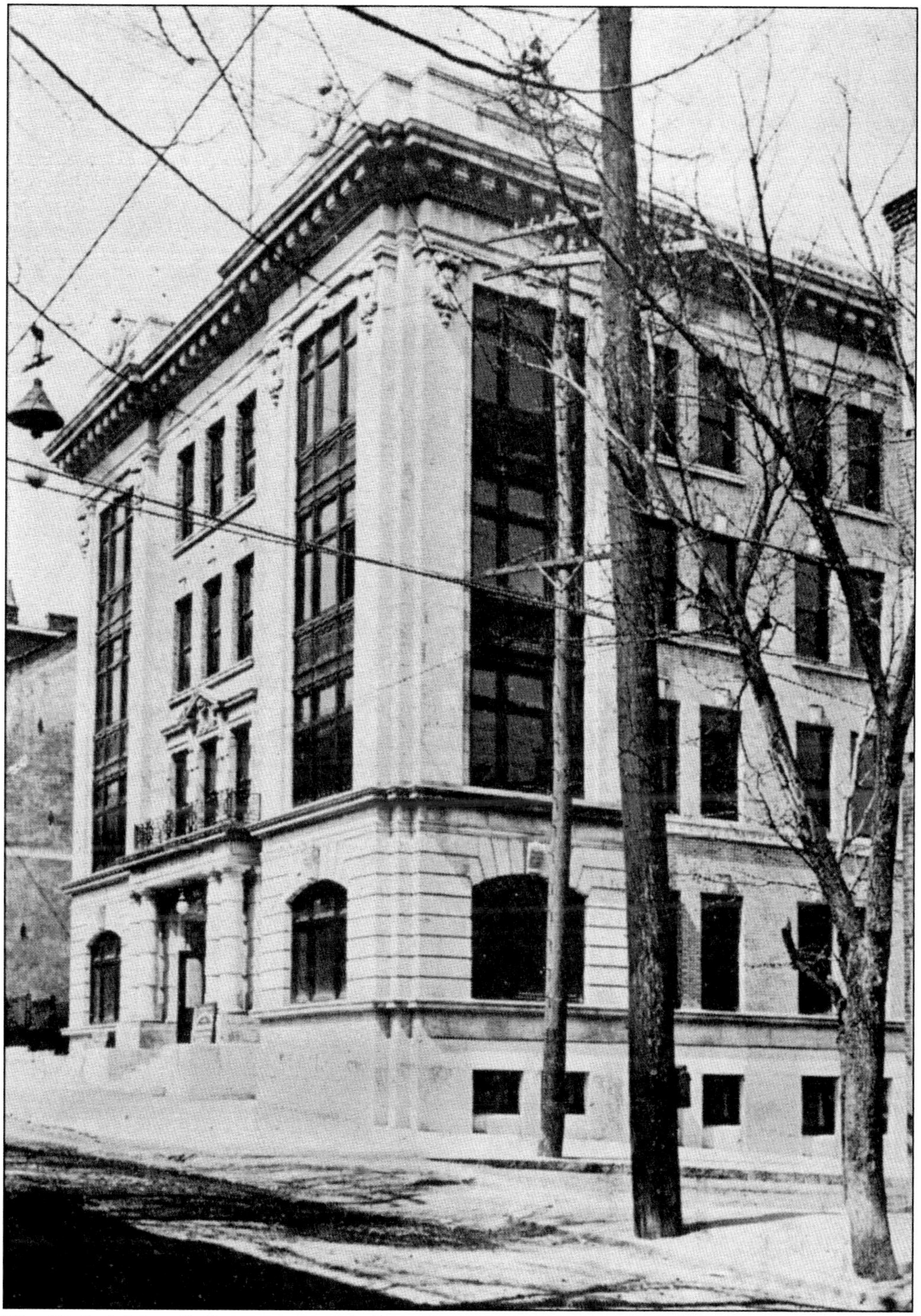

The Philadelphia & Reading Coal & Iron Company was organized in 1870 as an auxiliary of the Philadelphia & Reading Railroad. The company purchased 100,000 acres of coal land and grew to become one of the greatest and most powerful industrial organizations in the United States and the largest mining company in the world.

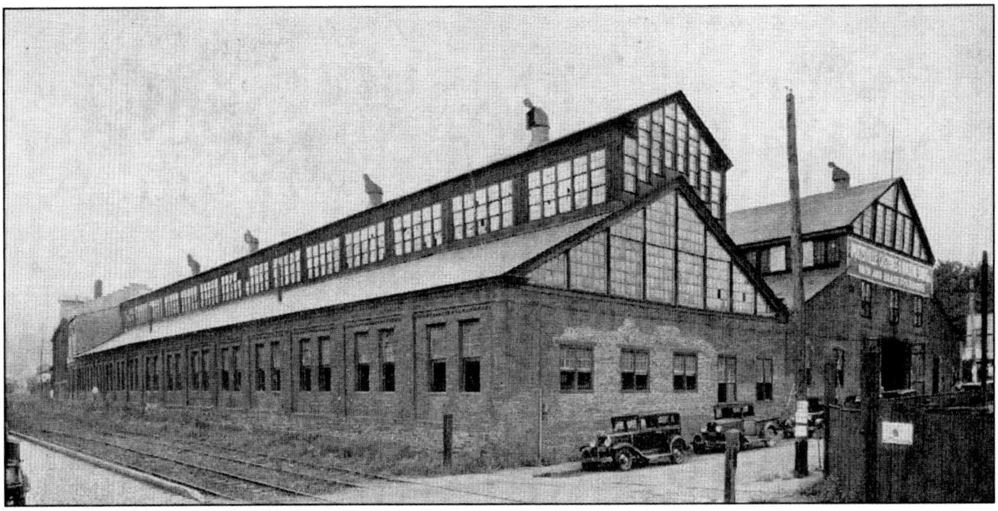

The upper shops of the Pottsville Castings and Machine Shops were located at Railroad Street, today's Progress Avenue, and East Arch Streets. The Pottsville Shops made machinery and equipment for the coal mines in Schuylkill County, and became part of the Philadelphia & Reading Coal & Iron Company in 1879. This image is not a postcard, but is an ink blotter instead.

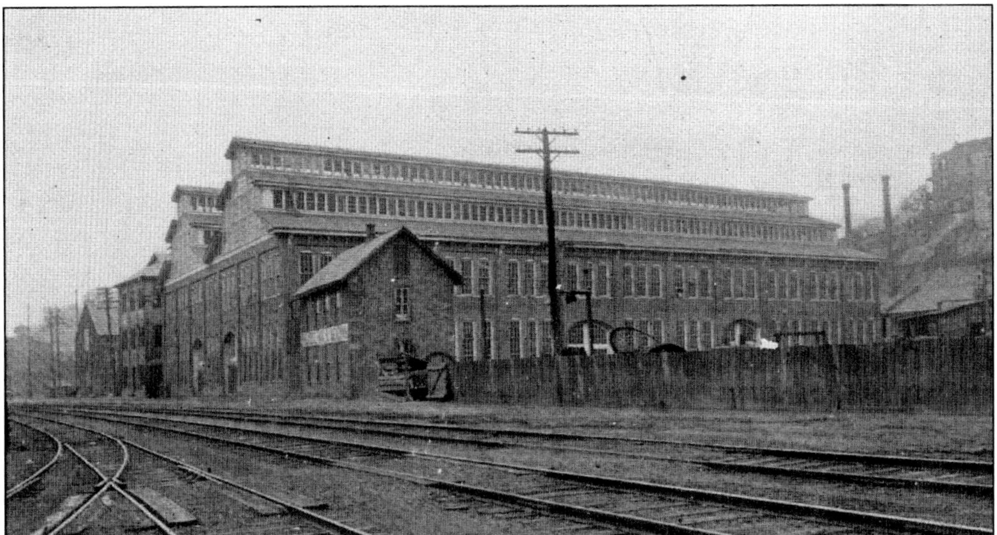

The lower shops were on Coal Street, now Route 61, and ran south from East Norwegian Street. The shops were well adapted to the needs of the mining industry, and manufactured special machinery and tools that were used in the collieries and coal mines. During WW II, propeller blades for ships were made here. Shortly after the war, the shops were closed.

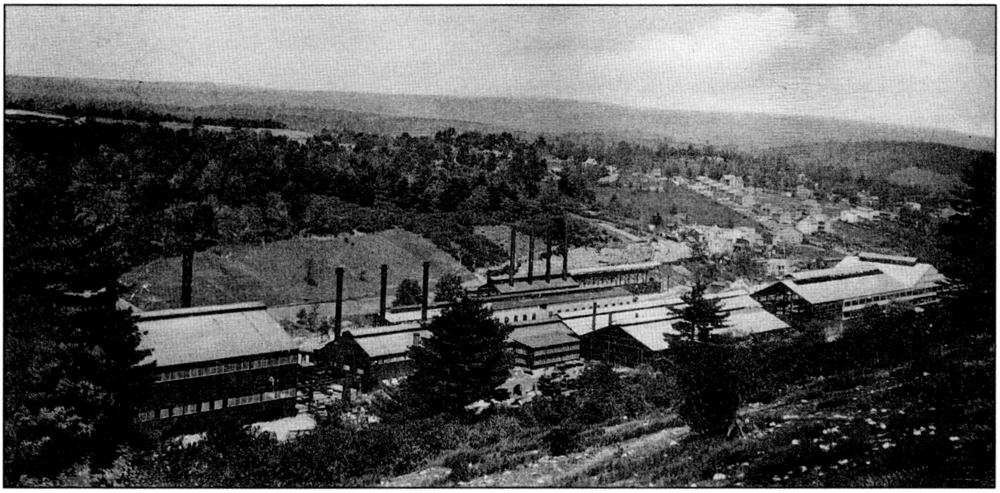

Charles M. Atkins came to Pottsville in 1853 and, with his two brothers, purchased a rolling mill. In 1864 Atkins purchased the Pottsville Rolling Mill in the Fishbach section of Pottsville. The business grew so much that the mills had to be expanded and eventually covered 8 acres. The name was changed, and it became the Eastern Steel Co. Mills.

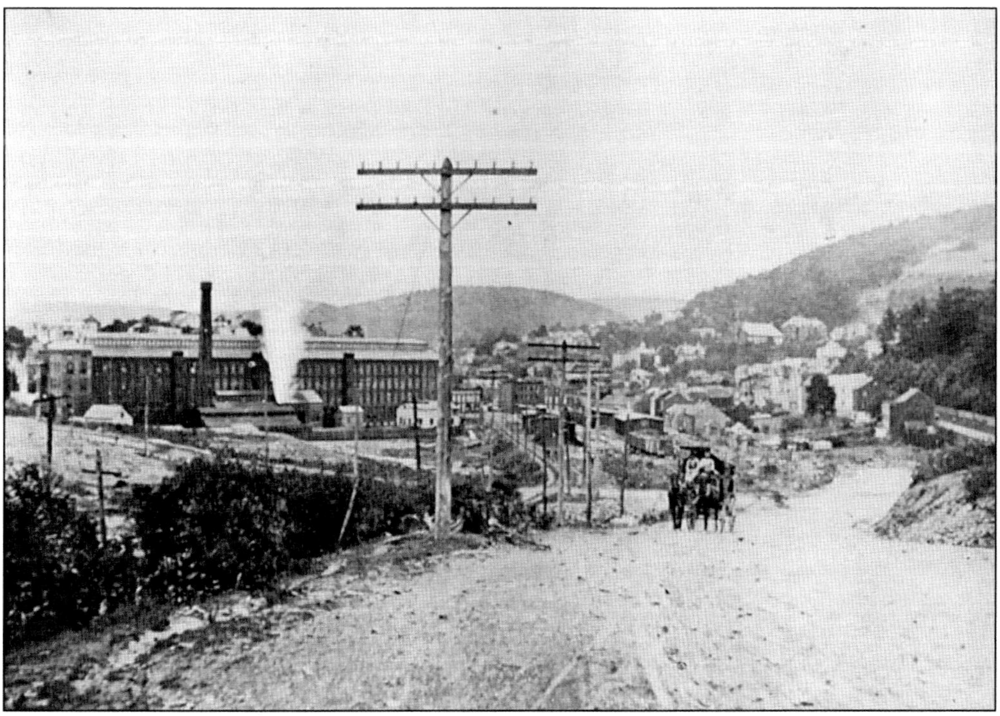

The Tilt Silk Mill is seen in this view looking east from near where the Pottsville Area Middle School is located today. It was brought to Pottsville by the board of trade after fierce competition from Allentown and Hazleton. It was completed and put into operation in 1888. At one time there were two thousand looms in it, and as many as 1,500 people were employed by the mill.

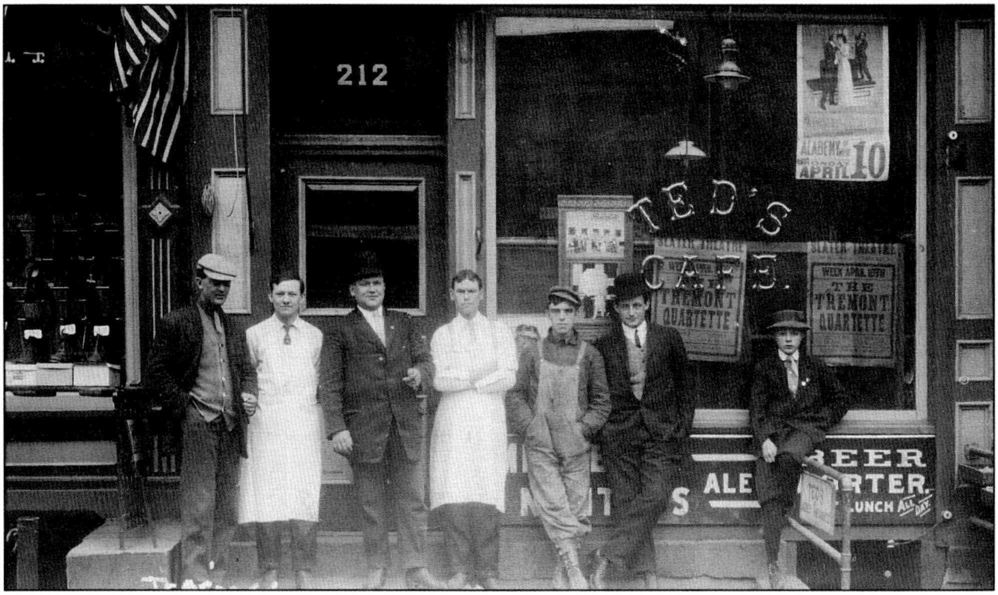

Ted Bushar's Sauer Kraut Band was a popular Pottsville musical institution. It was a comic band and was organized in 1907 when the old Moulders Band at the upper shops formed the Sauer Kraut Band. Ted Bushar became the director of the band, and it appeared in the Philadelphia Mummer's Parade until 1921. Ted can be seen in this view standing in front of his popular Ted's Cafe on Centre Street.

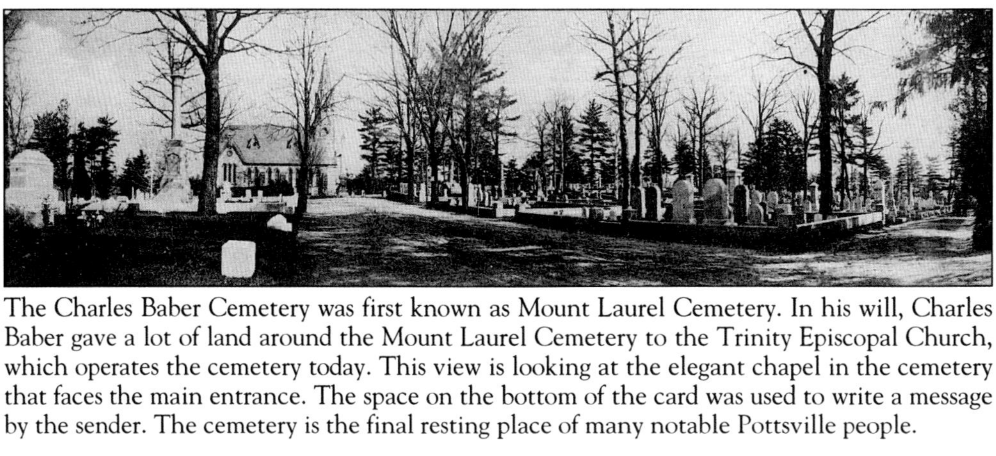

The Charles Baber Cemetery was first known as Mount Laurel Cemetery. In his will, Charles Baber gave a lot of land around the Mount Laurel Cemetery to the Trinity Episcopal Church, which operates the cemetery today. This view is looking at the elegant chapel in the cemetery that faces the main entrance. The space on the bottom of the card was used to write a message by the sender. The cemetery is the final resting place of many notable Pottsville people.

Three

Schuylkill County Houses of Worship

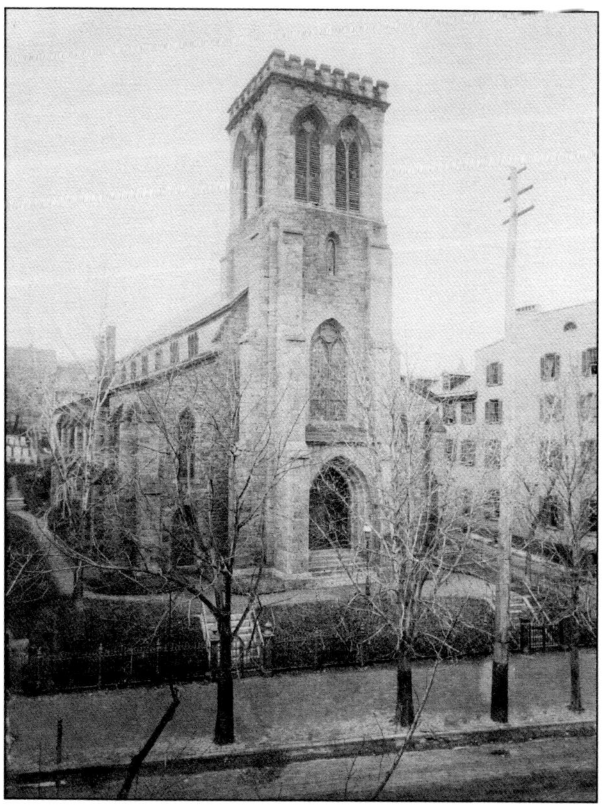

Trinity Episcopal Church in Pottsville is the city's oldest house of worship, constructed in 1830. This turn-of-the-century image shows a tree-lined street scene at the corner of Howard Avenue and Centre Street in Pottsville. Notice the old Penn Hall Hotel across Howard Avenue.

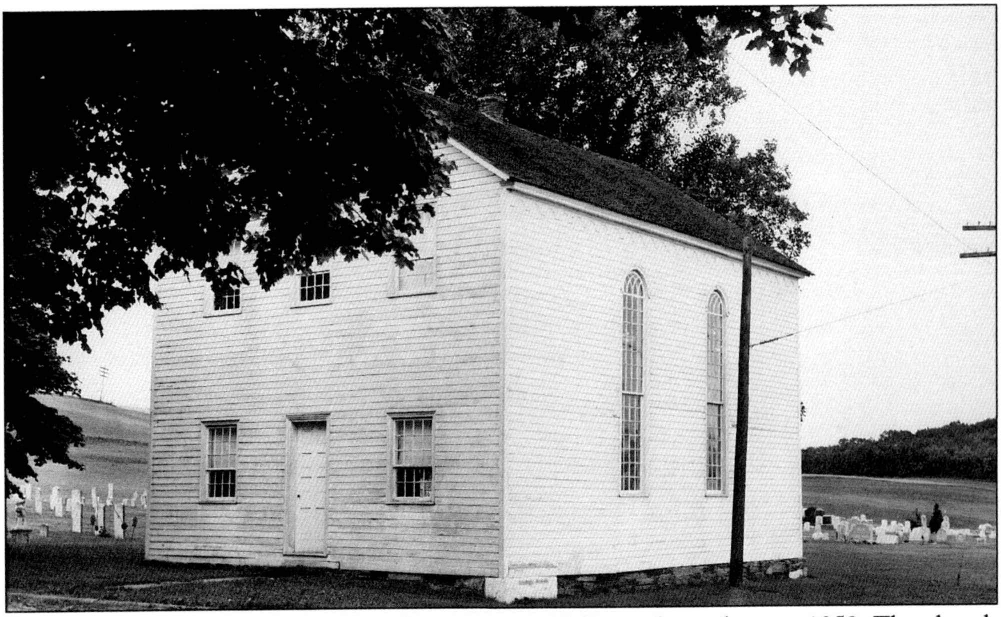

The "Old White" church situated in the Ringtown Valley is shown here in 1959. The church was built in March of 1842 and served both the Lutheran and Reformed denominations of the valley. The Old White, or "Union" church, was the first church built on the north side of the Broad Mountain in Schuylkill County.

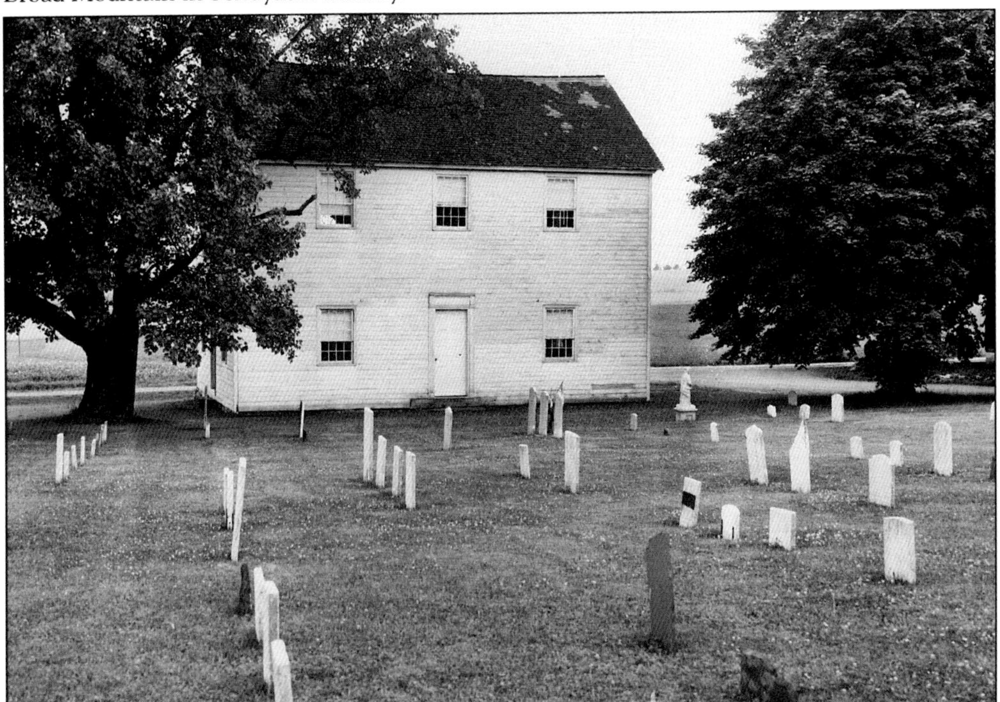

Looking east from the cemetery, the Old White church is pictured in this rural setting. The first burials in the cemetery preceded the construction of the church. Several Revolutionary War veterans and early settlers to the Catawissa Valley are buried here.

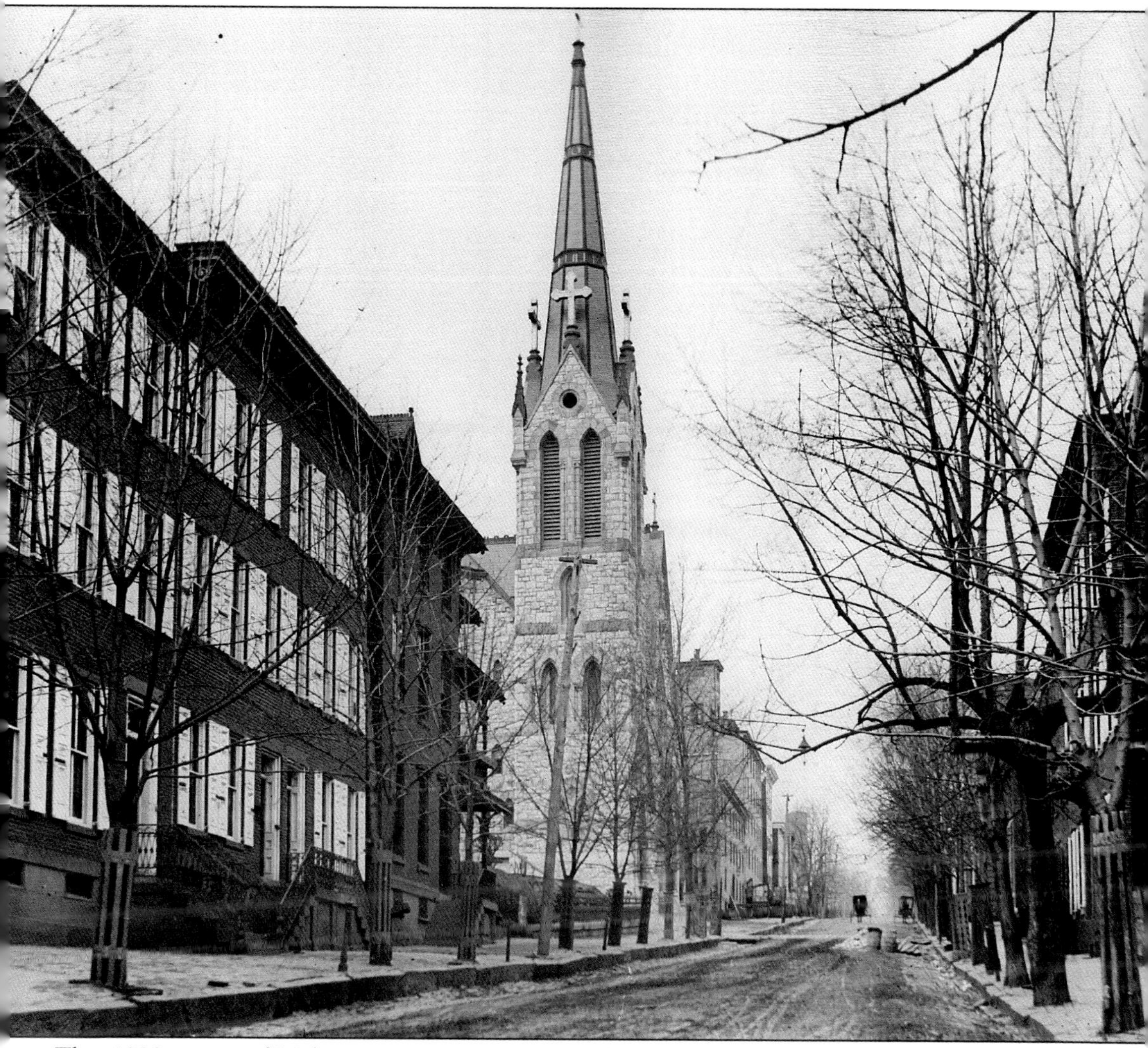

This 1890s scene of Mahantongo Street in Pottsville reveals the tall spire and facade of St. Patrick's Roman Catholic Church. The original church was built in 1828 on land donated by John Pott, founder of the city. The present church structure was built in 1891–92.

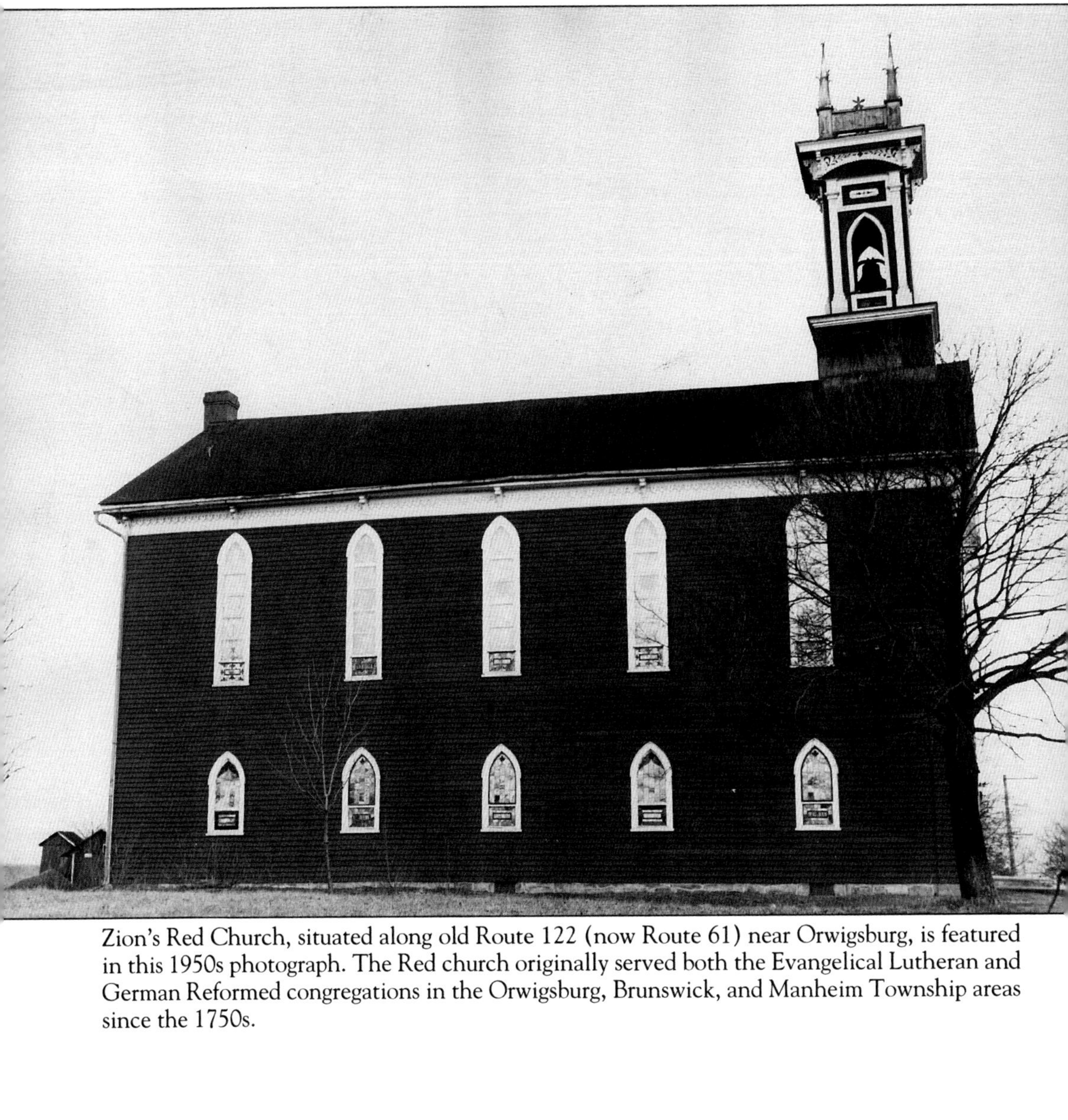

Zion's Red Church, situated along old Route 122 (now Route 61) near Orwigsburg, is featured in this 1950s photograph. The Red church originally served both the Evangelical Lutheran and German Reformed congregations in the Orwigsburg, Brunswick, and Manheim Township areas since the 1750s.

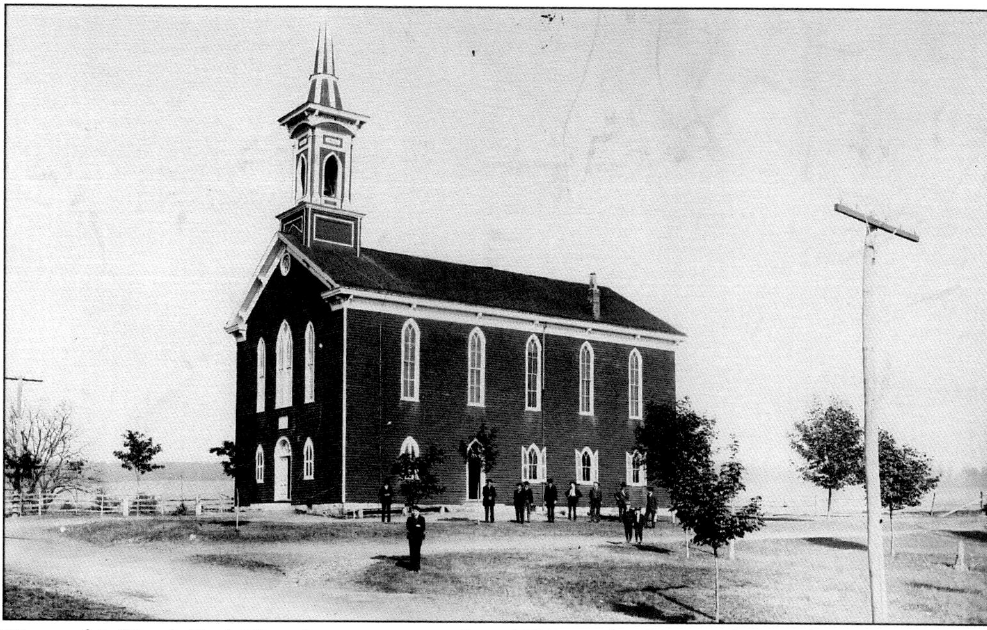

Pictured is Zion's Red Church as it appeared in 1890 south of Orwigsburg. This image is taken from the old Centre Turnpike looking north across where Route 61 follows today.

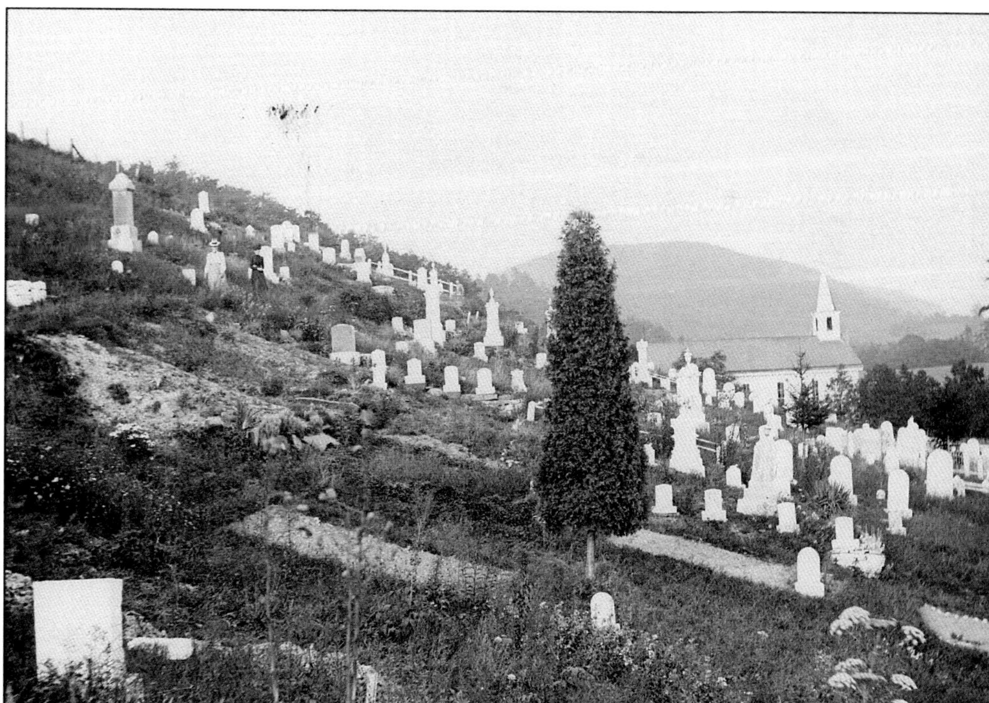

Frieden's Lutheran Church at New Ringgold is shown near the right center of this 1890s image. Frieden's was established here prior to 1830 and served the Lutheran and Reformed Congregations around New Ringgold, McKeansburg, East Brunswick Township, and the Lewistown Valley. Frieden's church building was constructed in 1875.

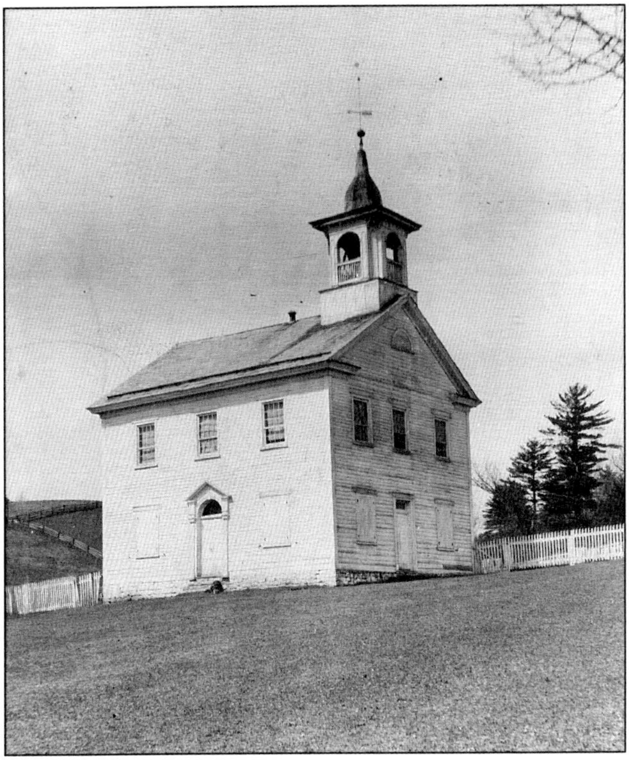

Established in 1780, Jacob's Evangelical Lutheran Church is located in Pine Grove Township and is one of the earliest churches in the county. Early residents of Pine Grove settled here beginning in the 1760s. The church was built in May of 1833 and today stands along Route 443 just to the west of Pine Grove near Interstate 81.

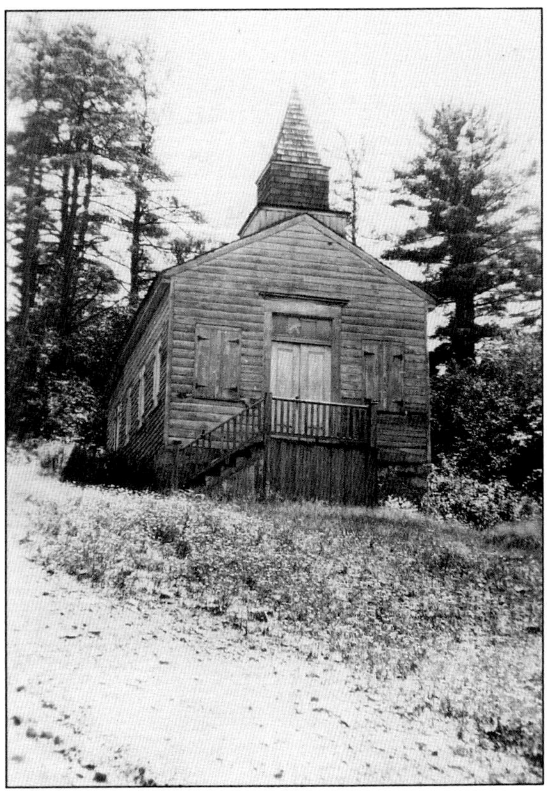

The Mechanicsville Chapel, as pictured in this 1929 photograph, stood at the corner of Park and First Streets in that borough. The chapel was constructed prior to 1881 and was served by the Episcopal church in Pottsville. It also provided Sunday School and church services for residents of Mechanicsville and Port Carbon.

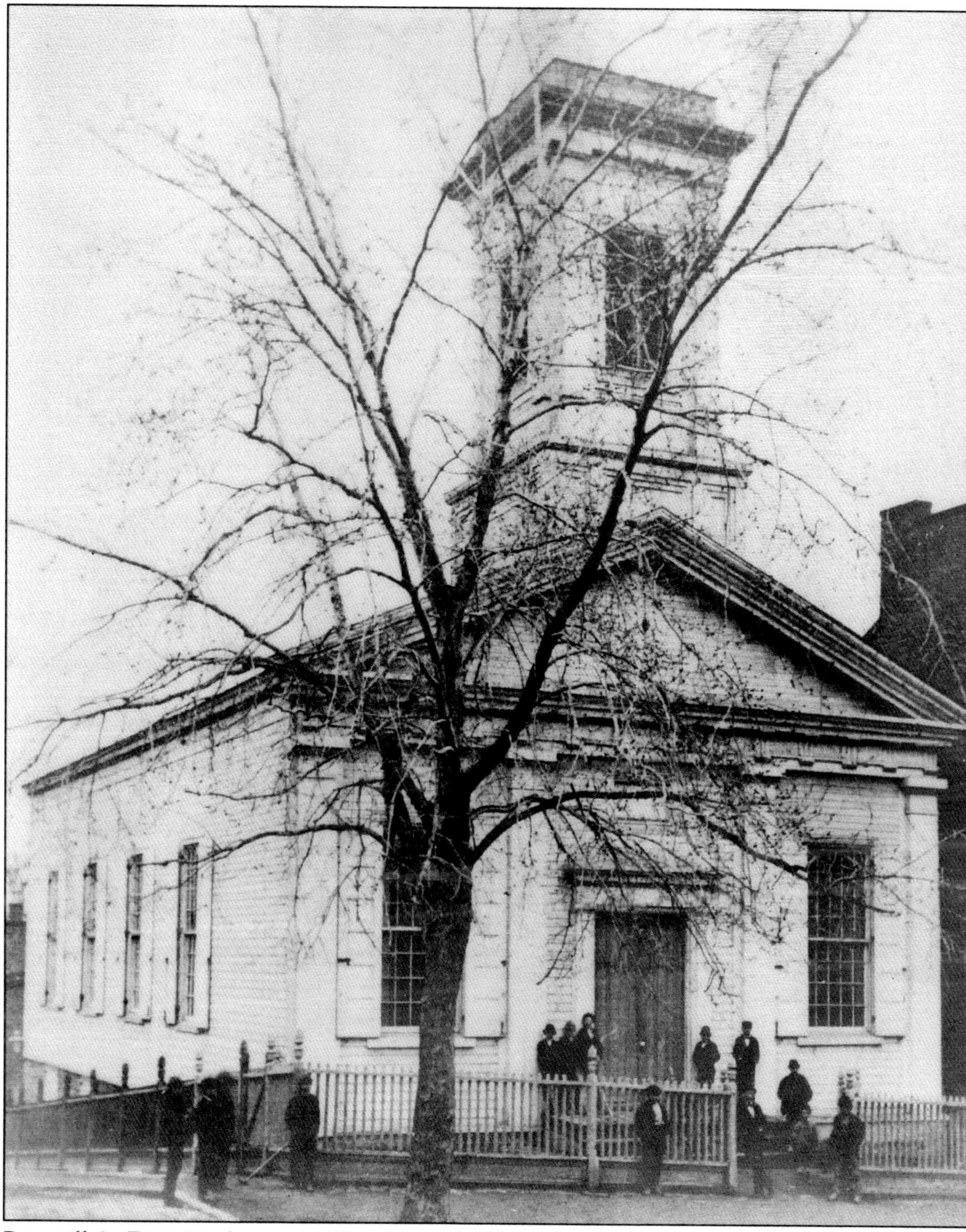

Pottsville's First Presbyterian Church is shown in this *c.* 1870s photograph. This image was taken just prior to the construction of the present-day structure on the corner of Third and Mahantongo Street. The cornerstone was laid in August of 1838 and construction was completed in 1842. This building was replaced by the present church in 1874.

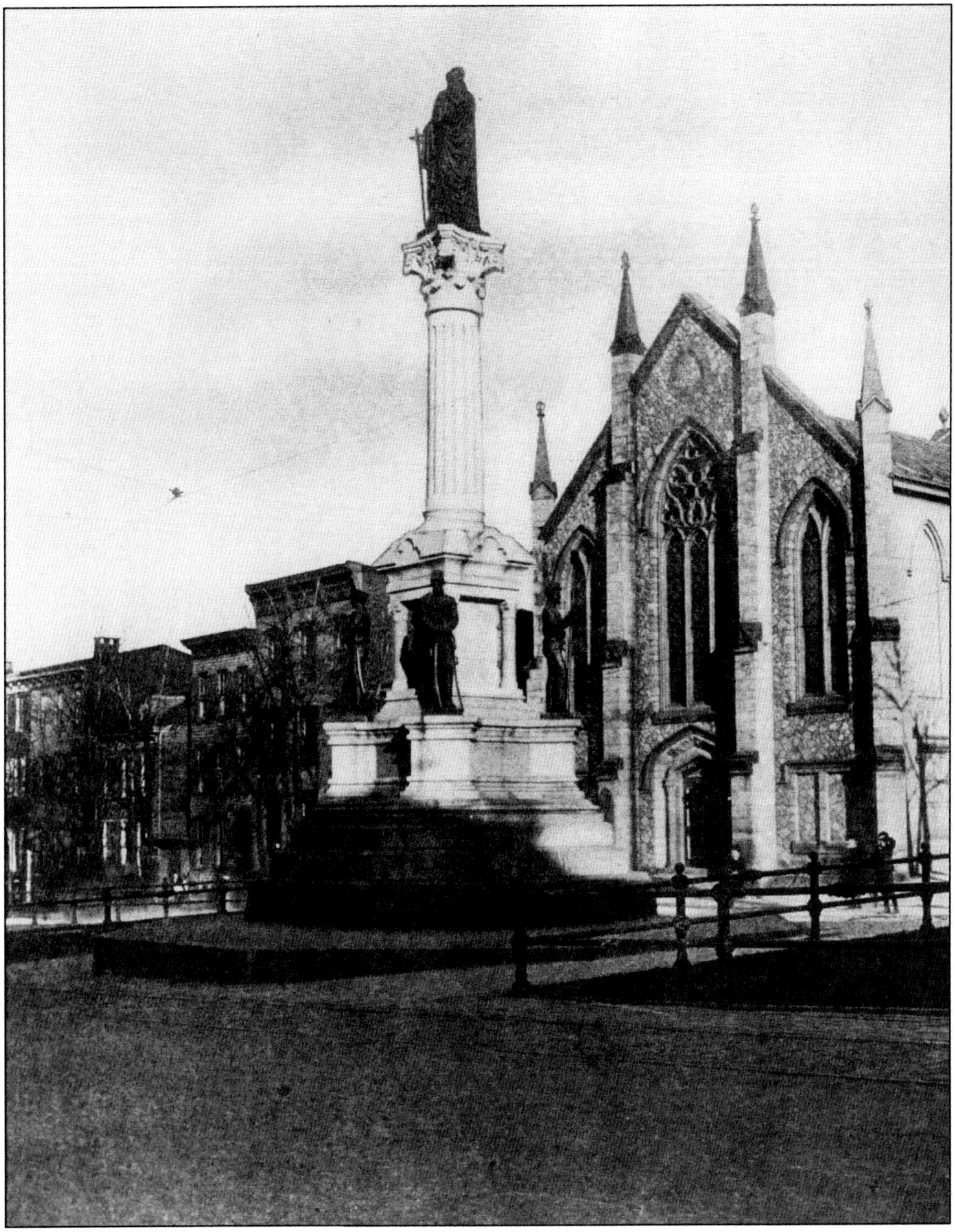

Pottsville's Second Presbyterian Church is featured in this late-afternoon 1906 image on Garfield Square. Originally, this church served the Second Methodist Episcopal congregation but was later occupied by the Presbyterian congregation in 1862. This building witnessed major renovations in the 1870s, 1896, and again in 1914.

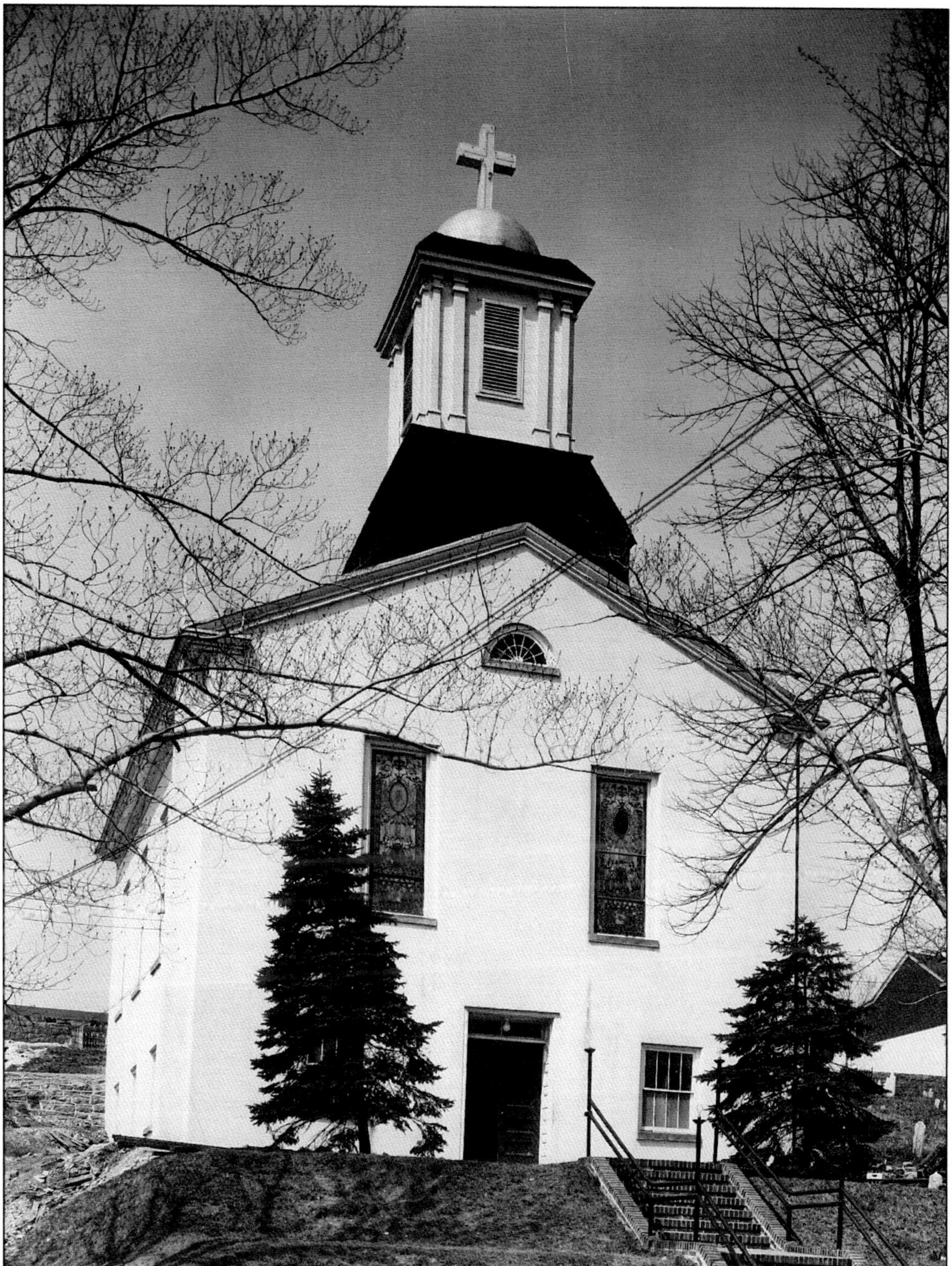

The Presbyterian Church of Port Carbon is featured here in this 1950s image. The church was built in 1833–34. Today's Port Carbon Presbyterians attend church in Saint Clair and Pottsville since the closure of the church in the 1960s. The structure is now used as the Port Carbon Borough Hall and a district court office.

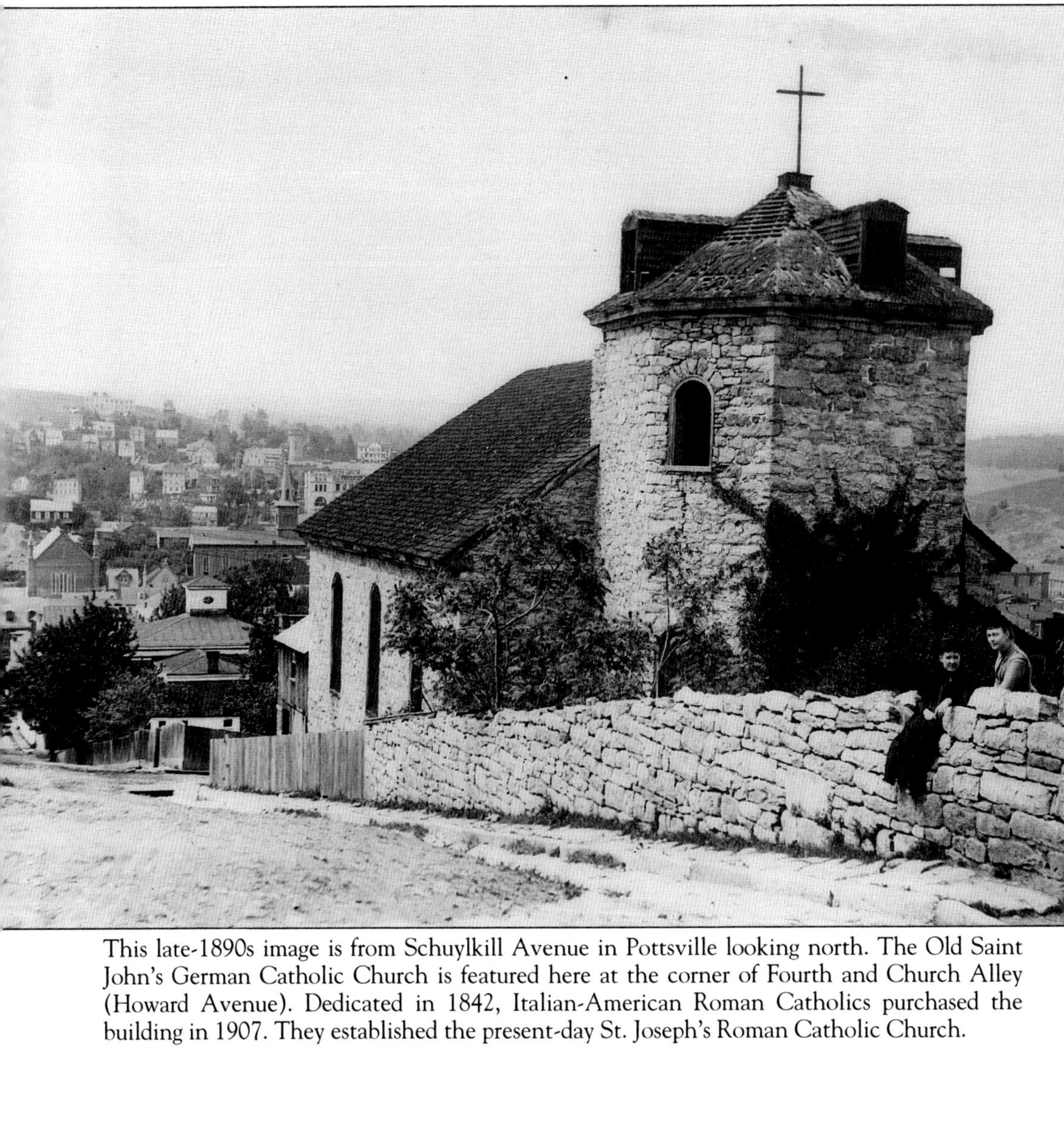

This late-1890s image is from Schuylkill Avenue in Pottsville looking north. The Old Saint John's German Catholic Church is featured here at the corner of Fourth and Church Alley (Howard Avenue). Dedicated in 1842, Italian-American Roman Catholics purchased the building in 1907. They established the present-day St. Joseph's Roman Catholic Church.

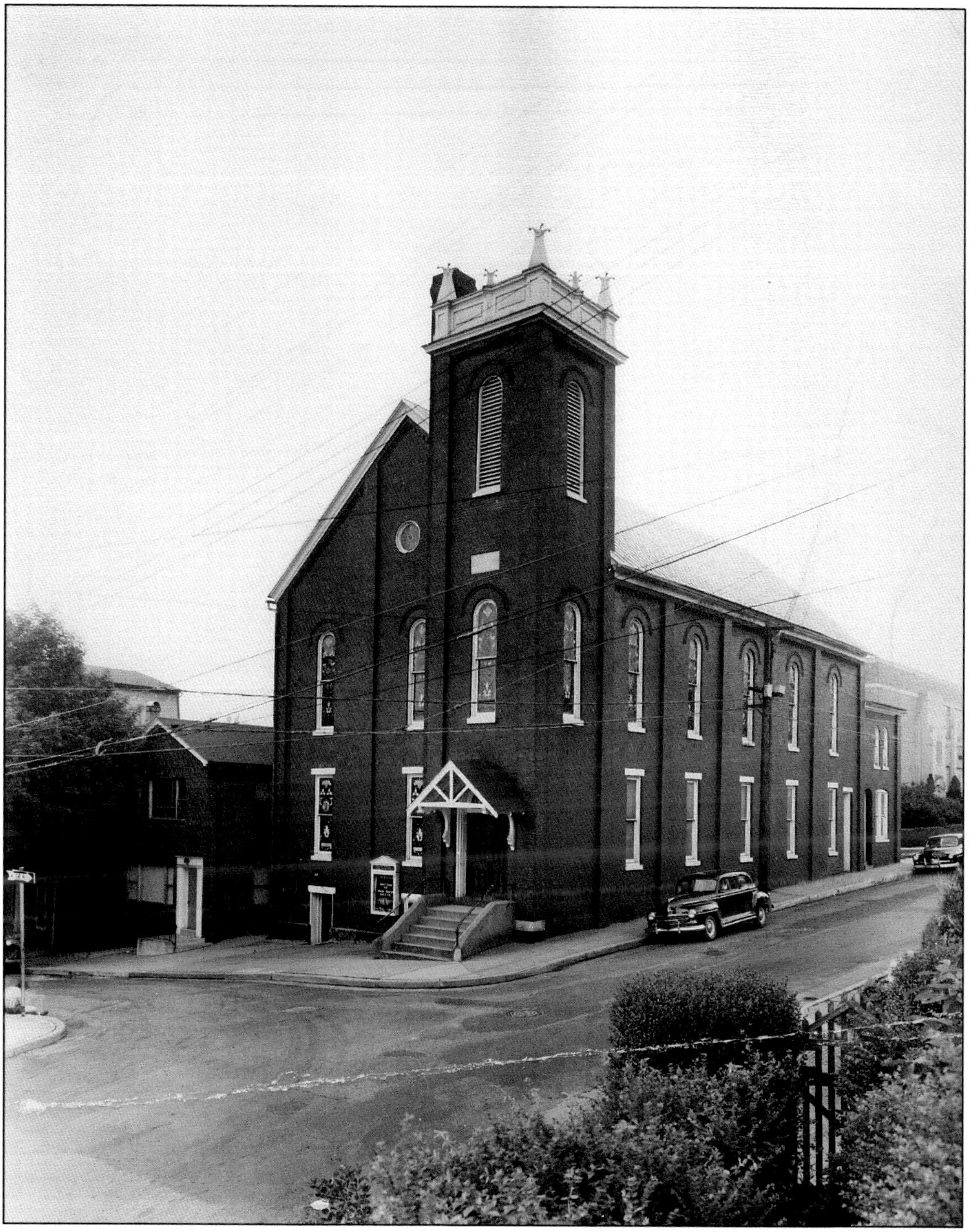

Grace Evangelical Church in Schuylkill Haven is featured in this 1950s image. Located at the corner of St. Peter and Union Streets, the church building was demolished in 1974. The present-day congregation attends services today at the new location at Jefferson and Earl Stoyer Drive. The congregation was established at Schuylkill Haven in 1830.

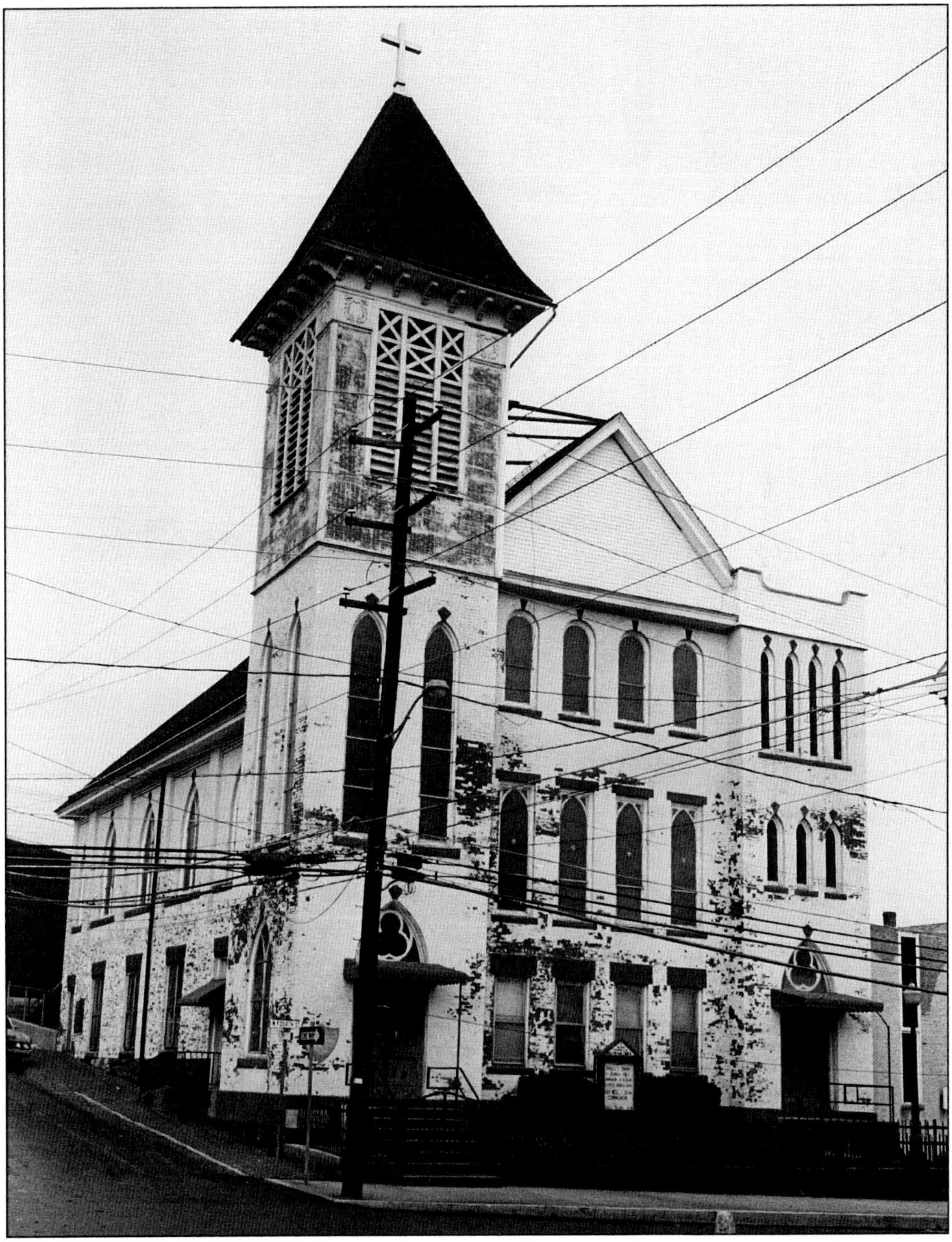

The Zion Lutheran Church located at the corner of Fourth and Lewis Streets in Minersville is seen here prior to its renovations during the summer of 1982. The Zion Lutheran Church was formed as the German Evangelical Lutheran Zion's Congregation prior to 1849.

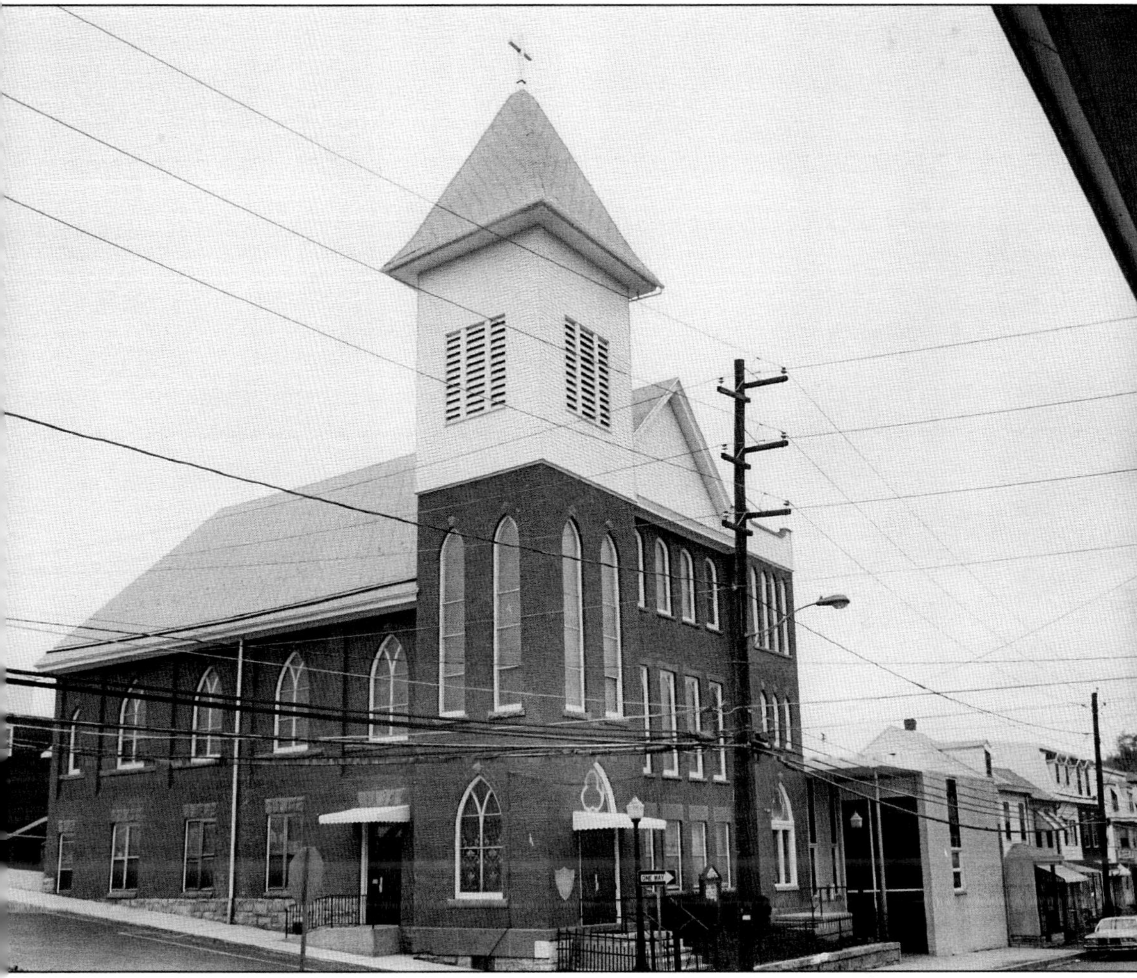

This is a later image of the Zion Lutheran Church in Minersville after renovations in October 1982. Restoration of the red brick and the unfortunate elimination of cornice and woodworking in the bell tower are noted changes. This structure was built in 1897 at the cost of $6,600.

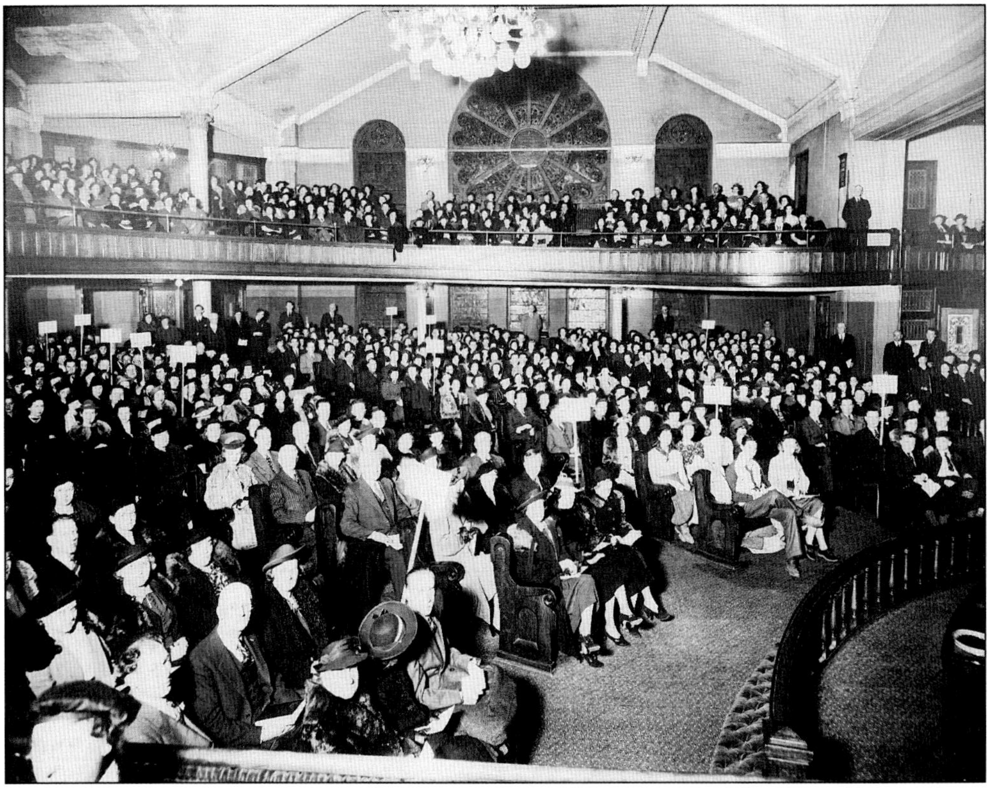

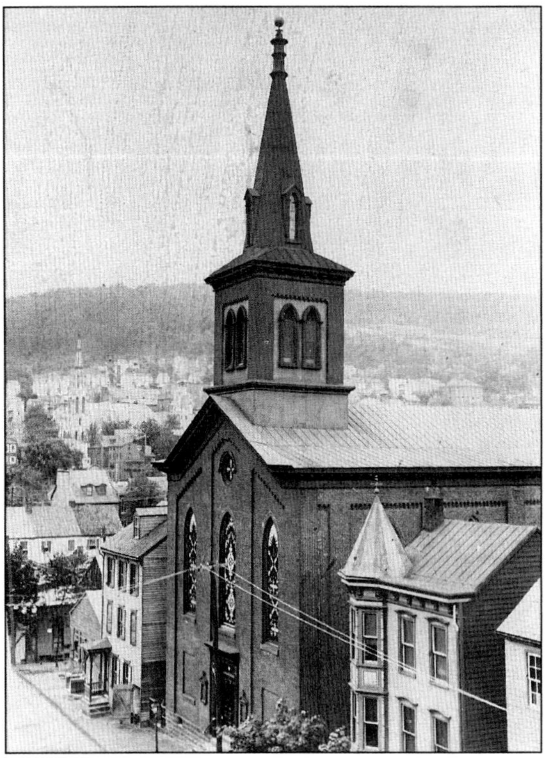

The interior of the United Methodist Church on Market Street in Pottsville is shown in this 1940s era image. Notice the configuration of the church pews and aisles and the large rose window in the top center of the photograph. The challenge in this image is finding a woman in the crowd who is not wearing a hat.

The Trinity Lutheran Church, located at Third and Race Streets in Pottsville, is shown in this 1890s image as seen from in front of the new Schuylkill County Courthouse building. The German Evangelical Lutheran Church was established in Pottsville in 1834. Built in 1867–68, this structure was replaced by the current structure located almost on the same site.

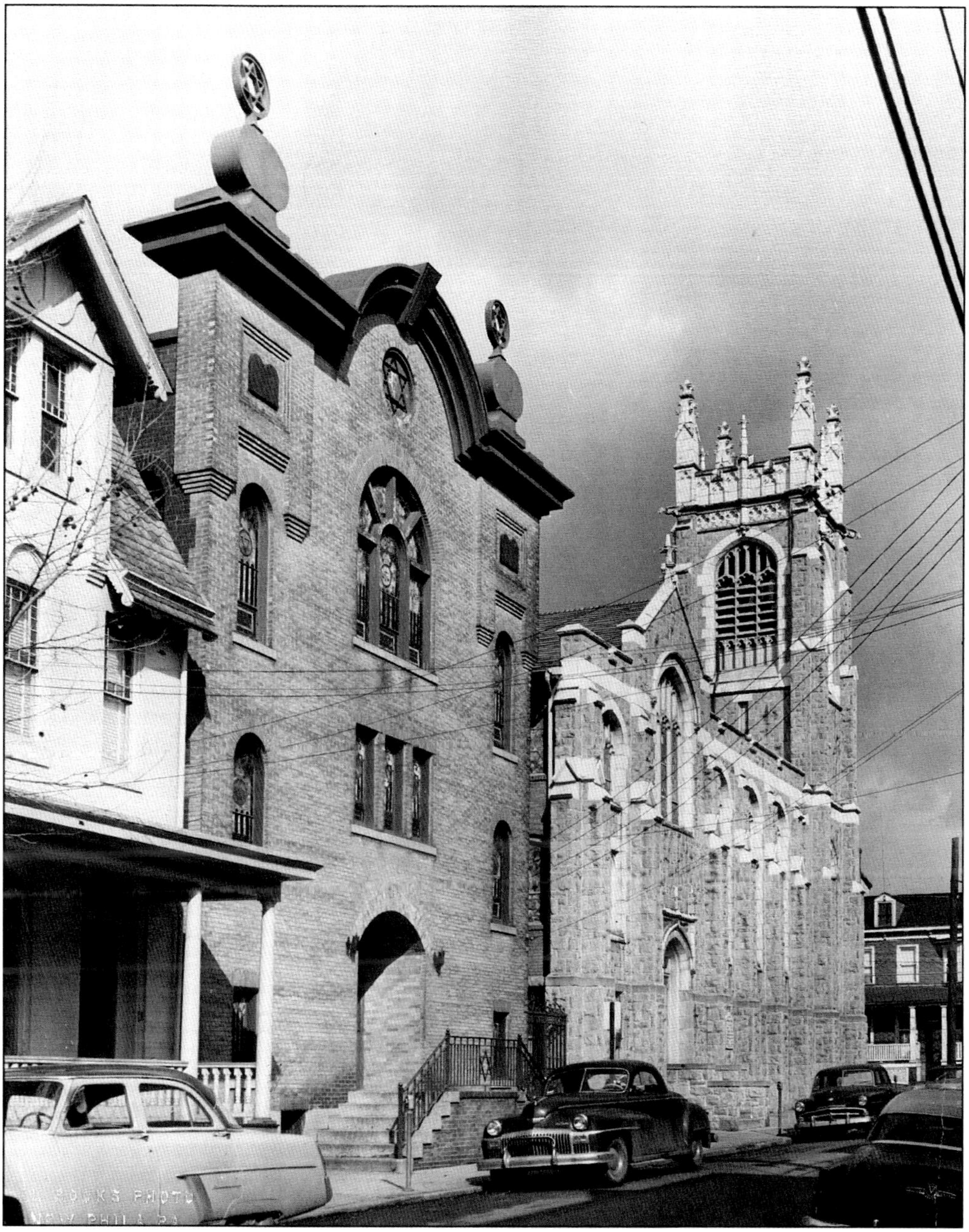

The Oheb Zedeck Synagogue, located along Arch Street in Pottsville, is shown in this 1956 image. The Jewish community established this synagogue in 1875. The Pottsville area Jewish community now worships at the new synagogue, which was built on Mahantongo Street. The present-day Trinity Lutheran Church is seen in this image.

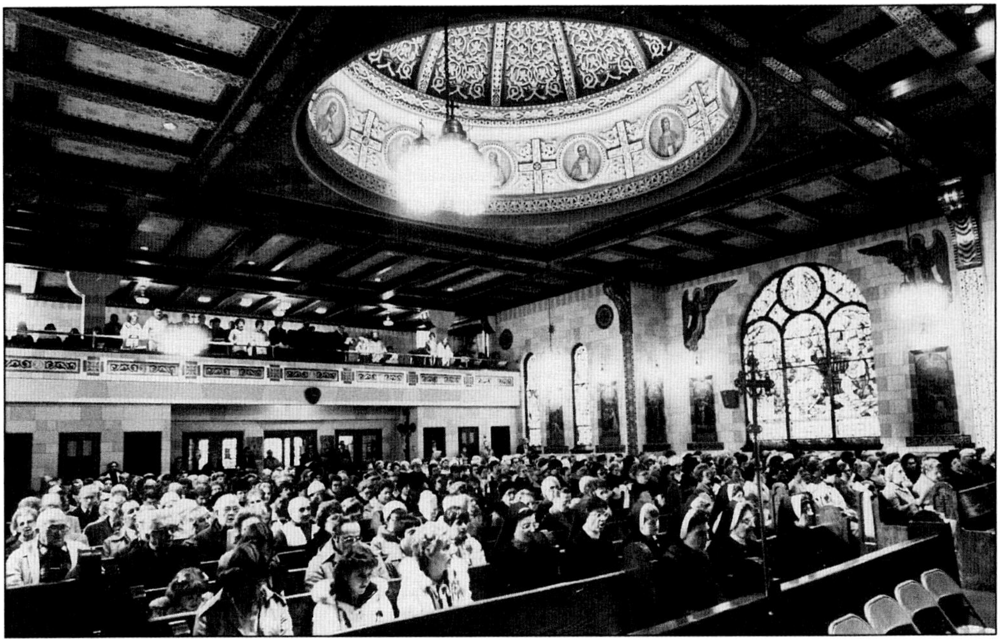

This 1981 image taken inside Saint Nicholas Ukrainian Catholic Church in Minersville provides a unique view of this beautiful church located along Front Street. Saint Nicholas Byzantine Catholic Church was established in 1916. The present-day church was constructed during the 1930s. Pay special attention to the ornate design on the dome of the cathedral.

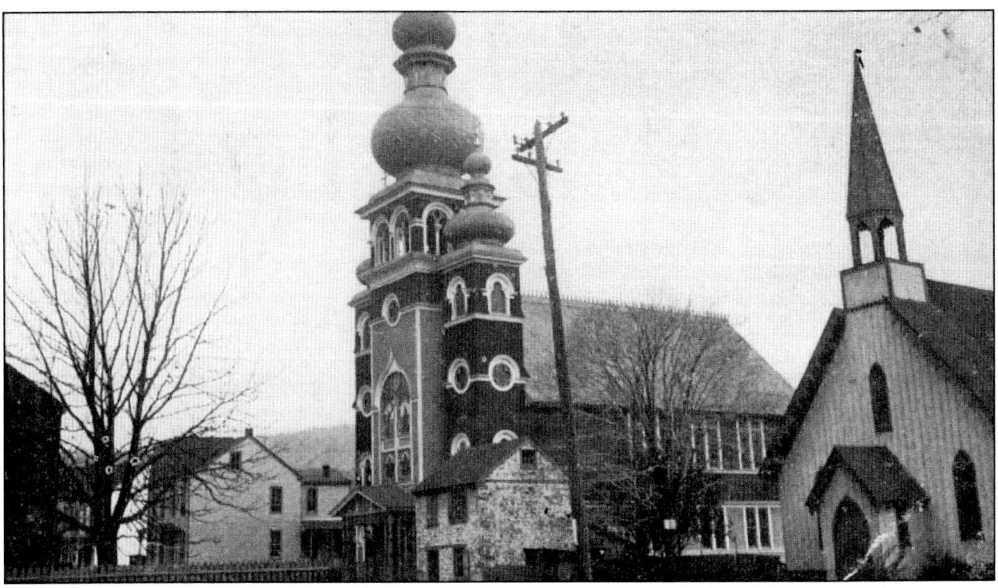

St. Michael's Russian Orthodox Church in Saint Clair is seen in this post-turn-of-the-century image along North Nicholas Street in the borough. The "onion" dome, typical of coal region Greek and Byzantine Catholic churches, is clearly visible in this photograph. The nearby Episcopal church is dwarfed in comparison to St. Michael's, which was established here in 1897.

Four

Scenes along Old Route 122

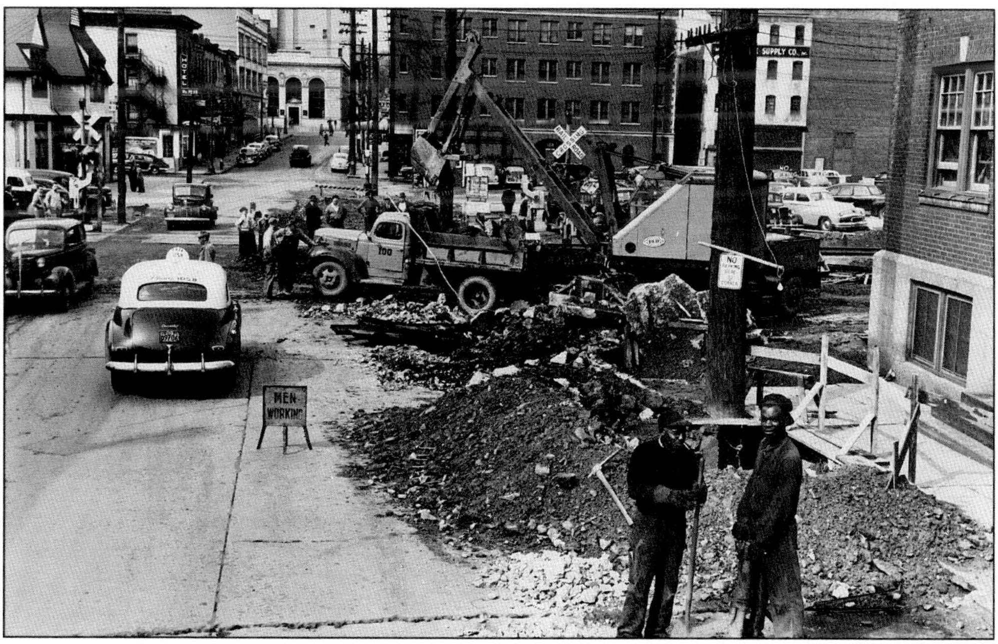

Looking west along Norwegian Street in Pottsville, highway construction at Coal Street (now Claude A. Lord Boulevard) marks the arrival of Route 122. The Reading Railroad Station is to the left of this 1950 image. Notice the Hotel William Penn and the front of the Pennsylvania National Bank. The Pennsylvania Railroad tracks are seen in the foreground.

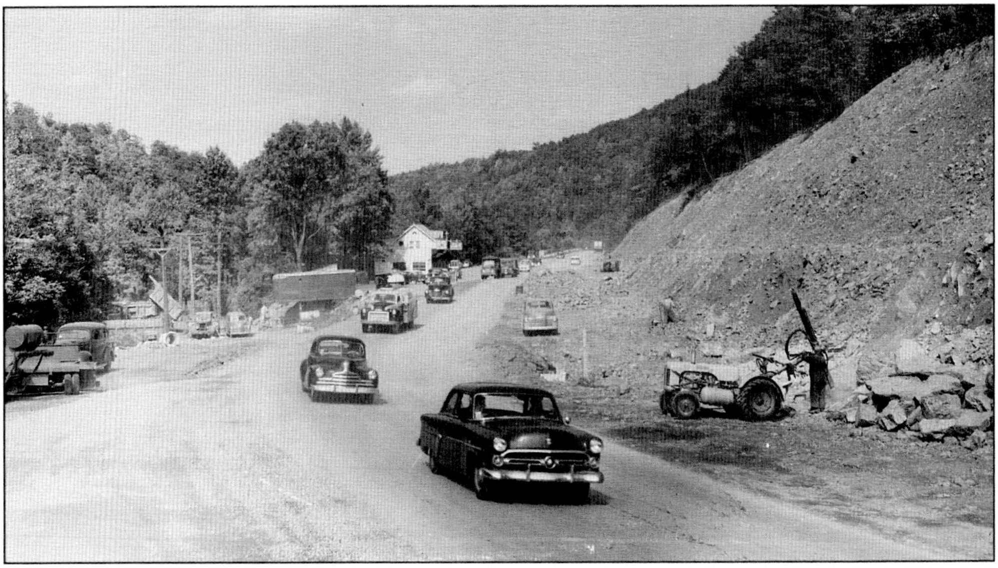

Construction of the new four-lane highway near Port Clinton is shown in this 1950s image. Excavation along the northbound lane has reduced traffic to one lane only. Following the path of the King's Highway and later the Centre Turnpike, Route 61 through Port Clinton remains a critical local transportation artery.

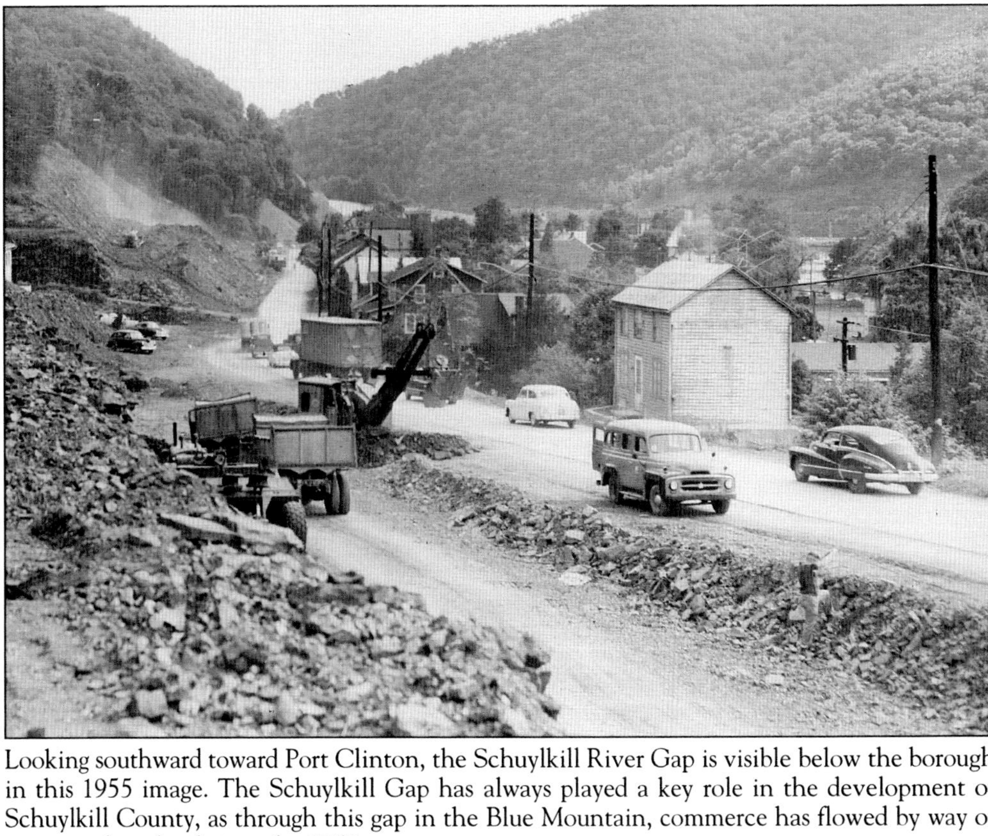

Looking southward toward Port Clinton, the Schuylkill River Gap is visible below the borough in this 1955 image. The Schuylkill Gap has always played a key role in the development of Schuylkill County, as through this gap in the Blue Mountain, commerce has flowed by way of river, road, and rail since the 1750s.

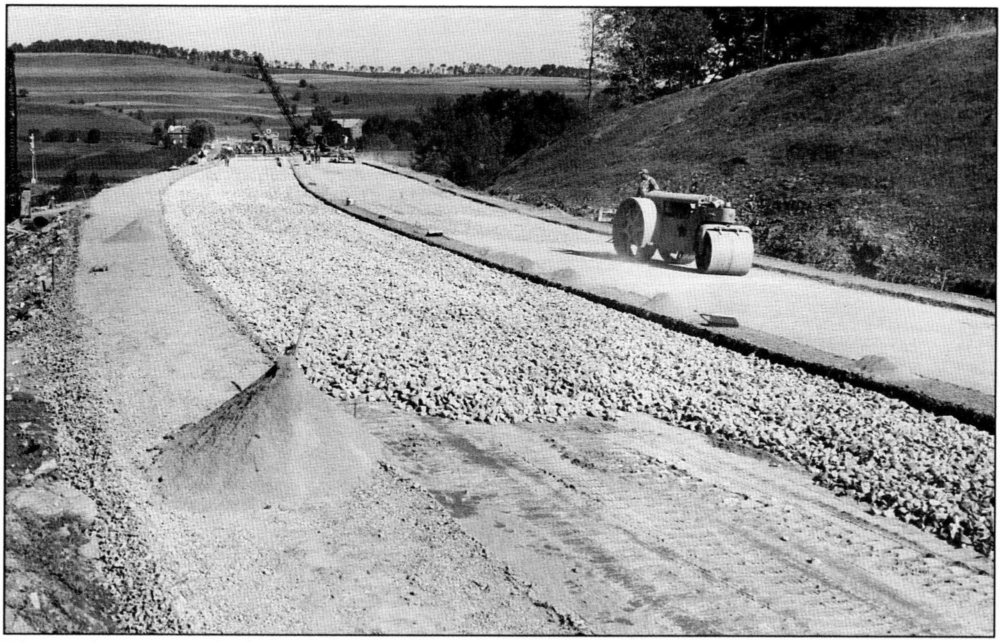

This 1959 image is looking north along Route 61 at Molino in Southern Schuylkill County. The last section of Route 61 nears completion in this image. The key to the project is the bridge over the Little Schuylkill. With the completion of this stretch of road in the fall of 1959, the four-lane highway connecting Reading with Pottsville was realized.

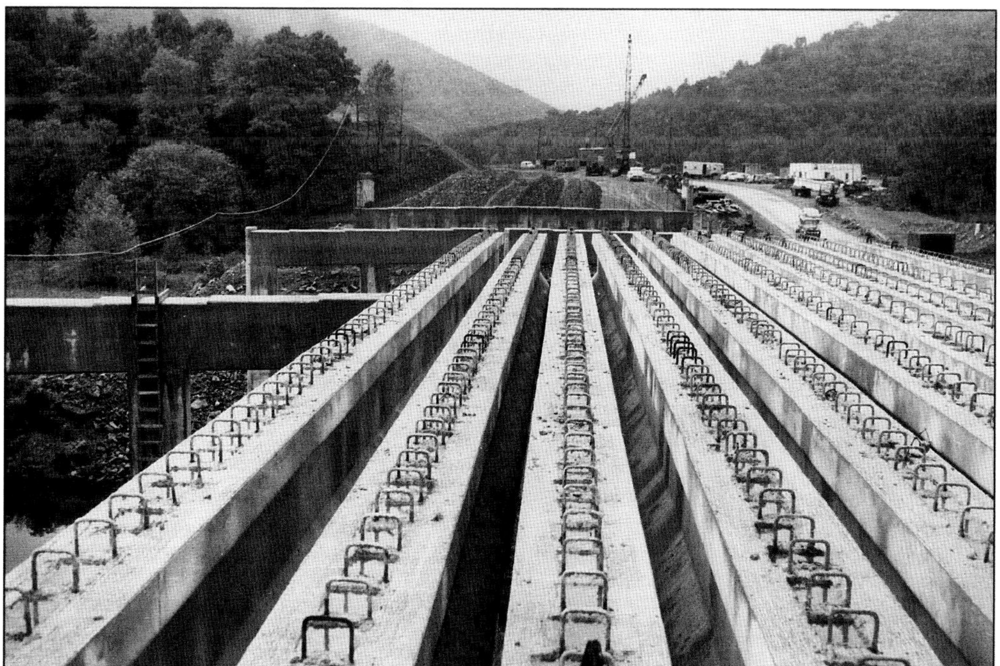

Spanning the Little Schuylkill at Molino, construction of Route 122 includes bridge construction in this 1959 photograph. Looking south along what is now Route 61, this image was taken below the Route 895 cut off for New Ringgold, in West Brunswick Township.

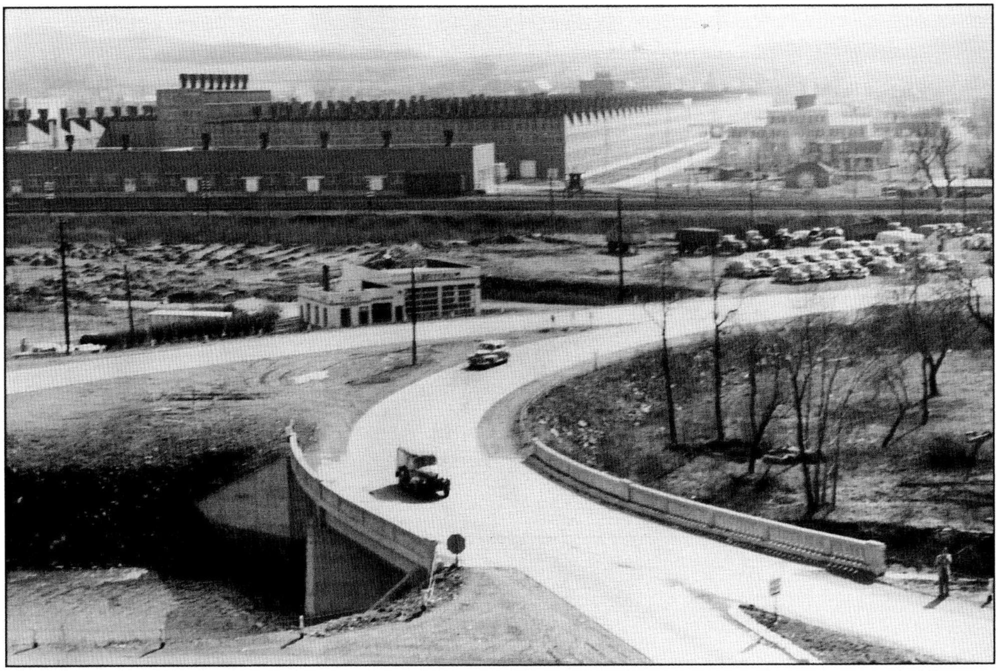

The "Aluminum Company of America Plant" (also known as Cressona Aluminum and Alumax in recent years) is seen in the distance in this image taken from Route 61 at Connor's Crossing between Schuylkill Haven and Cressona. The photograph is taken from atop the Lehigh Valley Railroad Trestle looking west in April 1953.

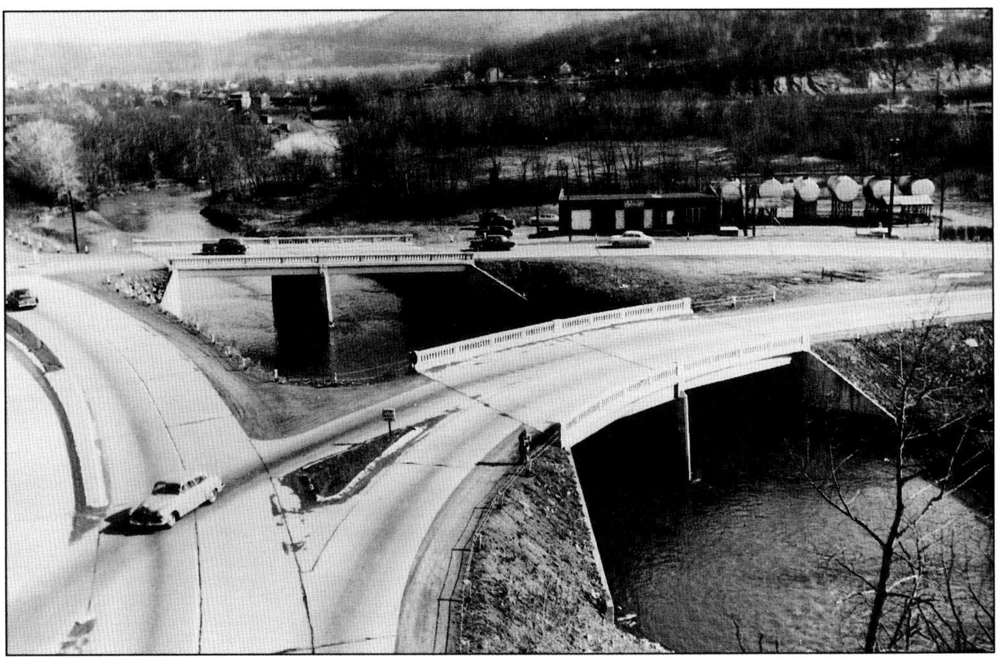

This is another view of the Connor's Crossing junction near Cressona looking southward at Route 122. This 1953 view is also taken from atop the Lehigh Valley Railroad trestle near Schuylkill Haven. The Schuylkill is seen flowing toward Schuylkill Haven in the distance.

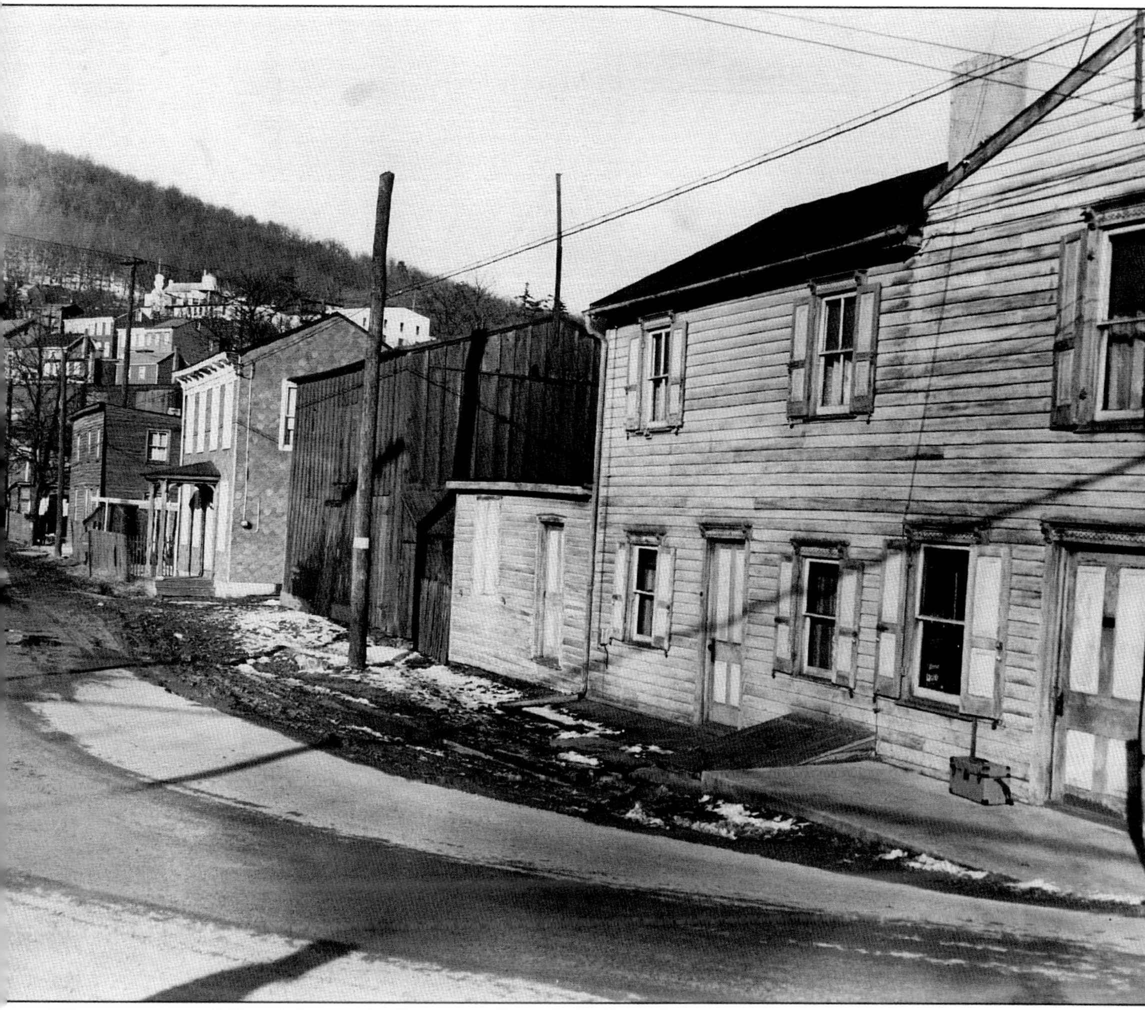

The majority of East Mount Carbon was demolished in the effort to make room for the new highway to Pottsville. These homes along Crow Hollow Road are only a few of those destroyed in the name of progress for Schuylkill County. The Brokhoff Dairy can be seen atop the hill in the left center portion of this 1950 image.

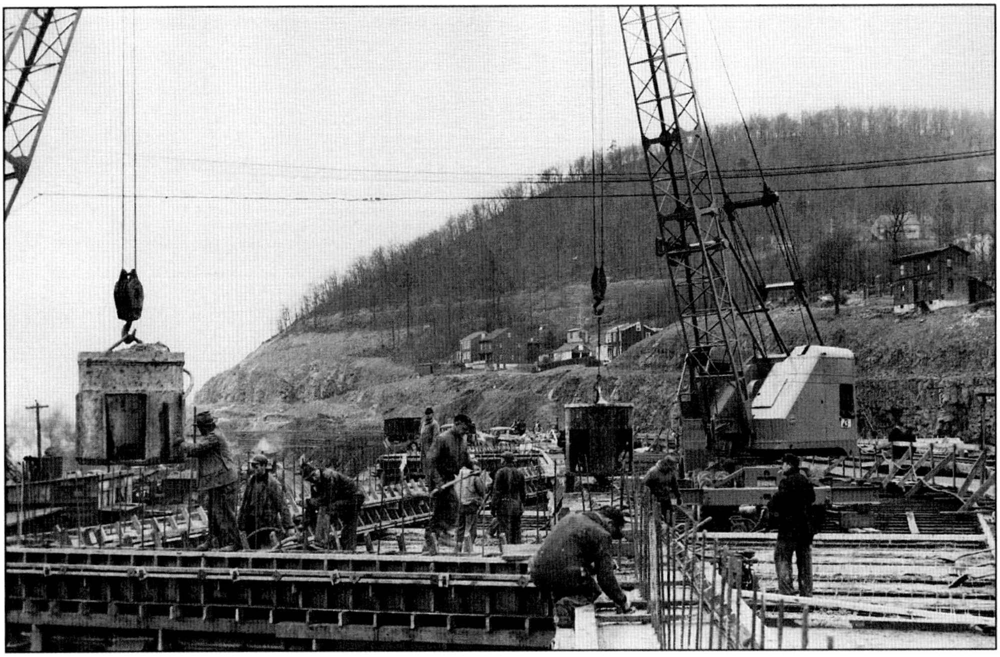

A new railroad overpass is being completed at East Mount Carbon to allow passage of the Pennsylvania Railroad between Pottsville and Schuylkill Haven. The Mount Carbon Arch would stand for nearly three decades, when in the mid-1980s it was demolished after the demise of the railroad.

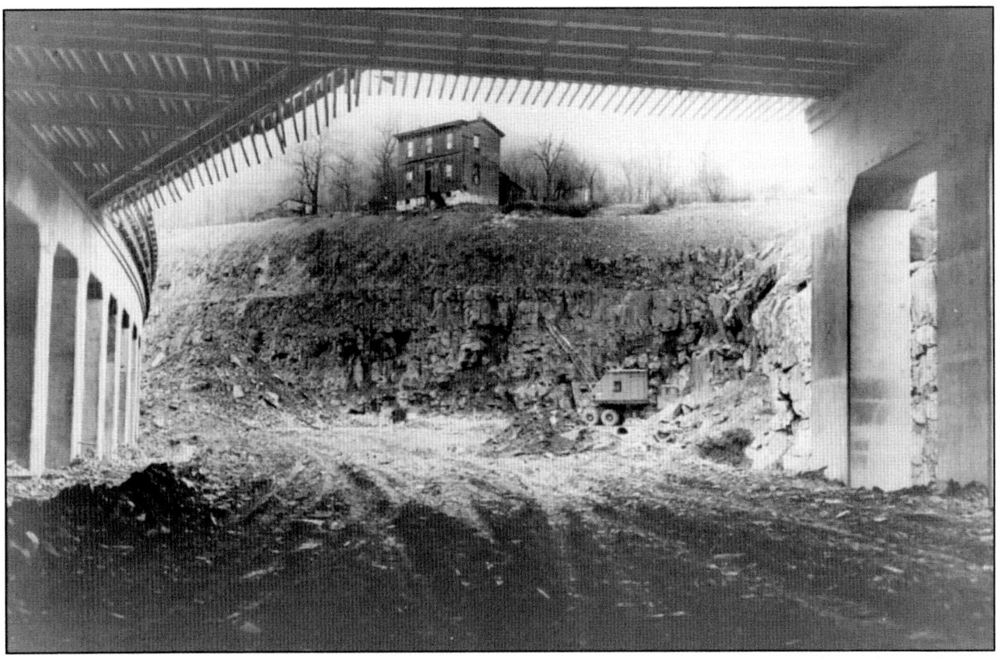

This unique view from underneath the northbound lane of the Mount Carbon Arch shows construction near the Tumbling Run Road turnoff. The completion of this overpass proved to be critical as Schuylkill County made the transition from a rail-based to a highway-based economy.

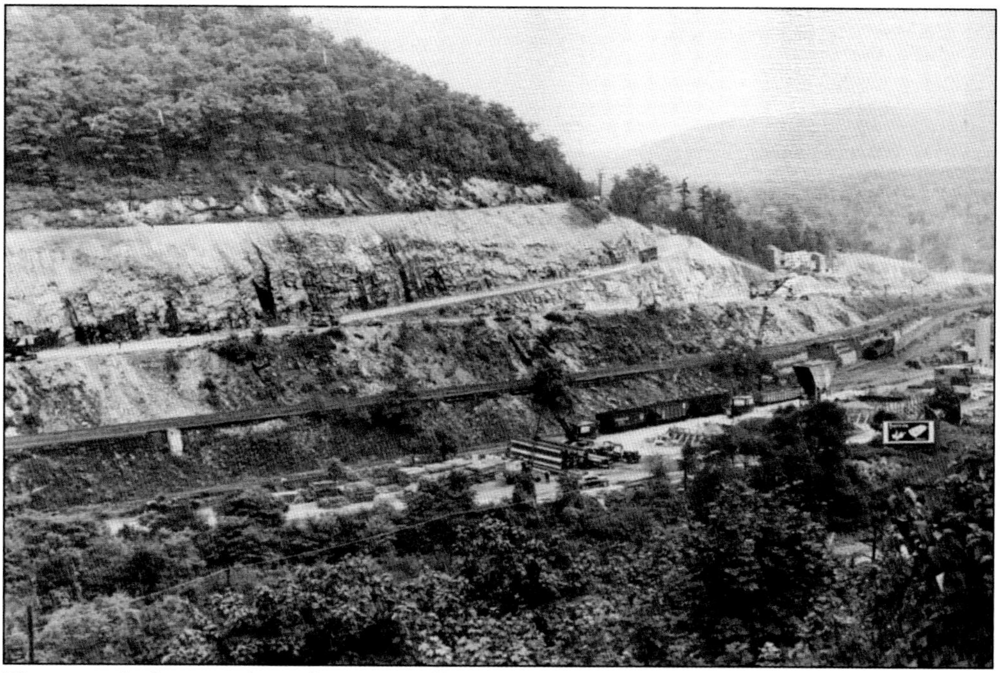

This image looking southeast from Pottsville in the summer of 1950 reveals highway construction along the base of Sharp Mountain. The Pennsylvania Railroad tracks are seen in the center of this image located near where the Pottsville Sewer Authority Plant is at Mount Carbon. A few houses remain at East Mount Carbon seen in the right center portion of this image.

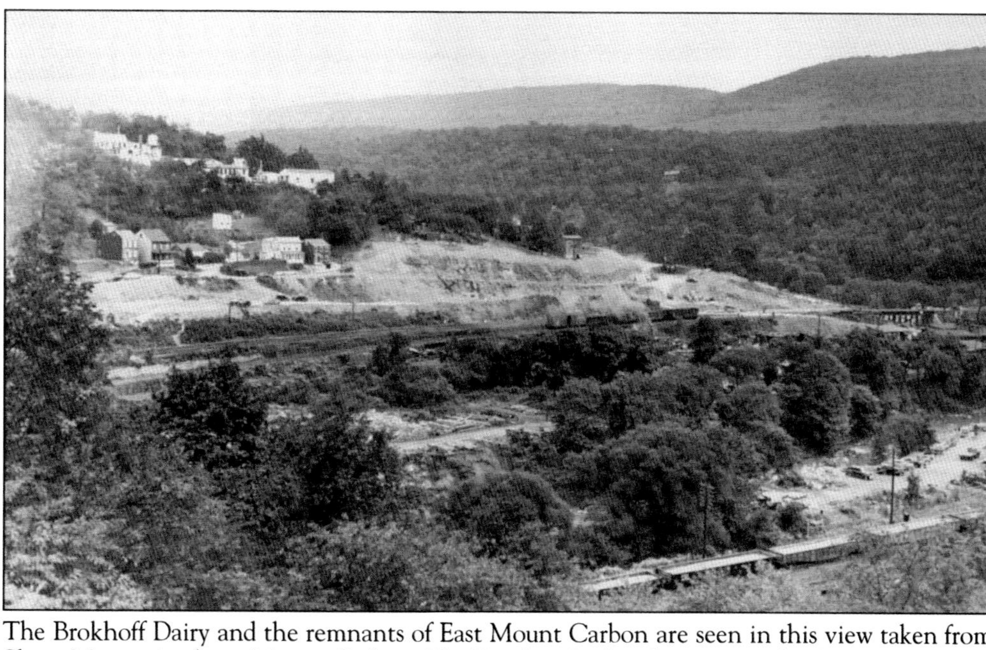

The Brokhoff Dairy and the remnants of East Mount Carbon are seen in this view taken from Sharp Mountain above Mount Carbon. The Reading Railroad is seen in the foreground, while the Pennsylvania Railroad runs from right to left beyond the Schuylkill River. The Tumbling Run Valley disappears beyond the dairy in this 1950 image.

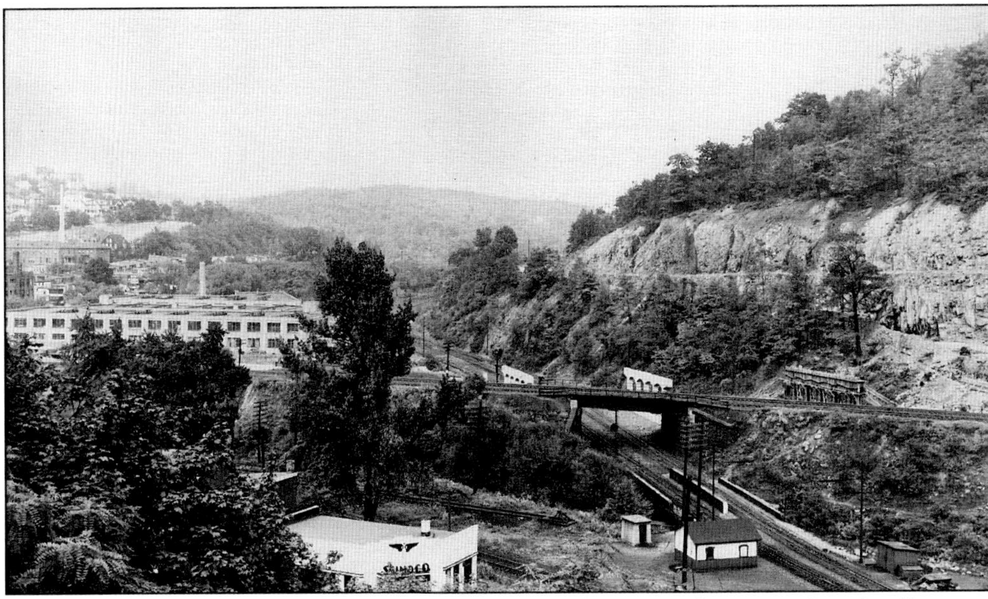

The Route 122 highway abutments are clearly seen in this image showing "The Island" section of Pottsville. The Pennsylvania Railroad tracks cross the Reading Railroad lines heading to Port Carbon and the Schuylkill Valley. The old Pottsville hospital can be seen in the background to the left of the photograph, while the road to Palo Alto stretches to the right.

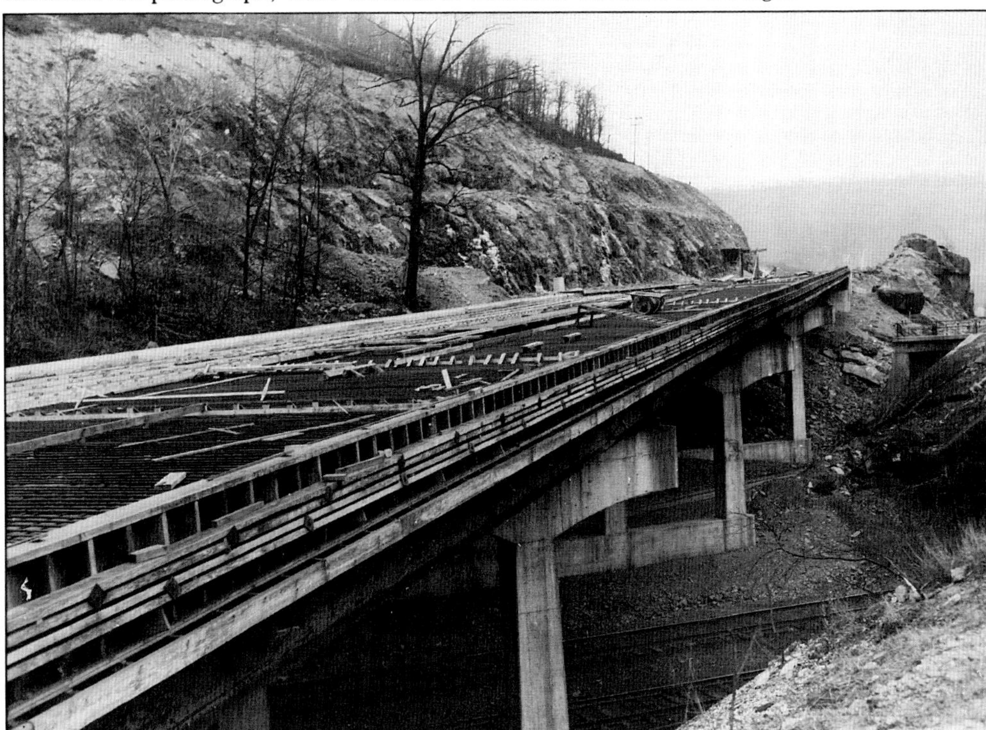

Bridge construction continues into the late fall of 1950 south of Pottsville. Route 122 crosses the tracks of the Reading Railroad leading to Mount Carbon. The Pennsylvania Railroad passes within 50 feet of the new highway bridge to the right of this image.

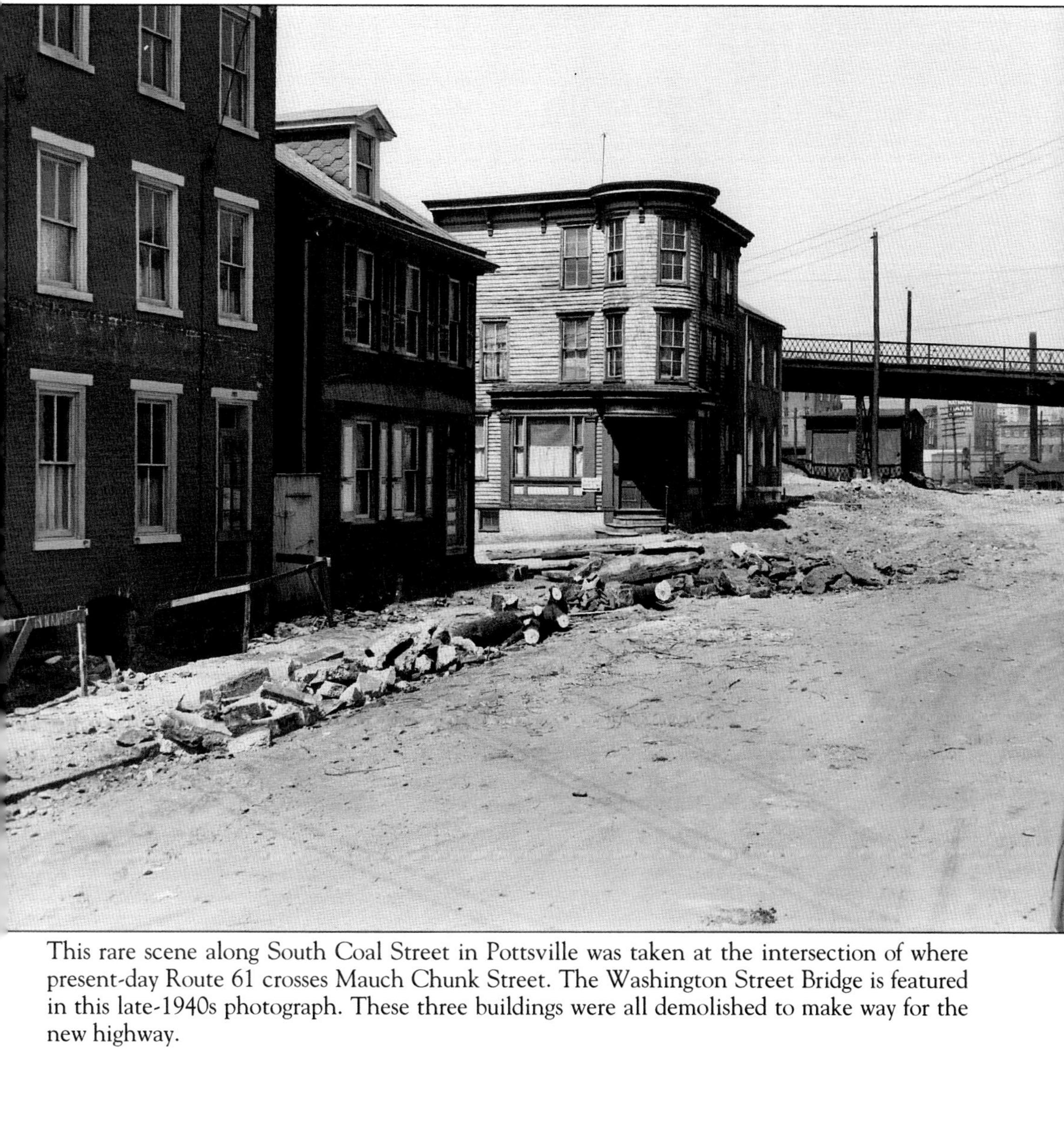

This rare scene along South Coal Street in Pottsville was taken at the intersection of where present-day Route 61 crosses Mauch Chunk Street. The Washington Street Bridge is featured in this late-1940s photograph. These three buildings were all demolished to make way for the new highway.

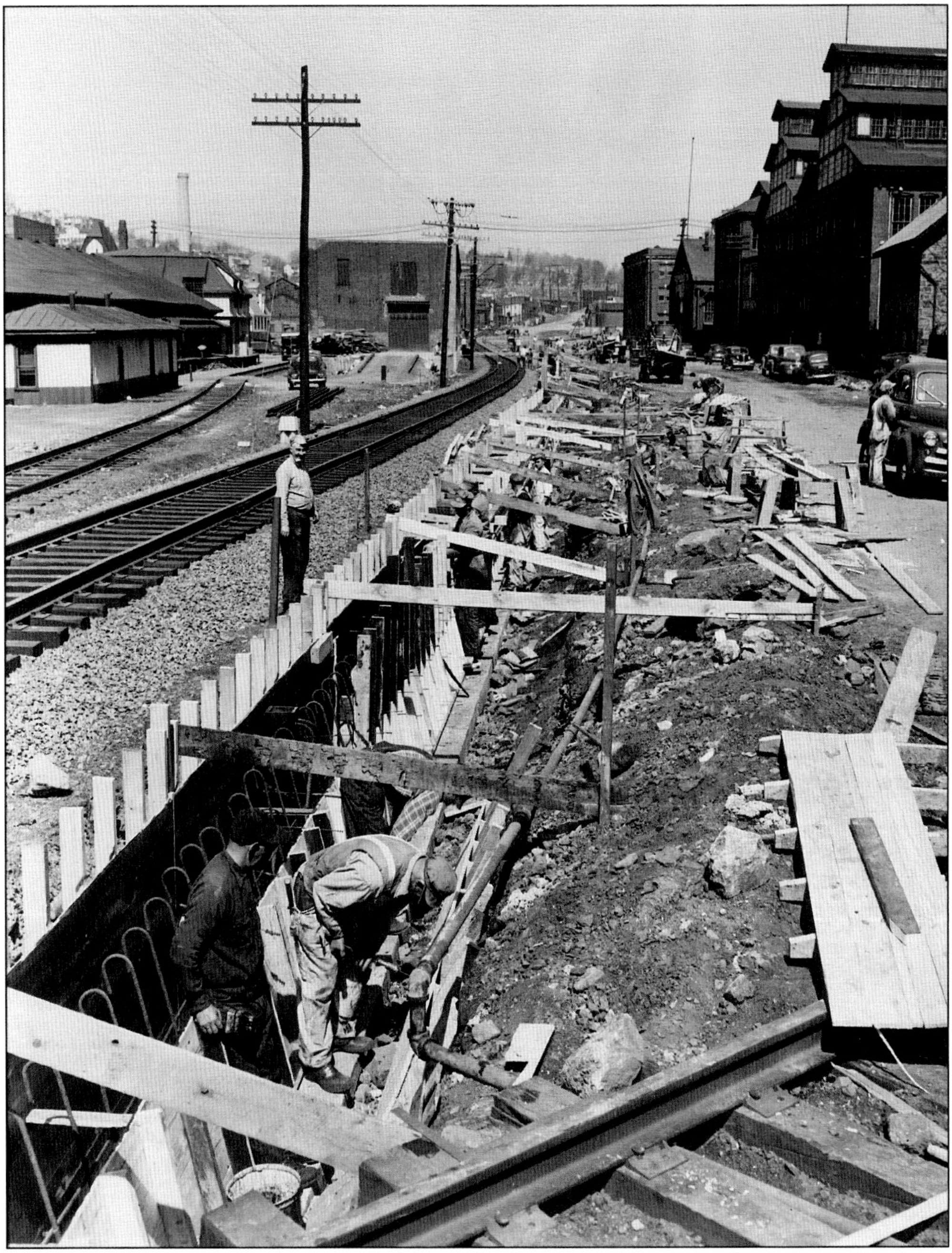

Road construction along Coal Street (now Claude A. Lord Boulevard) in Pottsville shows progress alongside the Pennsylvania Railroad tracks on the left and the Philadelphia and Reading Railroad Car Shops on the right.

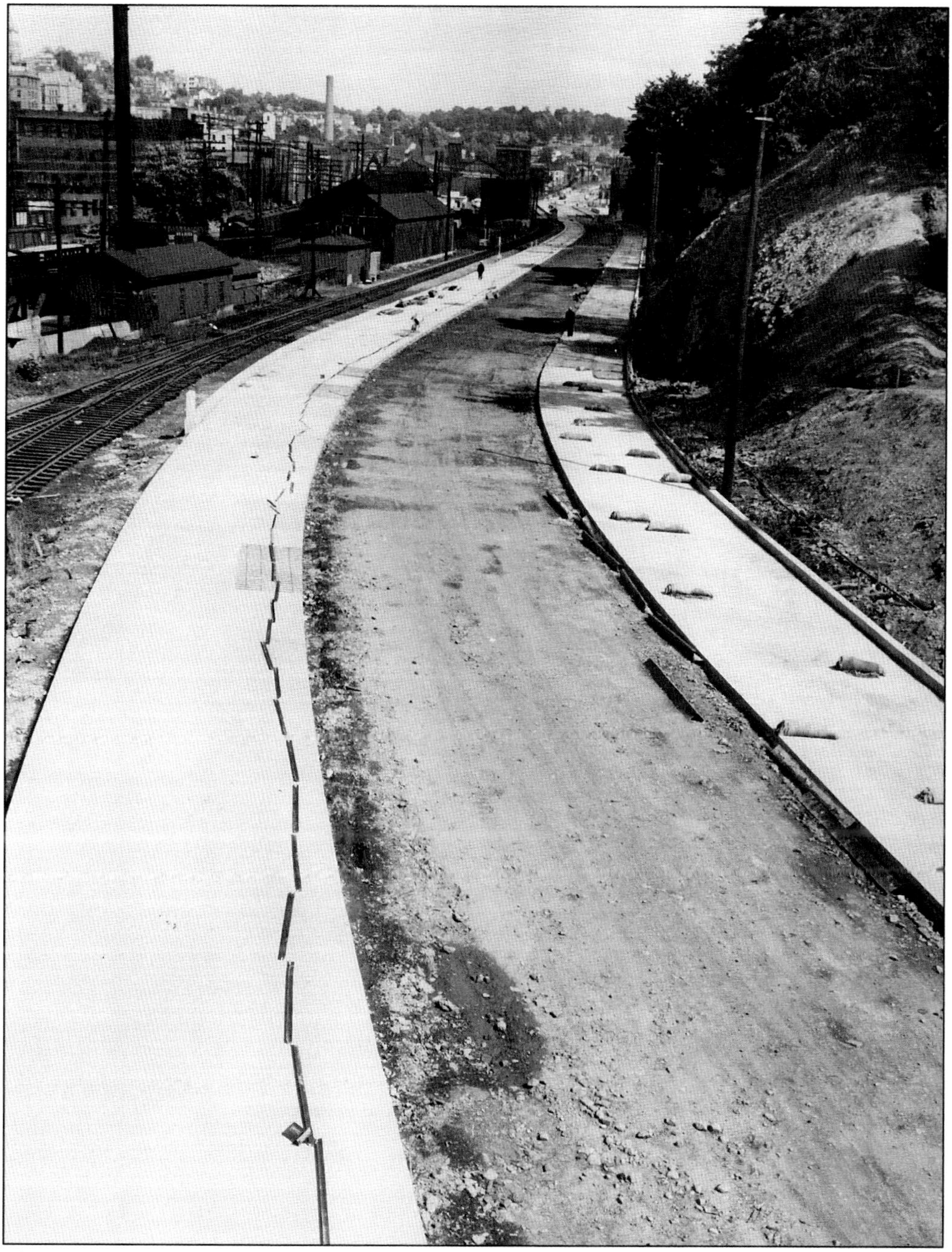

This rare view of Pottsville was taken from atop the Washington Street Bridge looking north along what is soon to become Route 122 (Now Route 61). The Pennsylvania Railroad tracks, the Reading yard, and the Schuylkill County Courthouse can be seen to the left of the highway in this late-1940s photograph.

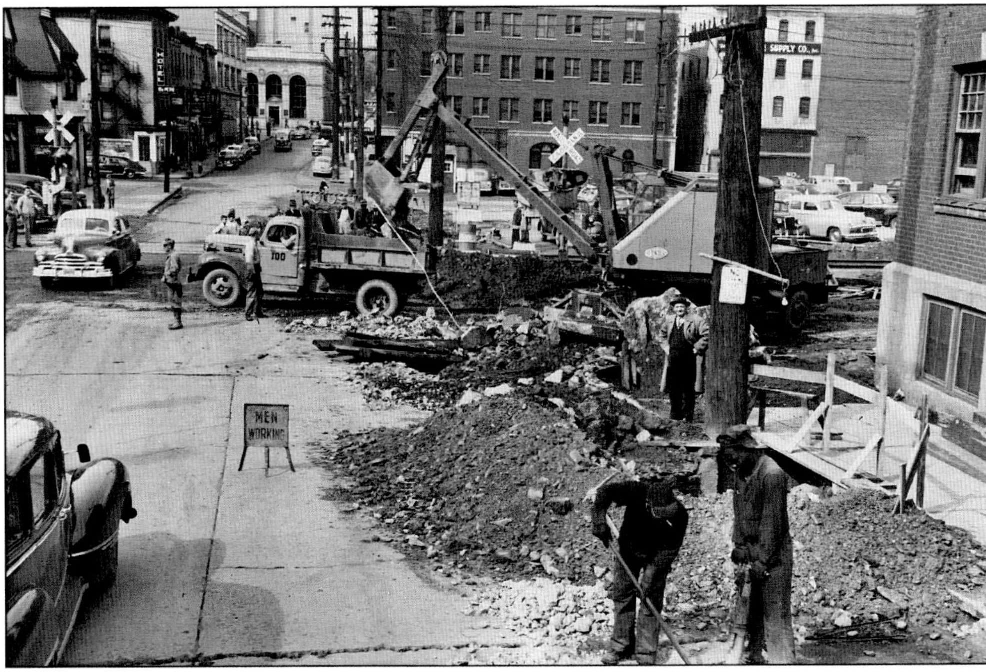

Construction crews prepare the intersection of East Norwegian and Coal Street for the laying of the new highway through Pottsville. The Reading Passenger station and the William Penn Hotel are seen to the left of this 1951 image. Beyond the shovel, the new bus terminal is to be built within following years.

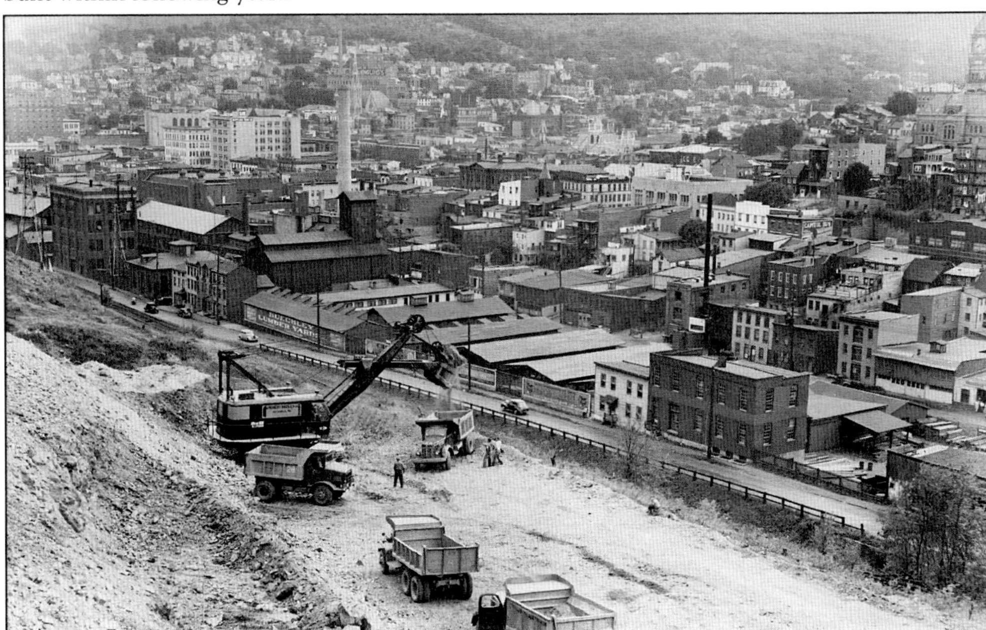

This classic panorama of Pottsville's cityscape shows J. Robert Bazley's highway construction above the Arch Street intersection. Coal Street is seen in the foreground. Prominent buildings visible in this afternoon photograph include the Schuylkill County Courthouse, city hall, the Yuengling Brewery, and the Thompson Building.

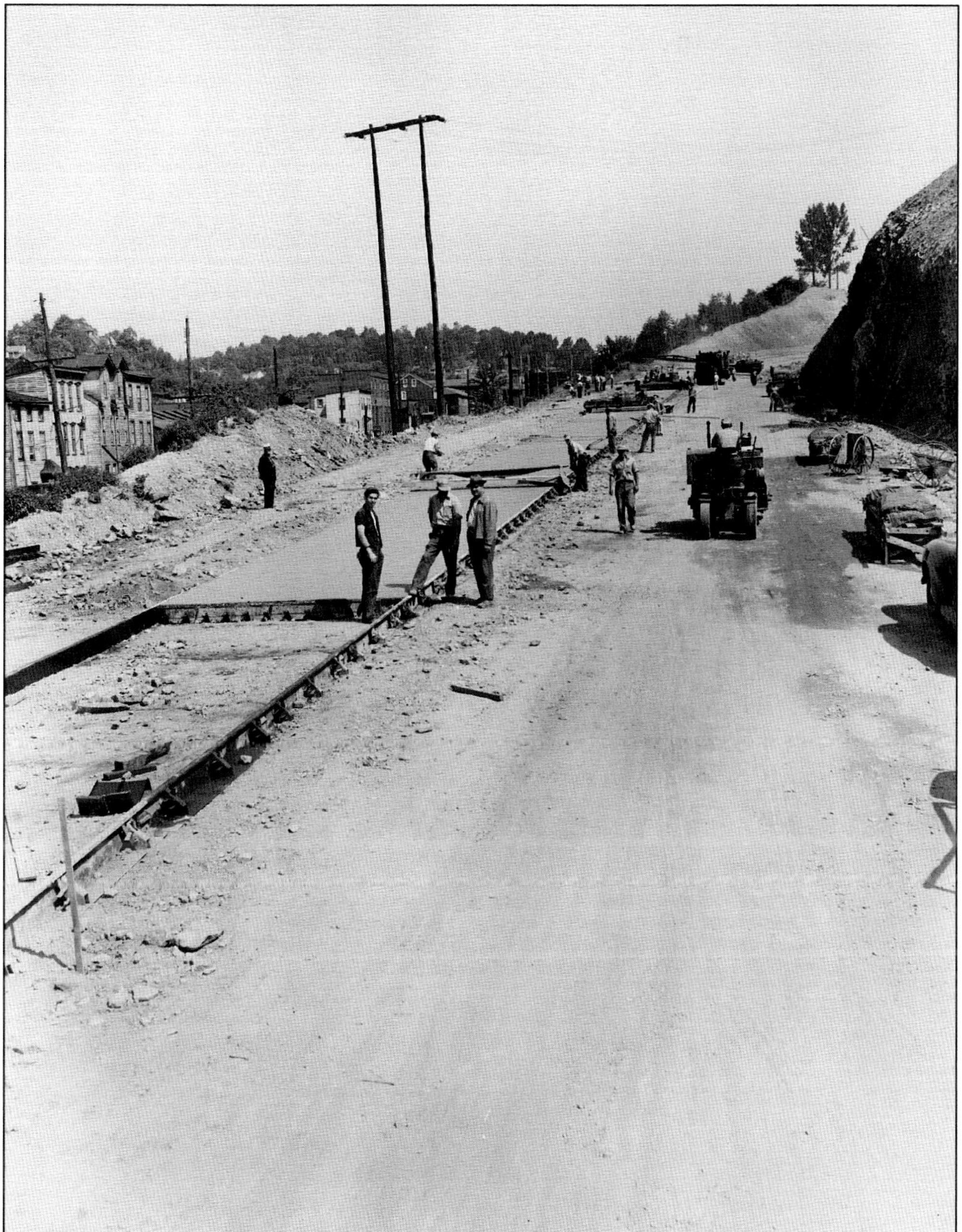

Route 122 construction continues along the Claude A. Lord Boulevard at Race Street in Pottsville.

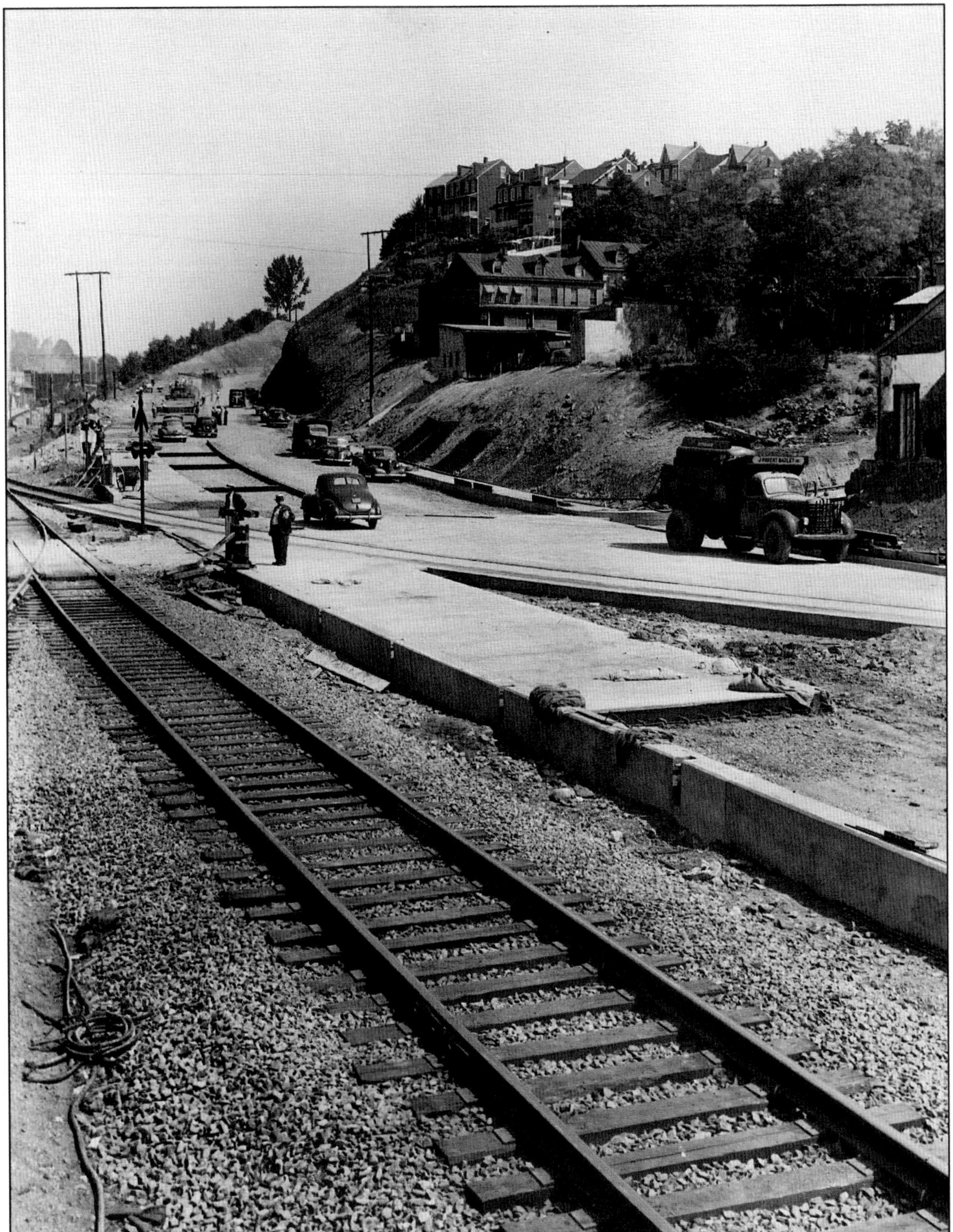

This is another view of highway work at the intersection of Arch and Coal Streets in Pottsville. The Pennsylvania Railroad tracks in the foreground were eventually covered over as the automobile replaced the locomotive in the 1960s and 1970s.

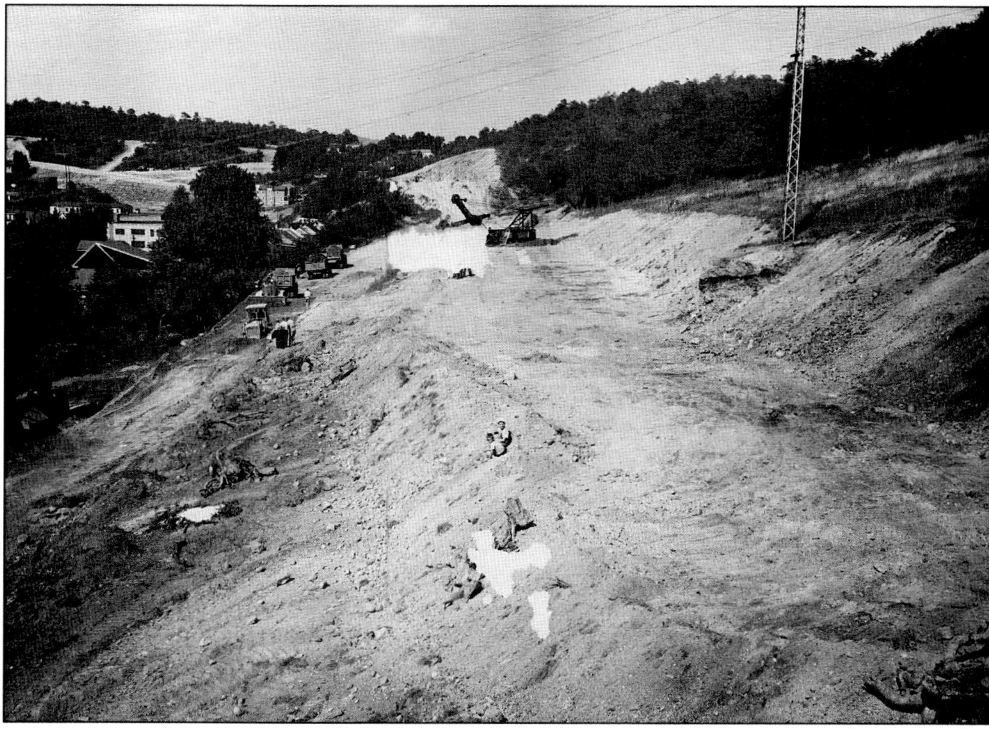

Bazley's construction equipment moves mountains along the future Route 122 near Mill Creek. Lawton's Hill climbs to the right, while Jalappa and Nichols Street is off to the left. The clearing on the right of this photograph is today (1998) home to an auto dealership, a motel, and office buildings. Whom are those children playing in the road?

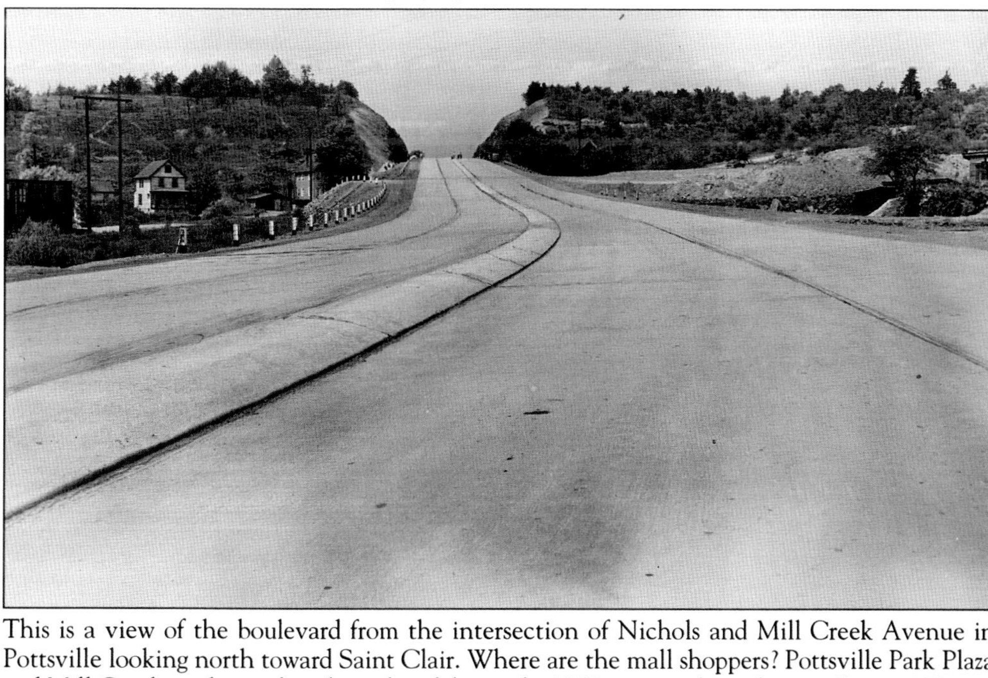

This is a view of the boulevard from the intersection of Nichols and Mill Creek Avenue in Pottsville looking north toward Saint Clair. Where are the mall shoppers? Pottsville Park Plaza and Mill Creek are located to the right of this early-1950s image along the new Route 122.

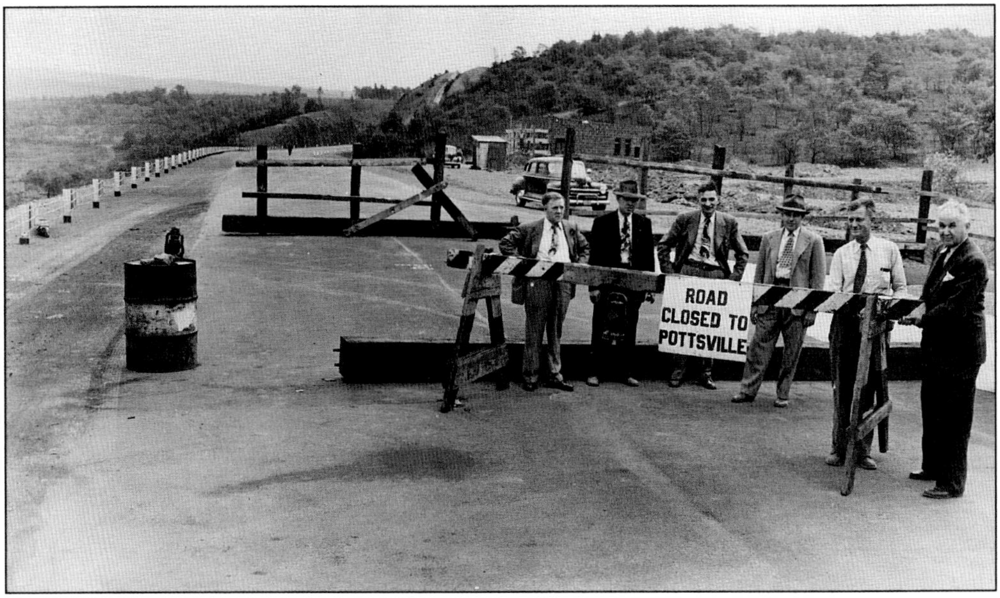

County and local officials prepare to remove barriers to traffic along Route 122 (Route 61) at Ann Street near East Mines north of Pottsville. Beyond the hilltop to the right of this image is where the Fairlane Village (1974) and Lowe's Hardware (1998) were constructed.

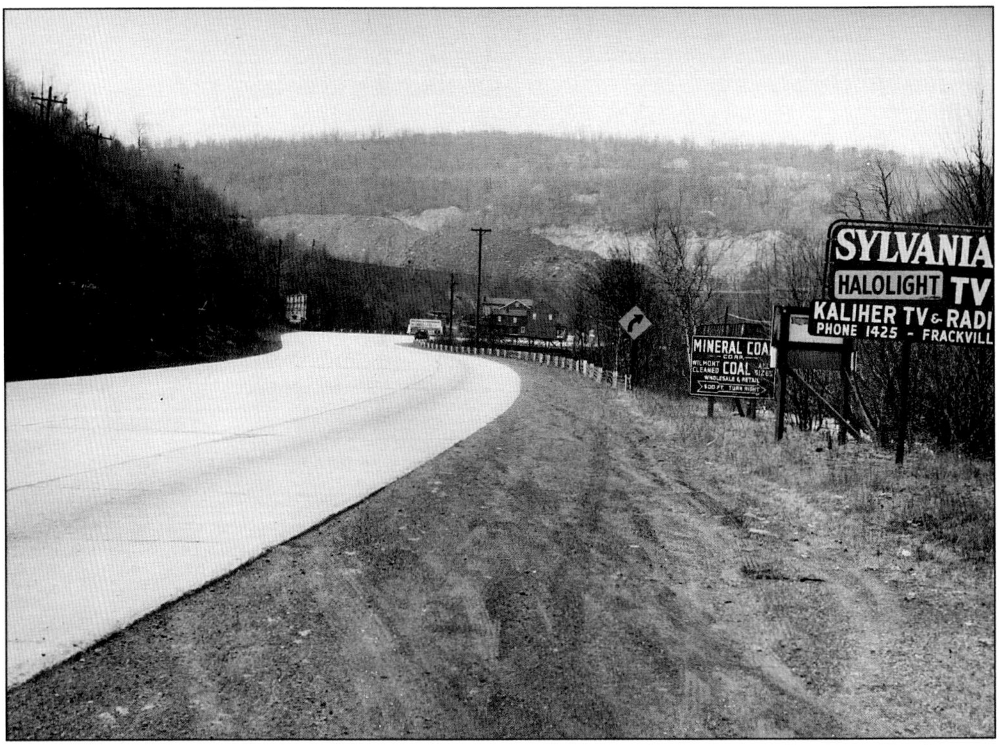

A lone northbound auto cruises away from the camera north of Saint Clair near Darkwater in this early-1950s photograph. The novelty of "Billboard Advertisements" quickly followed highway construction as witnessed in this image. The construction of Route 122/61 was, and still remains, key to the future of Schuylkill.

Five

Schuylkill Railroad Stations and Crossings

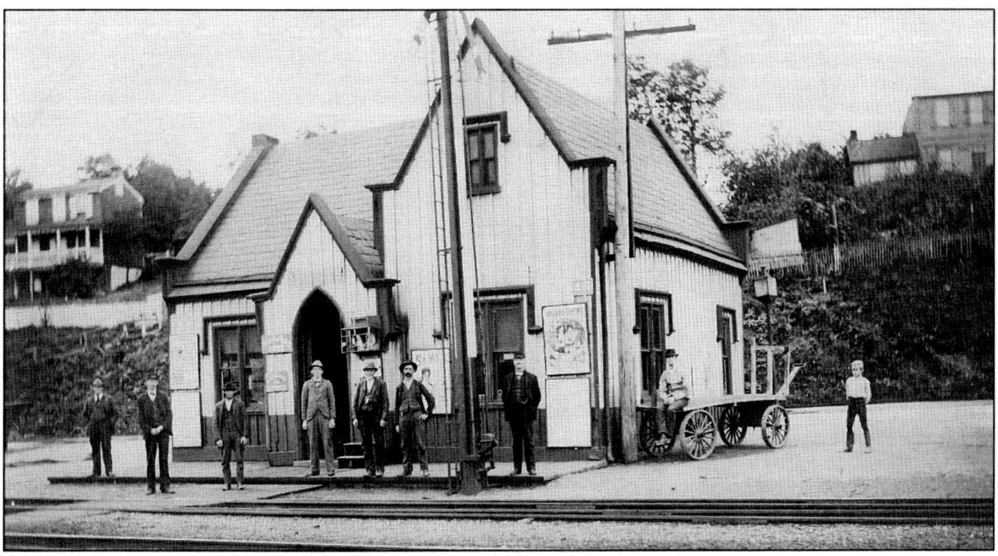

This rare 1903 image of the Philadelphia and Reading Railroad Station in Auburn provides a unique view to that community's railroading heritage. A key stop along the railroad line between Pottsville and Reading, this station stood between Front and Bear Creek Streets near the Schuylkill River.

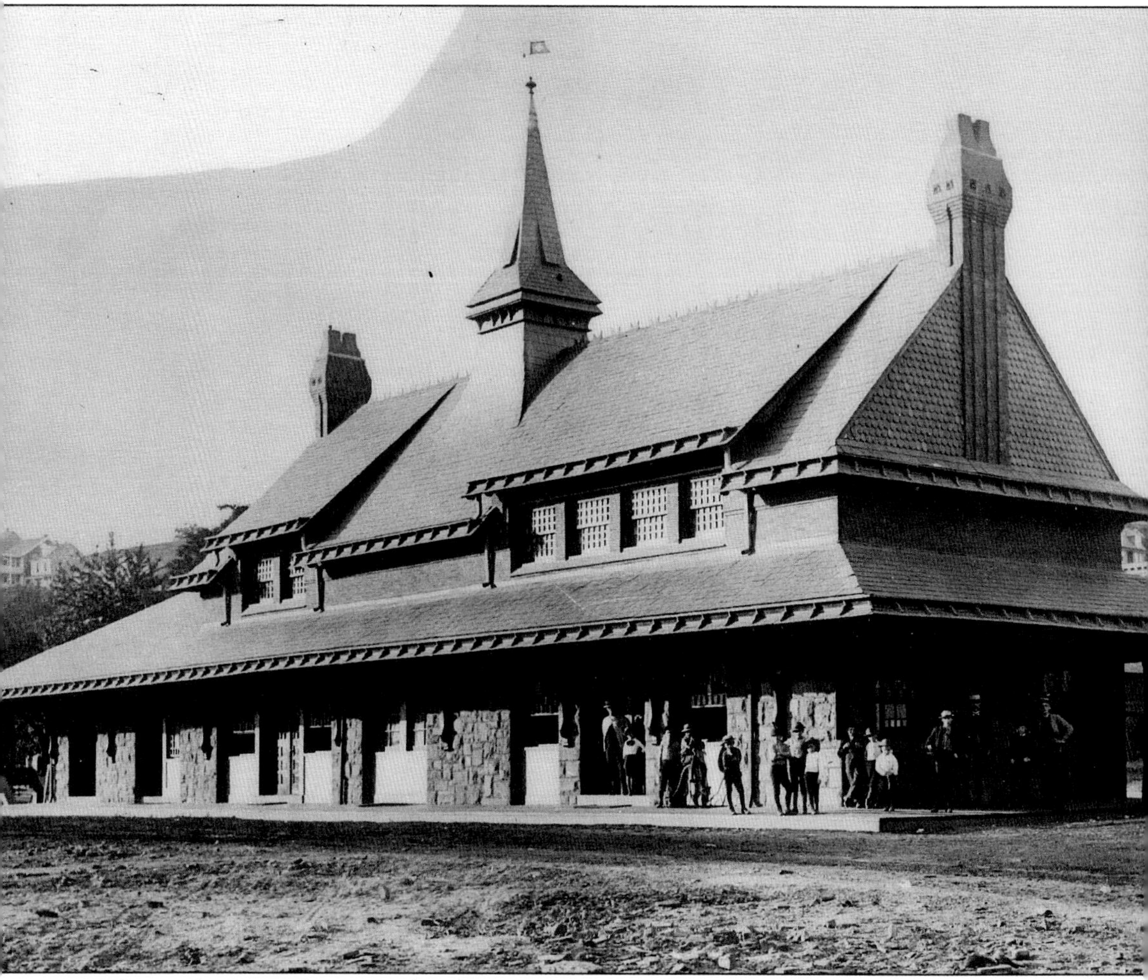

This is the Pennsylvania Railroad Station as seen in the 1890s along East Norwegian Street near Route 61 at Pottsville. The Pennsylvania Station was constructed directly opposite the Philadelphia and Reading Station.

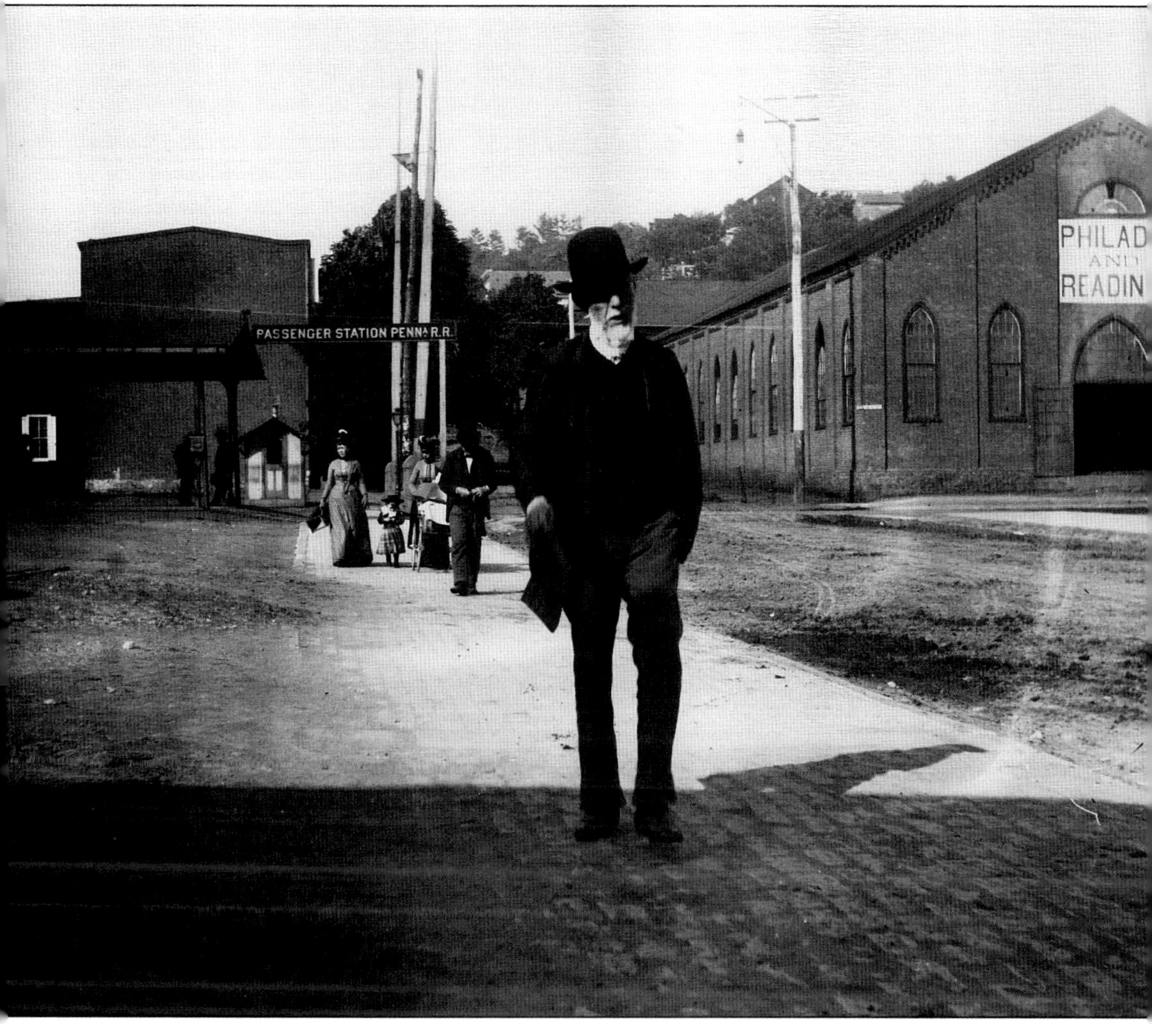

This 1890s scene looking east along East Norwegian Street was taken in front of the Pennsylvania Railroad Passenger station at Pottsville. The tracks of the Pennsy railroad are still visible today and can be seen jutting through the macadam at this now busy intersection in Pottsville.

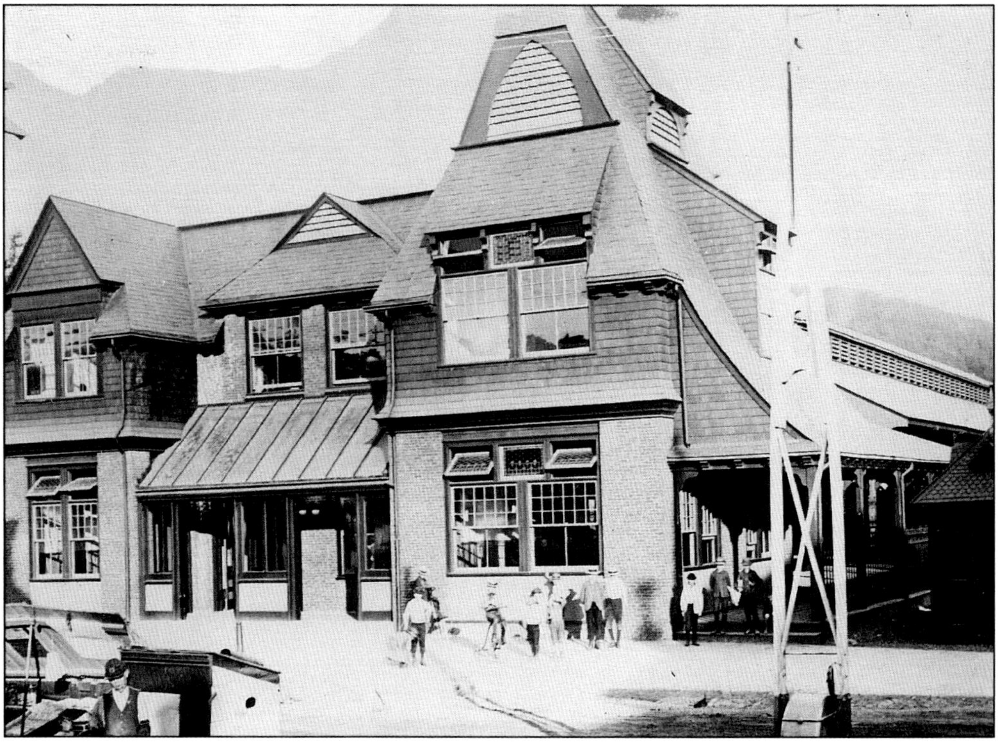

During its heyday, the magnificent Reading Passenger Station bristled with activity as seen in this turn-of-the-century photograph along East Norwegian Street in Pottsville. Take notice of the young lad riding the latest contraption on three wheels, as well as the disabled Civil War veteran in the foreground.

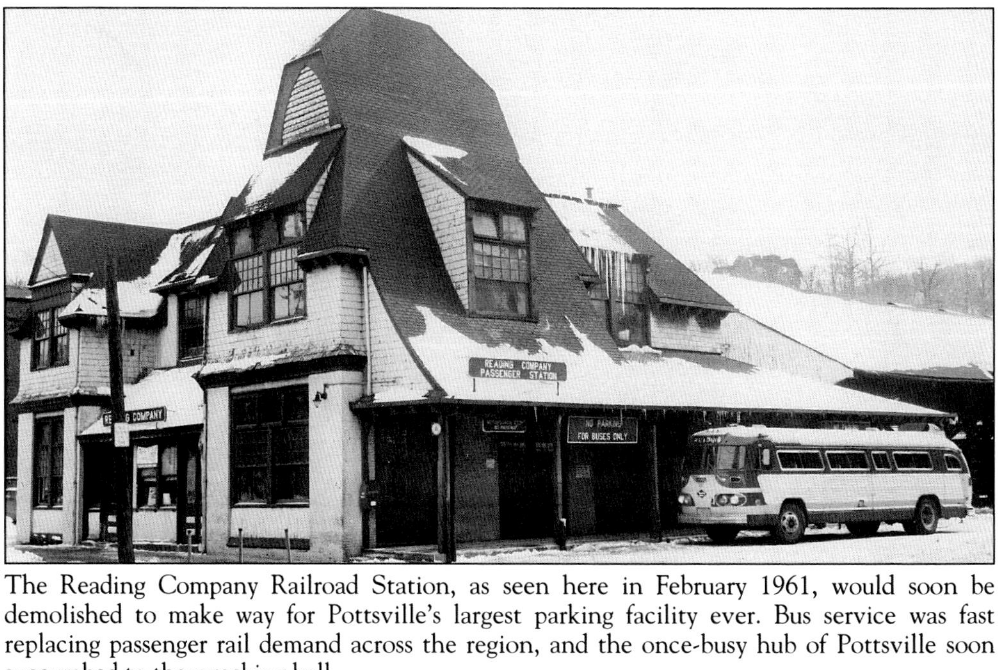

The Reading Company Railroad Station, as seen here in February 1961, would soon be demolished to make way for Pottsville's largest parking facility ever. Bus service was fast replacing passenger rail demand across the region, and the once-busy hub of Pottsville soon succumbed to the wrecking ball.

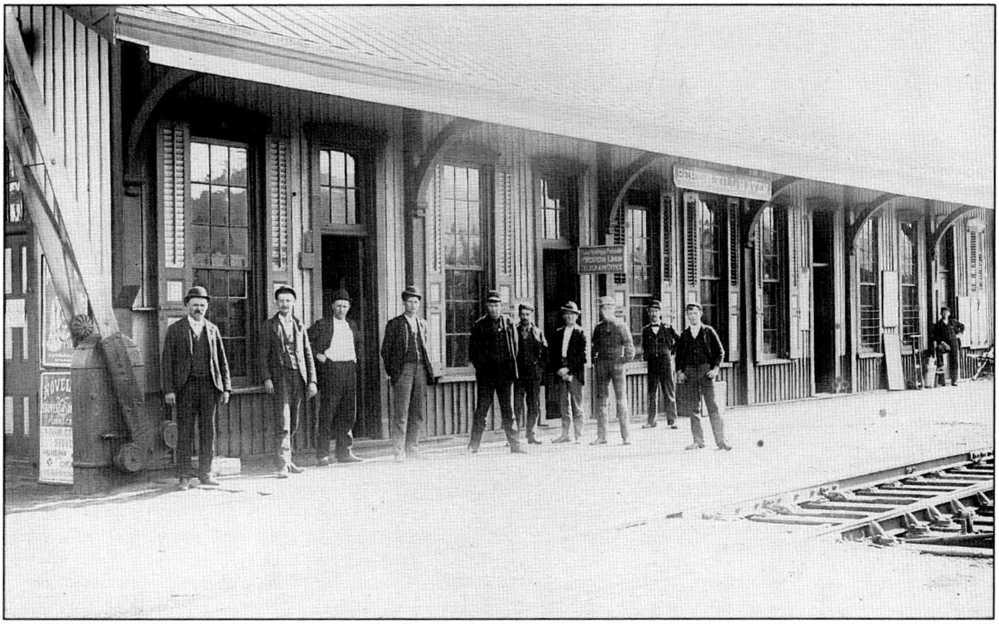

This 1904 image was taken at the Philadelphia and Reading Railway depot at Schuylkill Haven. The station was built around 1852 and extended from where the present station structure stands today to Main Street. This picture was taken shortly before the old building was abandoned.

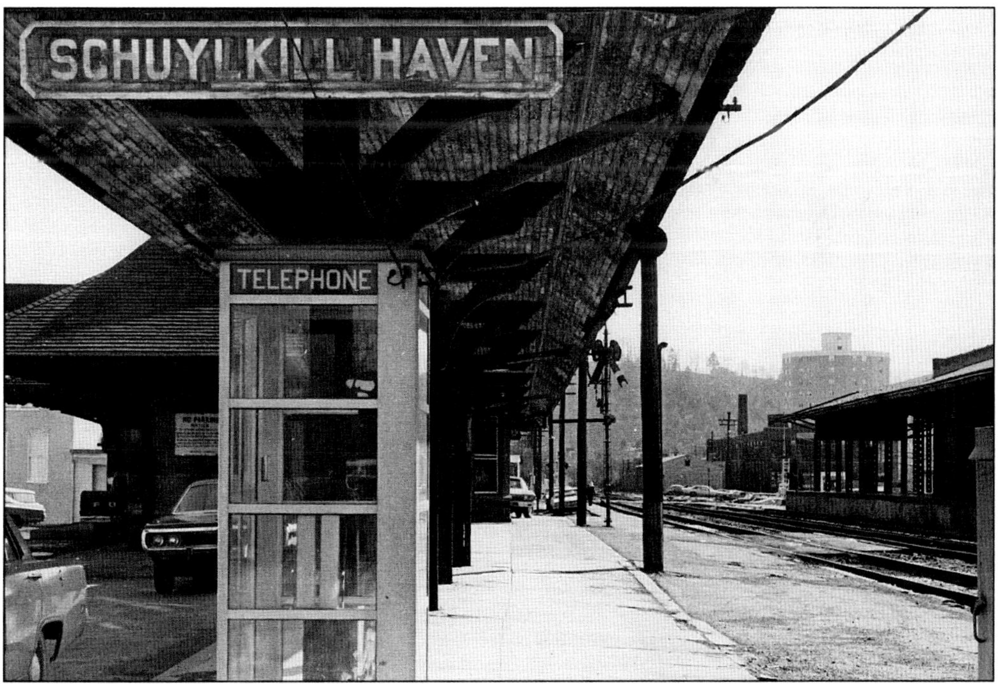

The Reading Railroad's Schuylkill Haven passenger station near Main Street is pictured in April 1976 prior to its renovation into the borough headquarters during the 1980s. Thankfully the deterioration, as seen in this image, was halted through the efforts of historically minded partners in Schuylkill Haven.

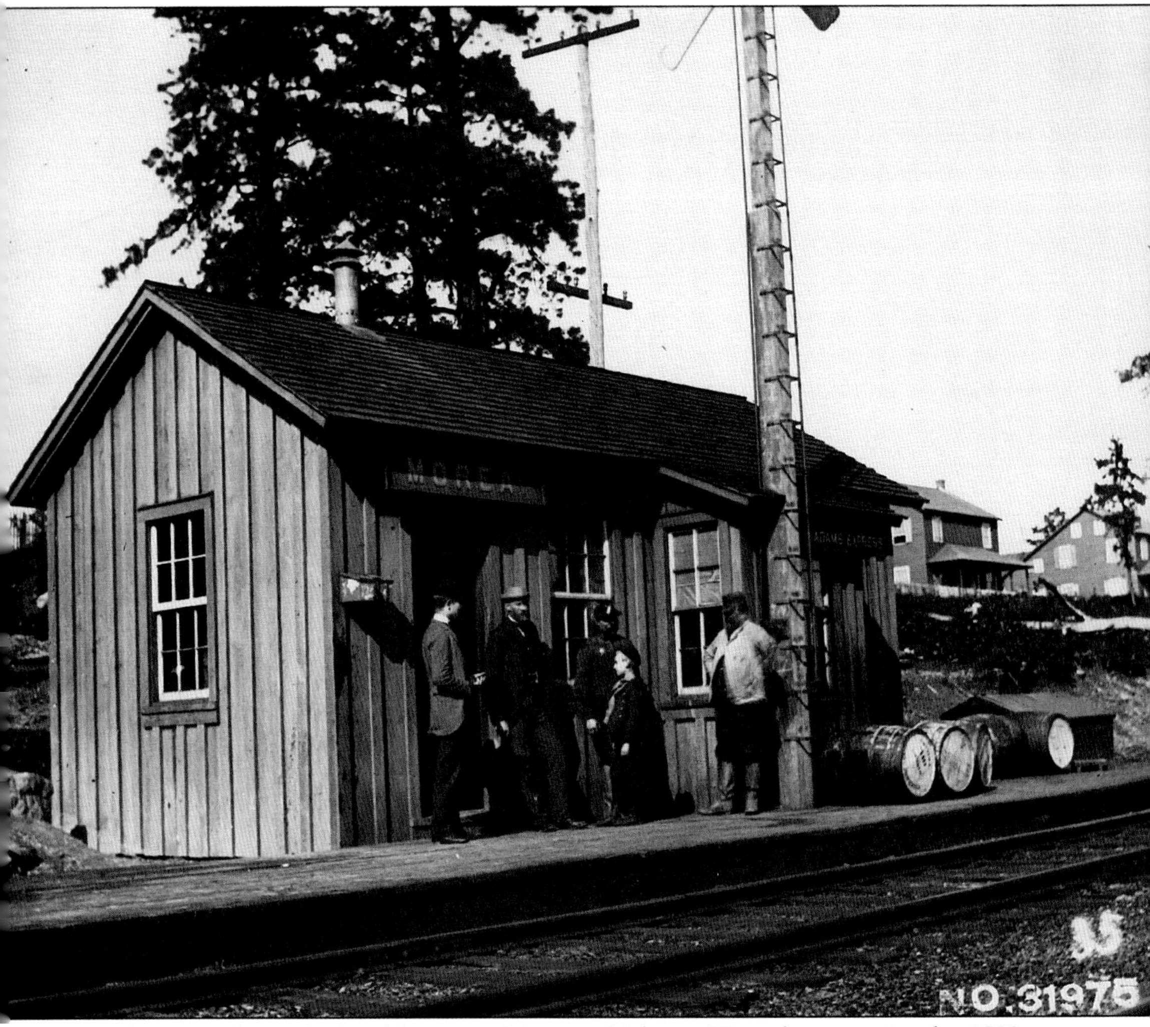

The Pennsylvania Railroad Station at Morea in Mahanoy Township is seen in this 1880s image. Morea rivaled many of the larger mining towns in the Mahanoy Valley in terms of the coal trade. From Morea, the Pennsylvania Railroad paralleled the Mill Creek southward to Saint Clair. Much of the railroad bed remains intact from Saint Clair to Morea today.

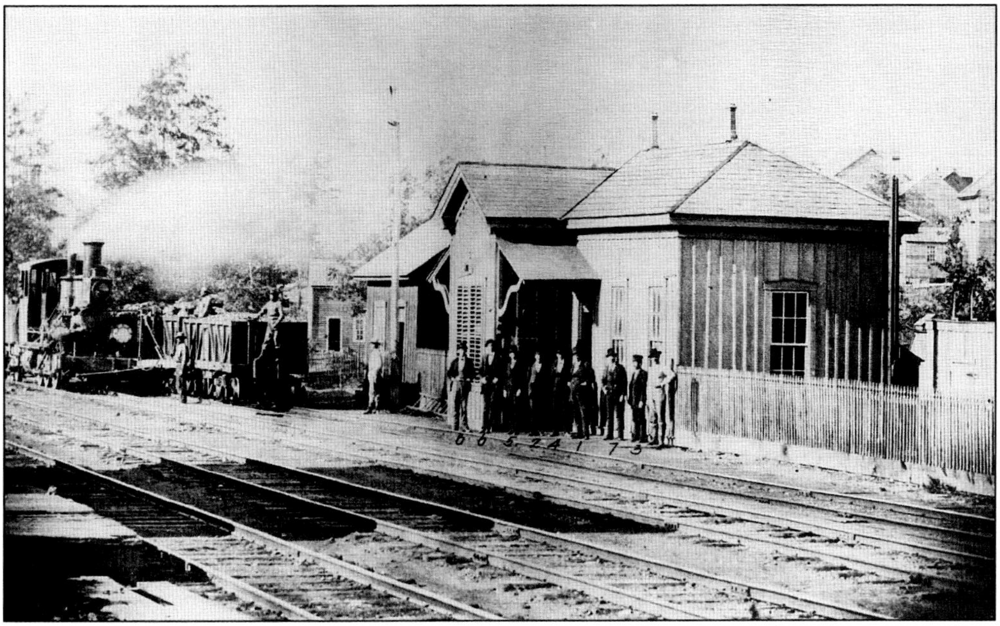

The Philadelphia and Reading Railroad's Frackville office is pictured in this 1870s image from atop Broad Mountain. This image is taken from the intersection of Frack and Mahanoy looking northeast not too far from where the railroad runs through town.

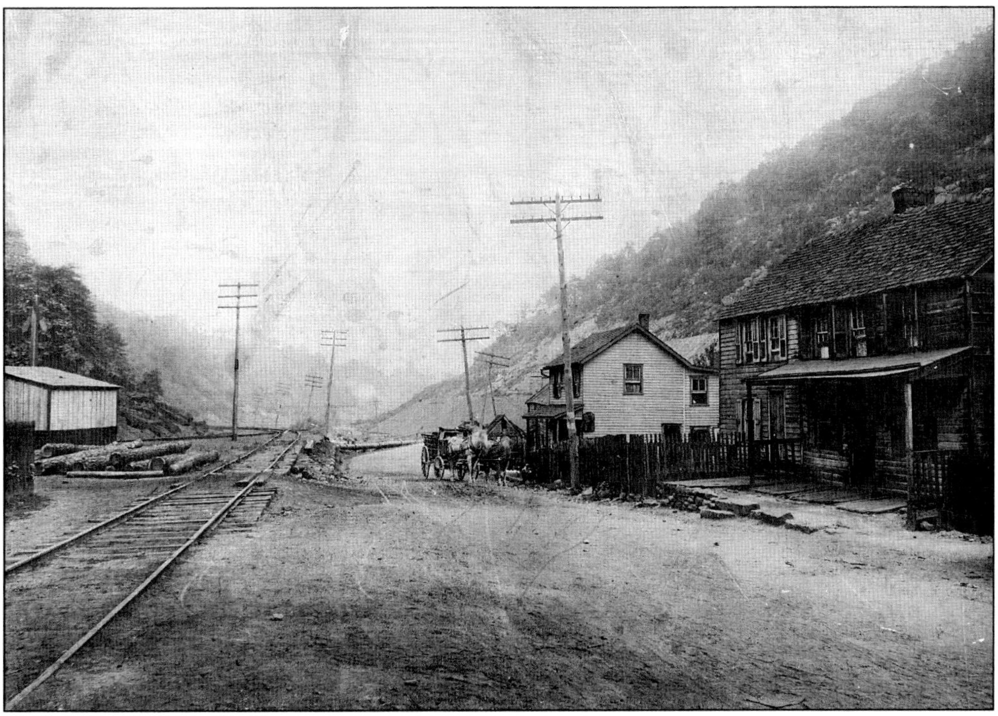

The dangerous railroad crossing at the bottom of the Frackville-Saint Clair Road is seen in this 1893 image. Located at the village of Broad Mountain (or Darkwater), the Mahoney Hotel, shown at right, witnessed an unending flow of coal and passenger traffic. Today, Route 61 passes through this location just north of Saint Clair.

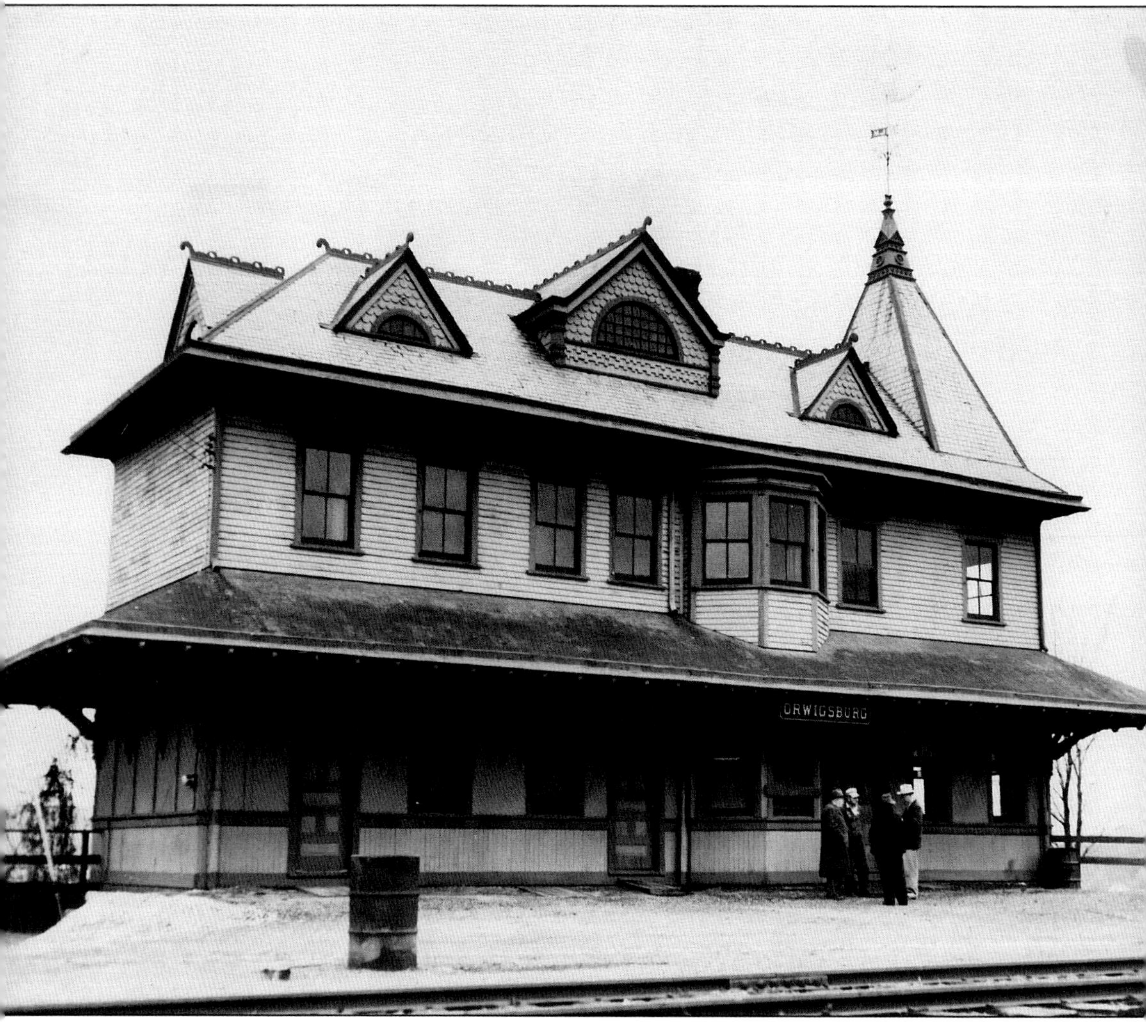

The Lehigh Valley Station at Orwigsburg on the northern edge of that borough is shown in this April 1953 photograph. Unfortunately, this Victorian-era station was demolished in the name of progress shortly after the photograph was taken.

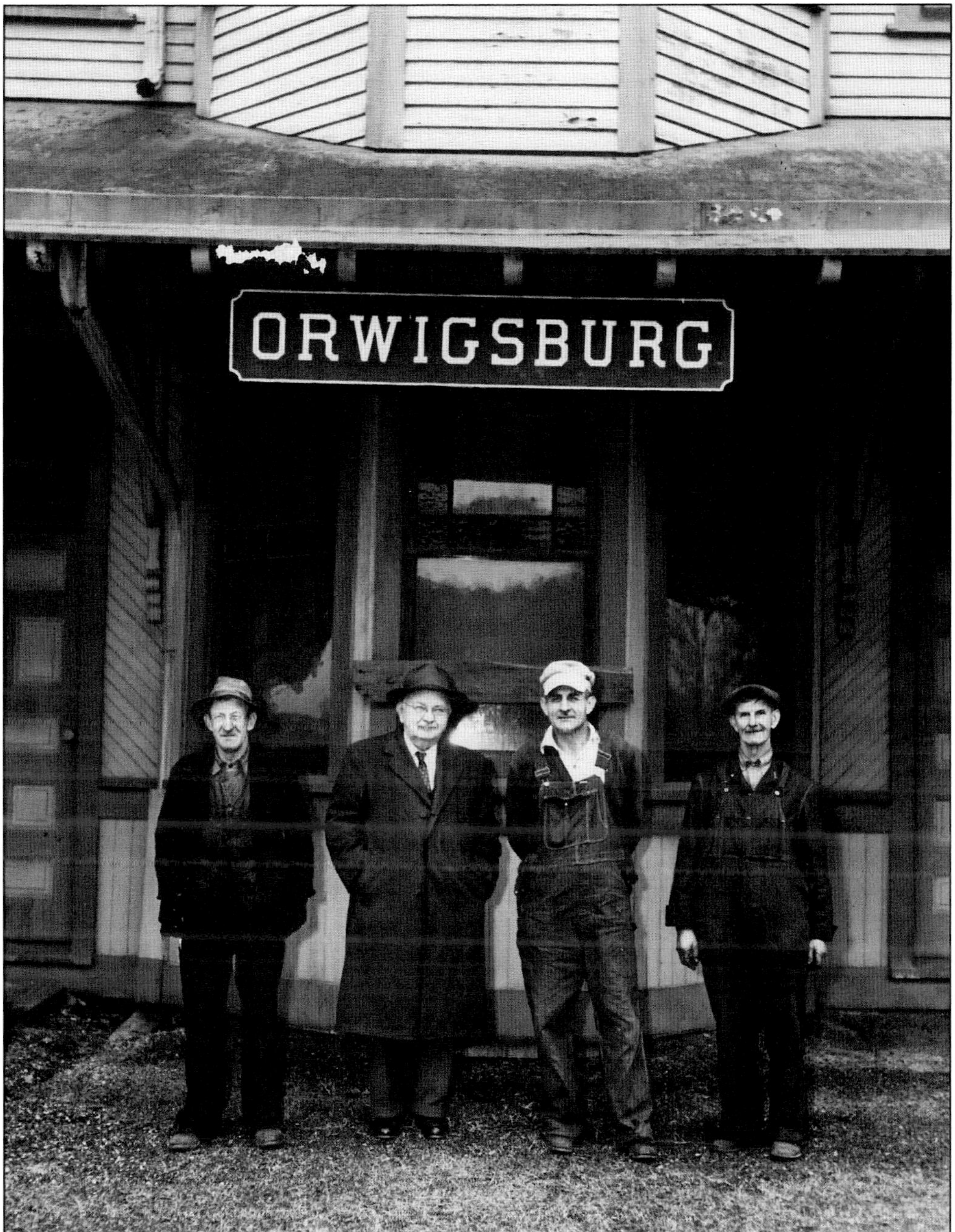

"Last Pose at the Historic Station" is the title of this 1953 photograph as mentioned in a local newspaper. Service to Orwigsburg came to an end after 63 years along the Lehigh Valley line. Standing from left to right are as follows: William Knittle, road gang foreman; W. Alfred Dietrich, veteran Orwigsburg patron; Lawrence Deibert, truck driver; and Calvin Riegel, laborer.

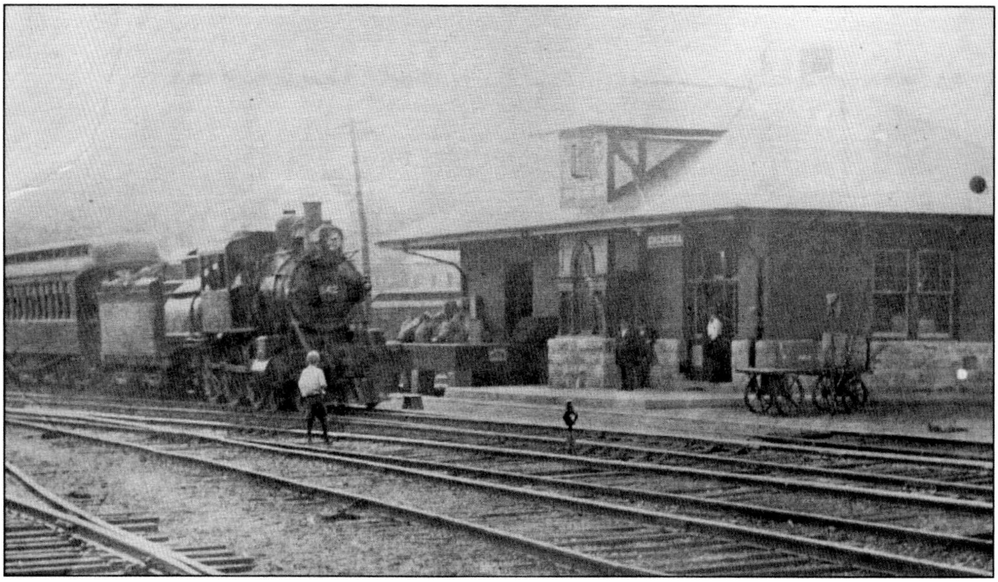

The "New" Philadelphia and Reading Railroad Station at Cressona is captured in this 1880s image that shows engine no. 542 waiting at the station as a curious lad looks on. This view was taken from Sillyman Street looking southwest from the crossing. Within 50 years, the present railroad bridge was constructed over Route 183 at this location.

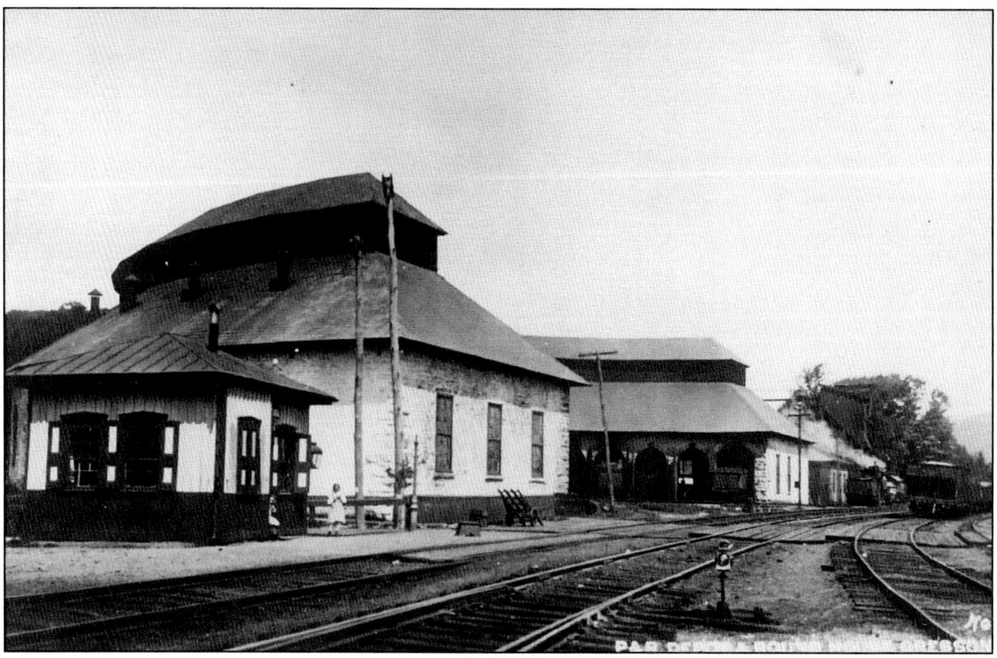

This early image of the Philadelphia and Reading Depot and Roundhouse at Cressona provides an interesting look into this unique and important railroad structure. Looking to the north from the Sillyman Street crossing, this photograph depicts the railroad yard operations near where the Blue Mountain Elementary School in Cressona stands today.

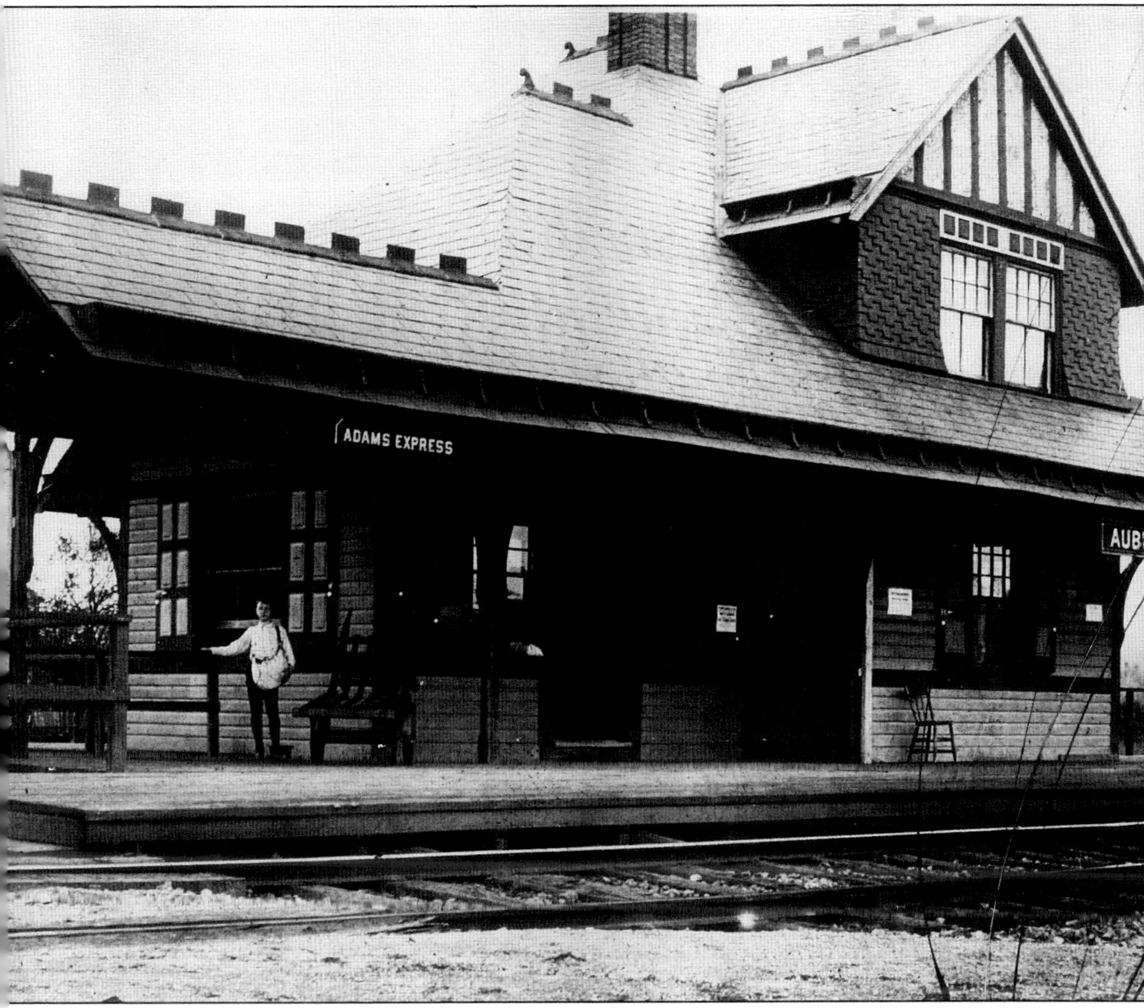

The Philadelphia and Reading Railroad's Passenger Station in Auburn is pictured in this turn-of-the-century photograph. The depot and freight house were located between Bear Creek and Front Street not too far from the Schuylkill Canal.

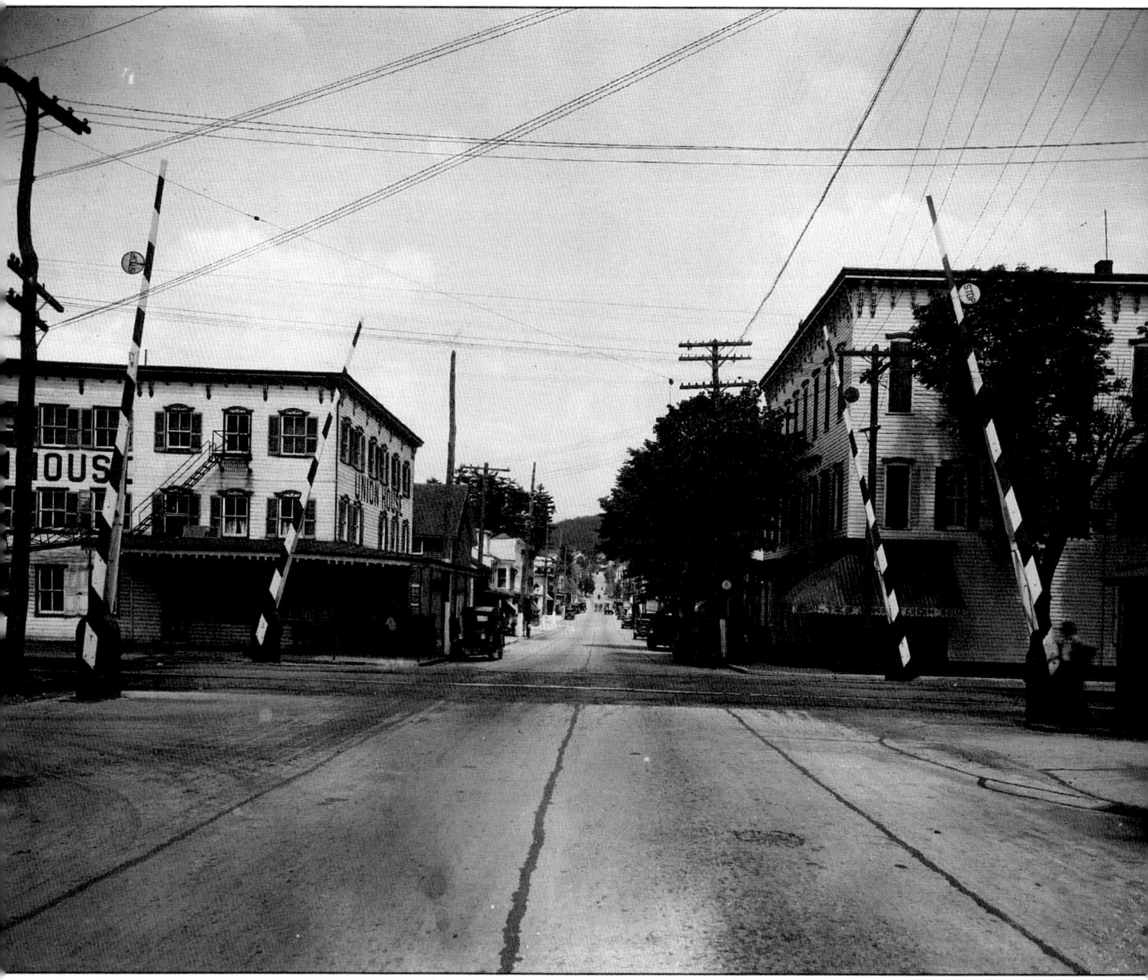

Downtown Tremont is captured in this unique railroad-crossing scene from the summer of 1928. Looking east along Main Street from near Crescent, a tree-lined Route 209 stretches eastward toward Pottsville. The Union House Hotel is pictured at the left and Schultz's Drug Store and Ice Cream Shop is to the right at the crossing.

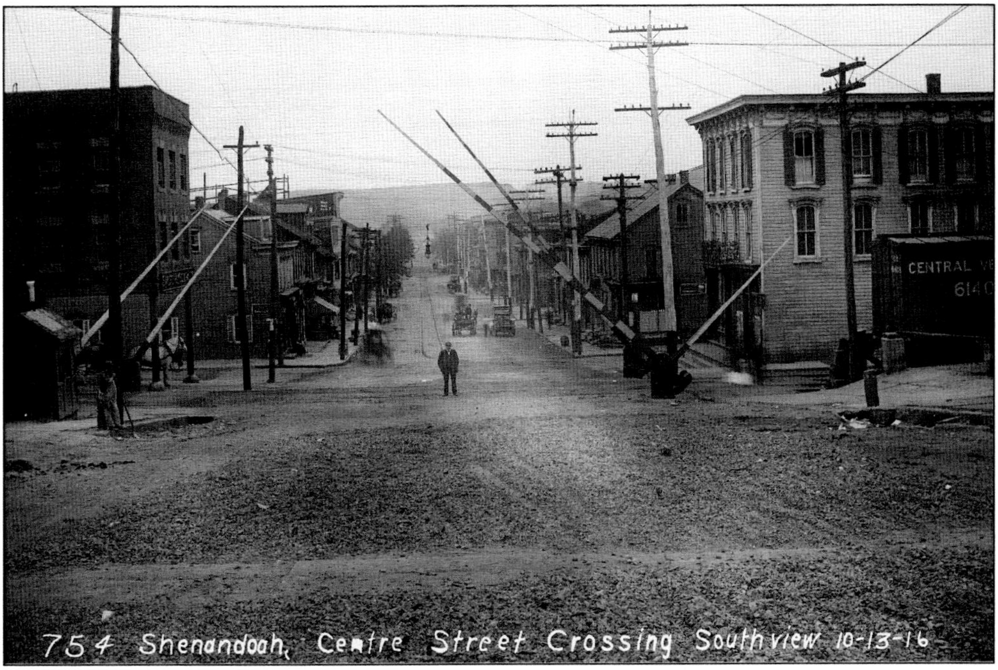

With few exceptions, this scene looking east along Centre Street in Shenandoah is familiar to many. Taken from Main Street this image shows the Centre Street Crossing as it looked in October 1916. This is the old Lehigh Valley and Mahanoy Railroad Crossing. Across the tracks on the right stood the Washington Hotel maintained by P.J. Ferguson.

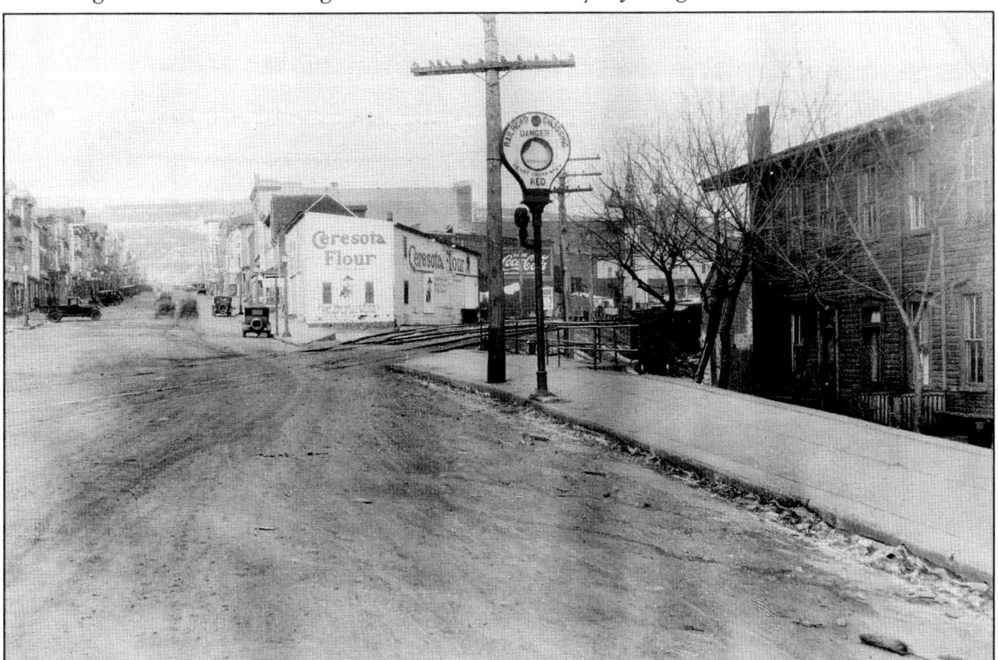

Looking north along Main Street in Shenandoah, this fading view of the downtown reminds us that the old Lehigh Valley Railroad ran through the area as late as December 1927, when this image was captured.

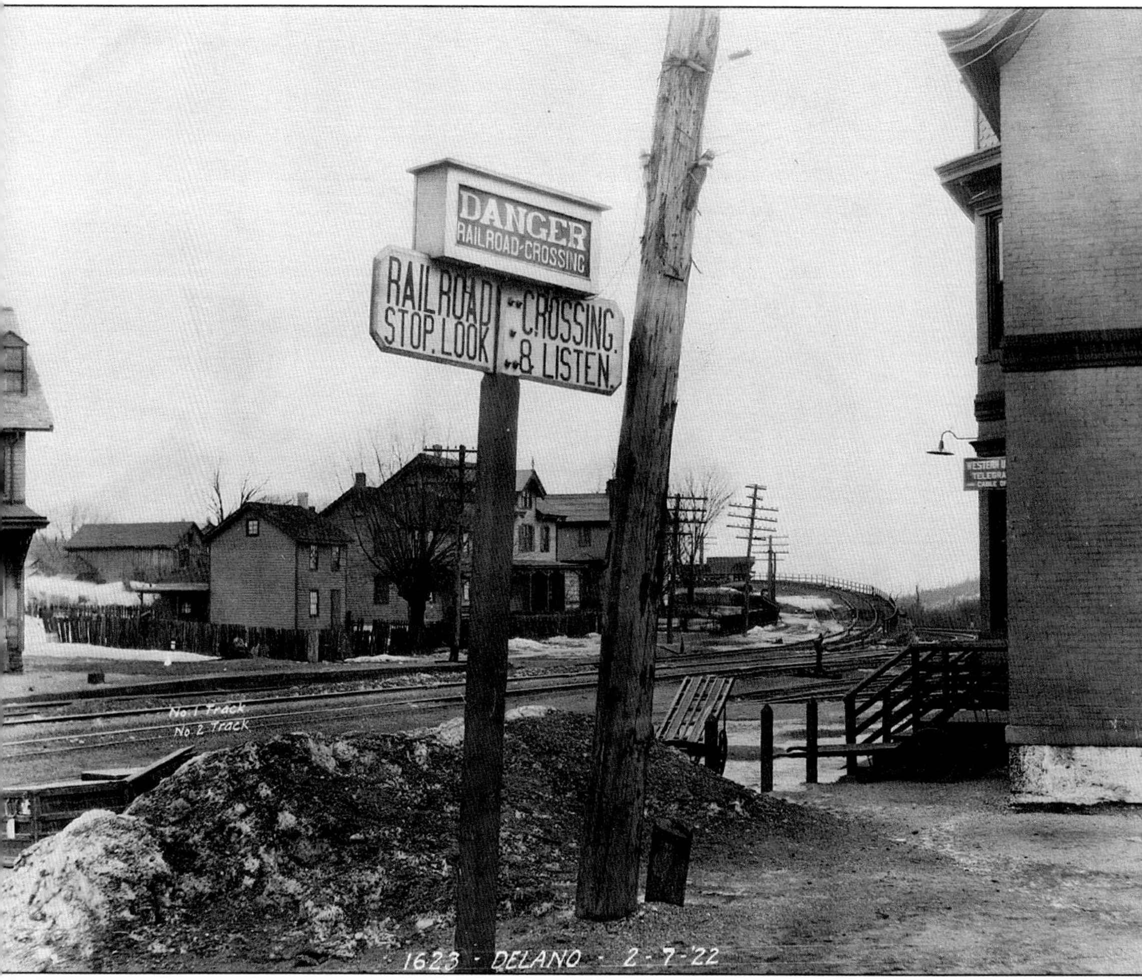

This 1922 view of the crossing at Delano is rare. The Delano station is situated to the right of the photograph, as the perspective is looking southeast across the tracks. The Delano Railroad yard lies off to the right of this image. Delano grew in importance as a railroad town at the end of the 19th century and the first half of the 20th century.

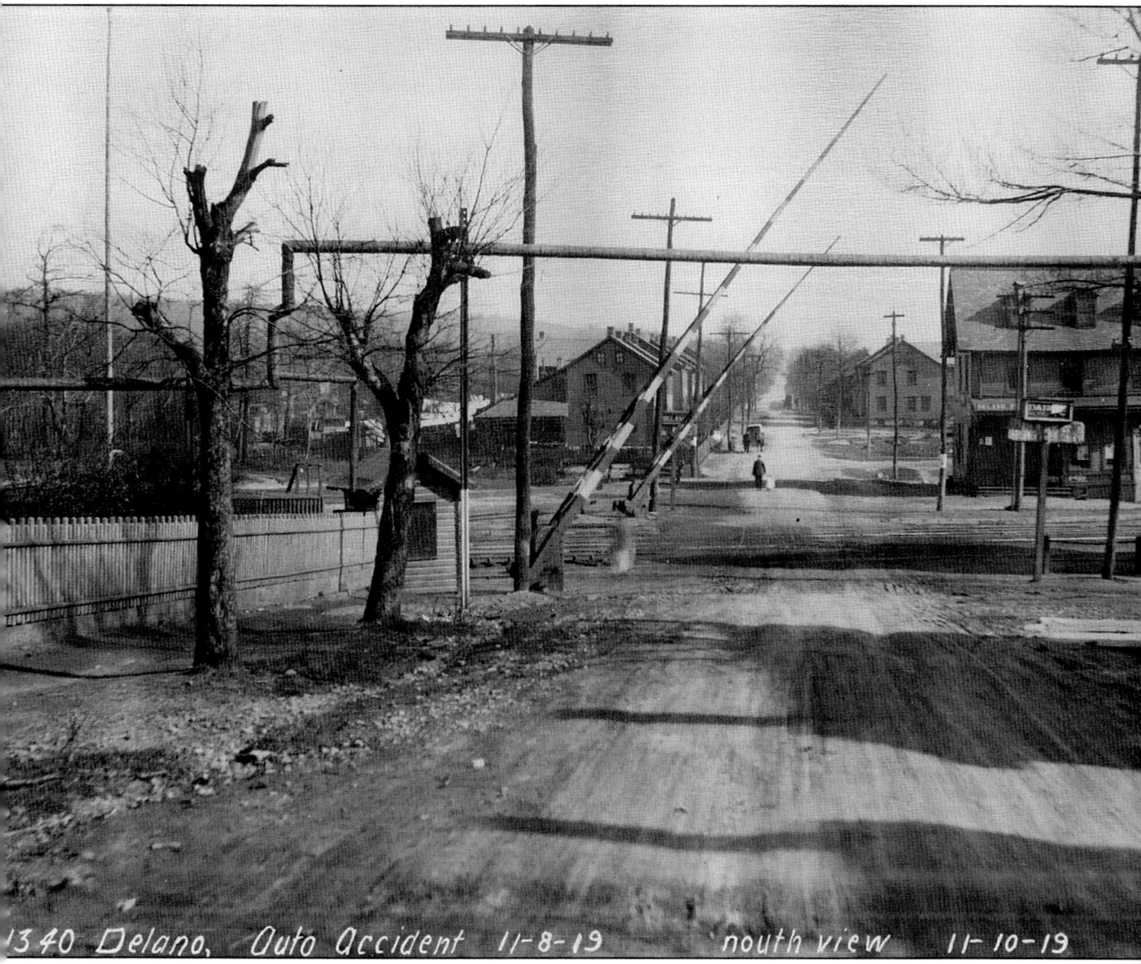

Another view of this crossing shows the Delano depot in this 1919 image. Delano is named after Warren Delano, Franklin Delano Roosevelt's maternal grandfather. This view was taken looking east showing the line of Coal Company homes on the street in the distance.

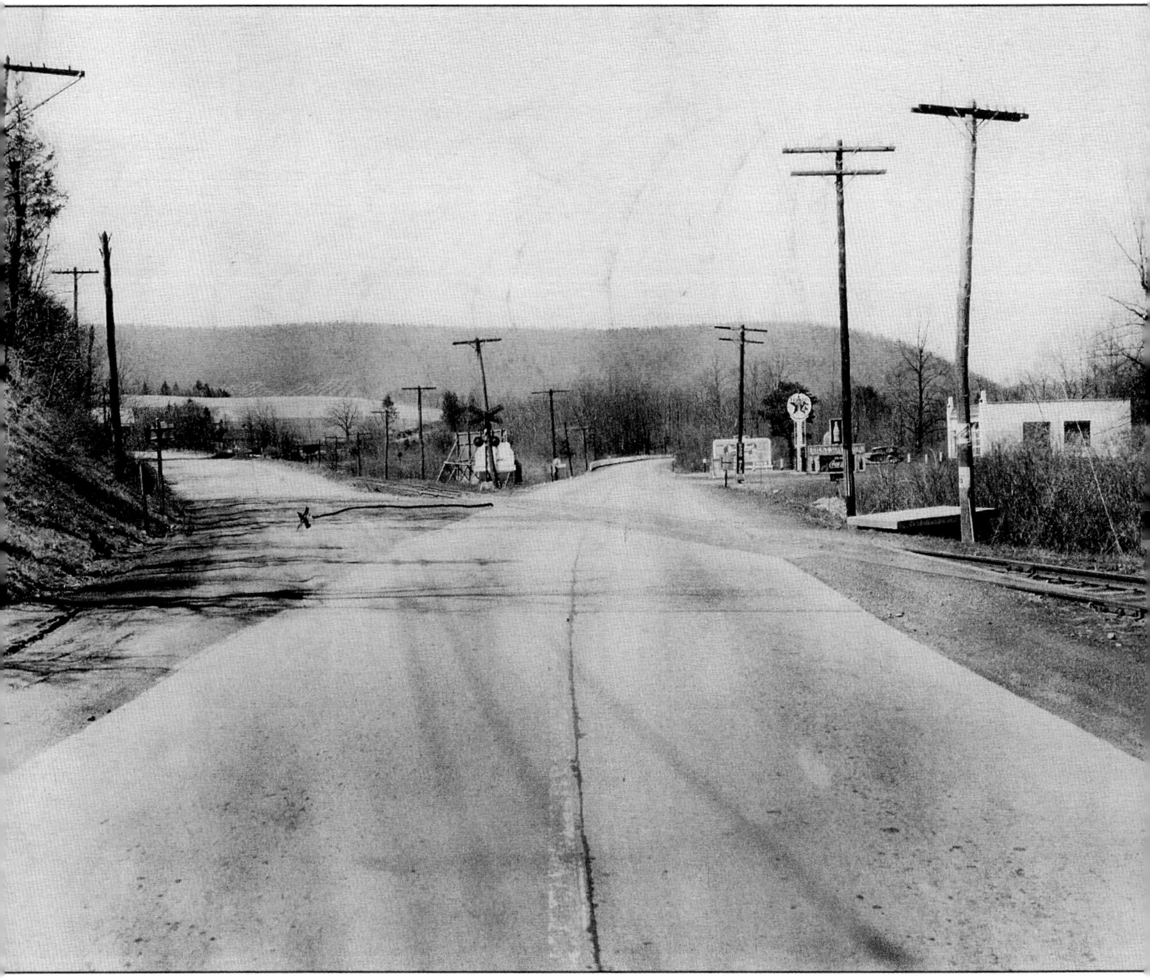

This 1946 image at Pine Grove shows the Philadelphia and Reading Railroad crossing along today's Route 125. This rail line was once operated by the Schuylkill and Susquehanna Railroad.

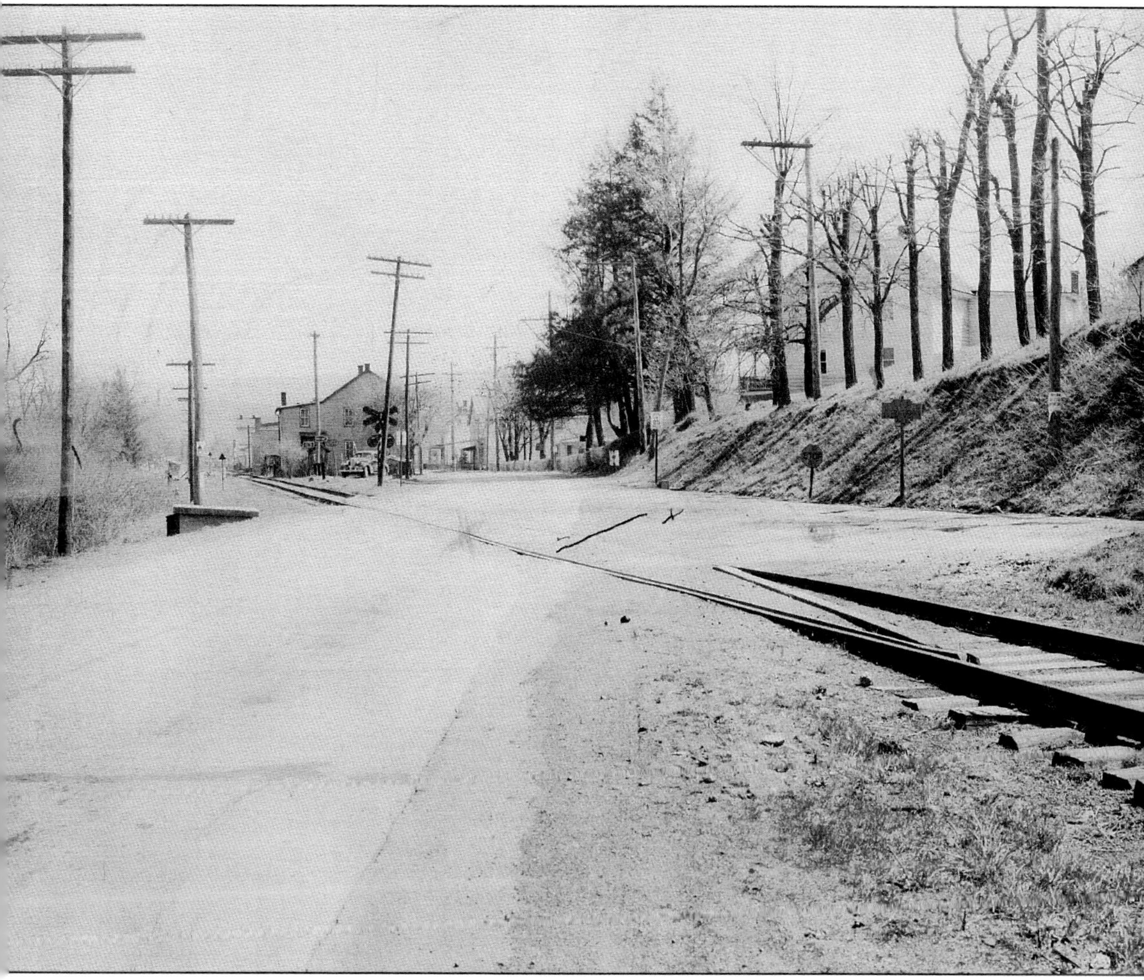

And, in reverse, here is a view looking south along State Route 125 at the same Railroad Crossing at Pine Grove on a sunny September day. Tulpehocken Street homes are seen in the distance. In the 18th century, this same road was known as the Tulpehocken Trail.

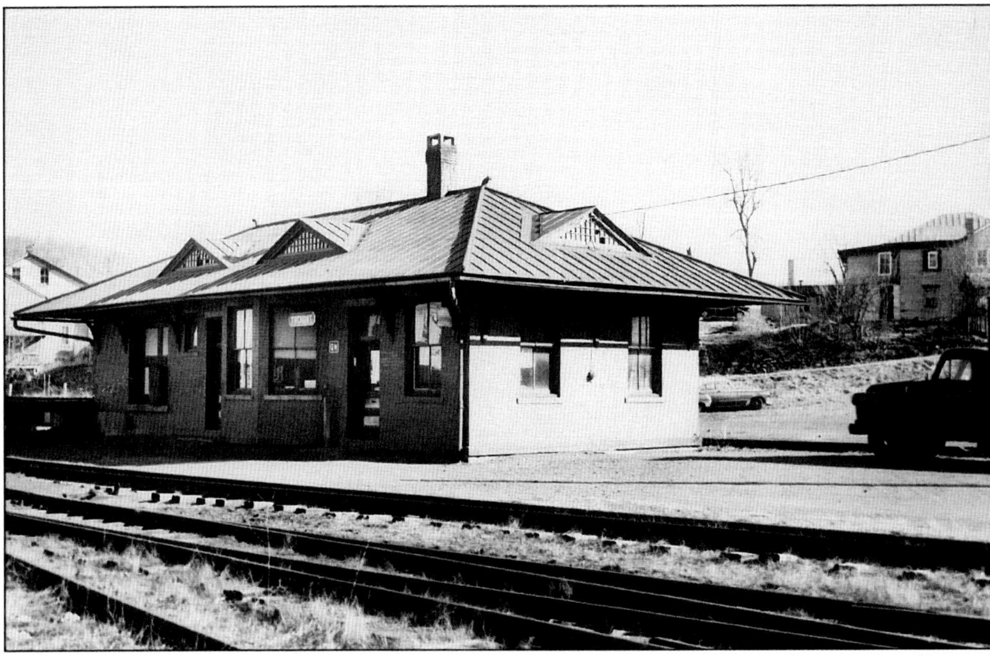

As a symbol of the region's railroad heritage, the Tremont Depot and Freight House still stand along Crescent Street, along the road to Donaldson. The railroad, as pictured here in 1963, is the former Tremont extension of the Mine Hill and Schuylkill Haven Railroad. This road tapped the tremendous coal reserves in the Schuylkill County west end.

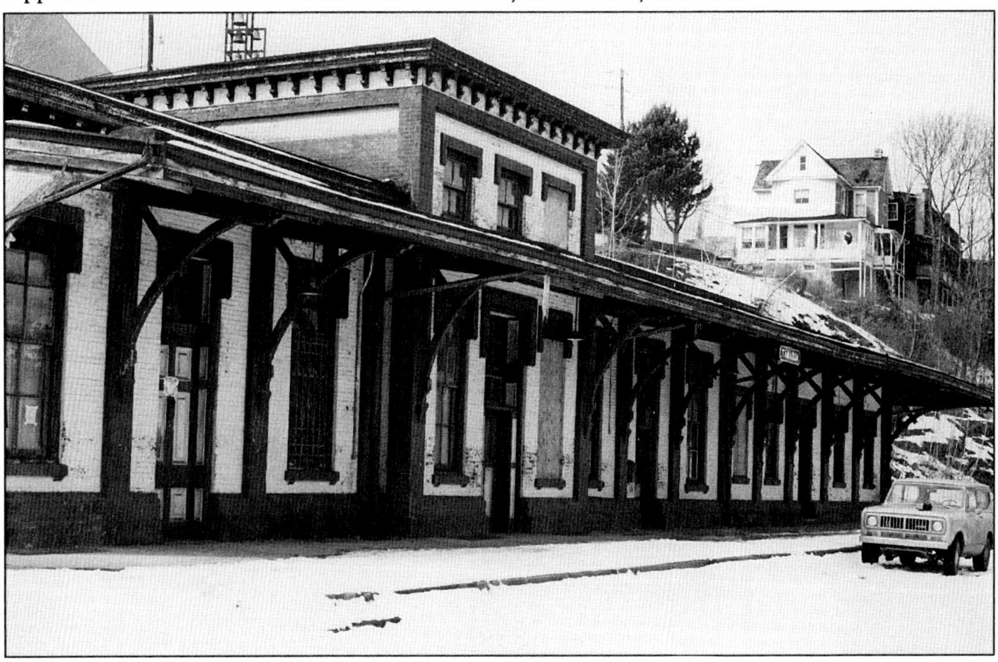

The Philadelphia and Reading's Railroad Station at Tamaqua was constructed in 1874, but is a mere shadow of its former self in this 1976 photograph. Fortunately for railroad fans, the Tamaqua Station is being saved, renovated, and preserved for future generations thanks to the efforts of Tamaqua Save Our Station and the Tamaqua Historical Society.

Six

Unique Views From Schuylkill County

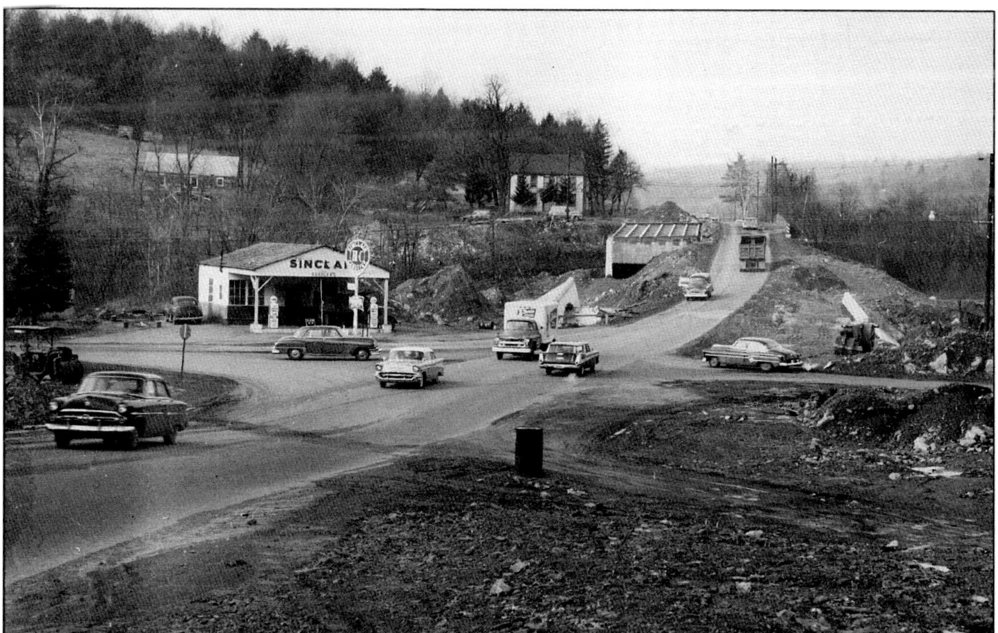

In 1959 this intersection witnessed development as the Pottsville-Minersville Highway was resurfaced and widened. Today's image of this Route 901 and 209 intersection in the Westwood section of Pottsville has changed considerably. Hey, where's the traffic light?

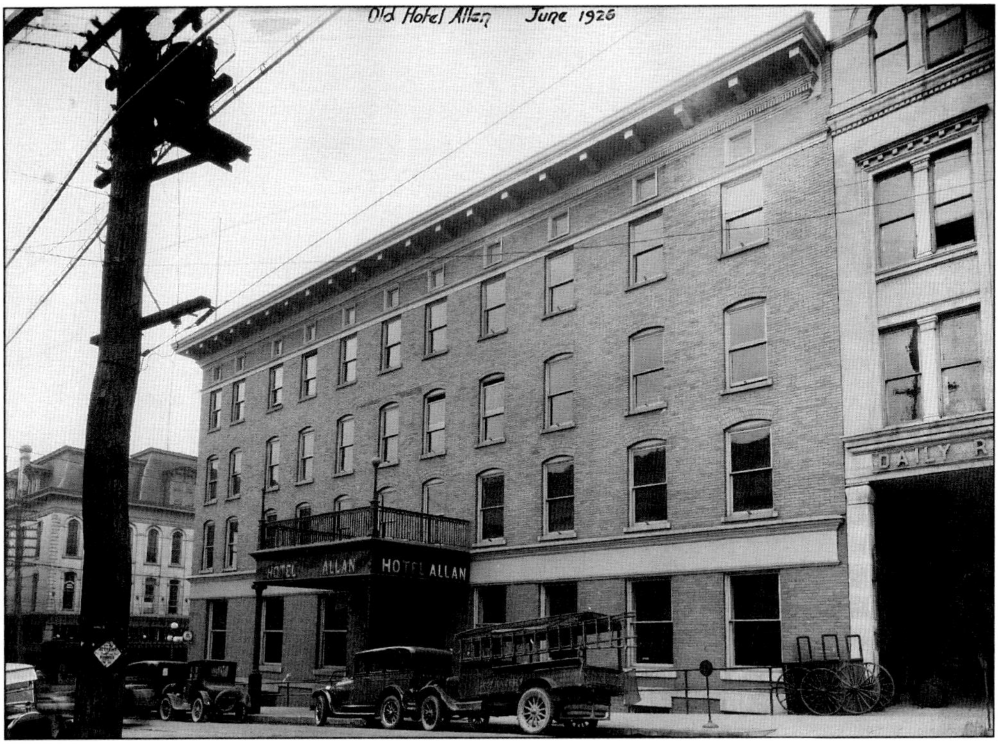

Oddly enough, the old Hotel Allan was not named after Necho Allen, but rather Thomas Allan, the establishment's proprietor. This June 1926 view is taken a year before the Necho Allen was built on the same spot. This property has been a lodging business since the White Horse Hotel was built in the first half of the 19th century.

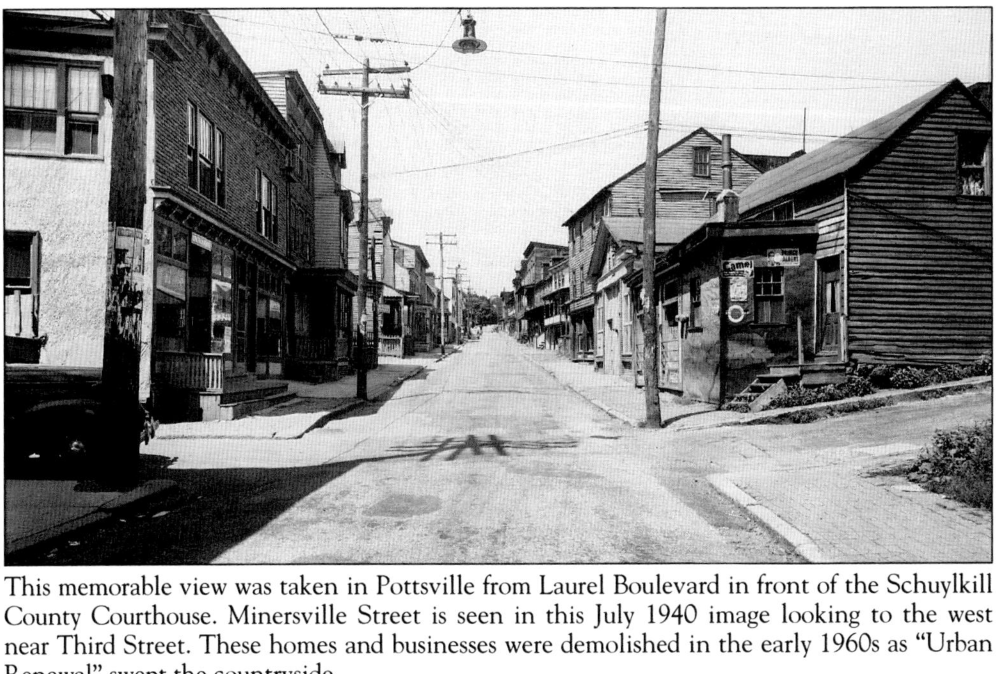

This memorable view was taken in Pottsville from Laurel Boulevard in front of the Schuylkill County Courthouse. Minersville Street is seen in this July 1940 image looking to the west near Third Street. These homes and businesses were demolished in the early 1960s as "Urban Renewal" swept the countryside.

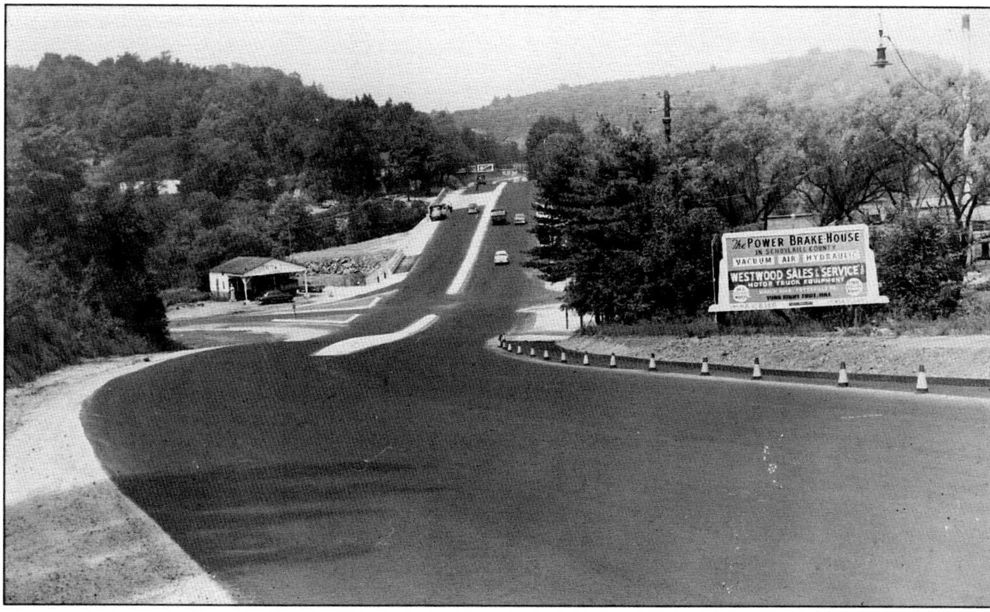

This is another view of the Pottsville-Minersville Highway near where the old Yorkville Arch stood in the Westwood section of town. This summer-of-1959 image shows the completion of the railroad bridge over the Reading Railroad line connecting Cressona and Minersville. Repaving is completed, but the traffic signal would not arrive until the mid-1980s.

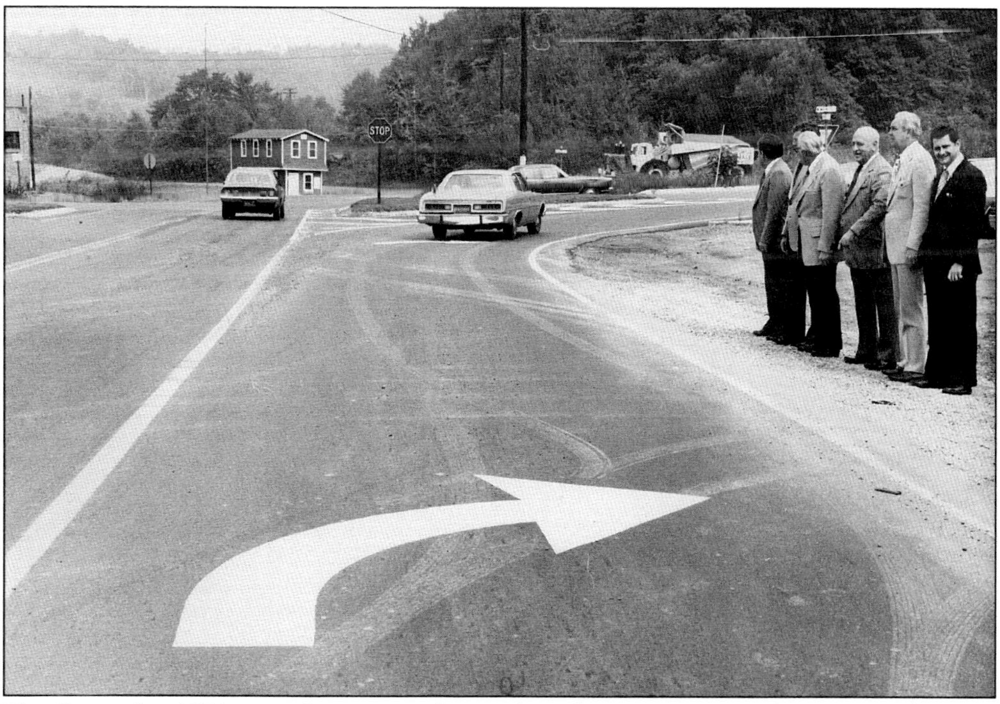

This September 1971 image features another angle to the intersection at the Westwood section of Pottsville. Taken from the Gordon Nagle Road approach to West Market Street, this image features, from right to left: Representative James Goodman, Charles Dimmerling, John S. Clarke, and three other local officials surveying development nearby.

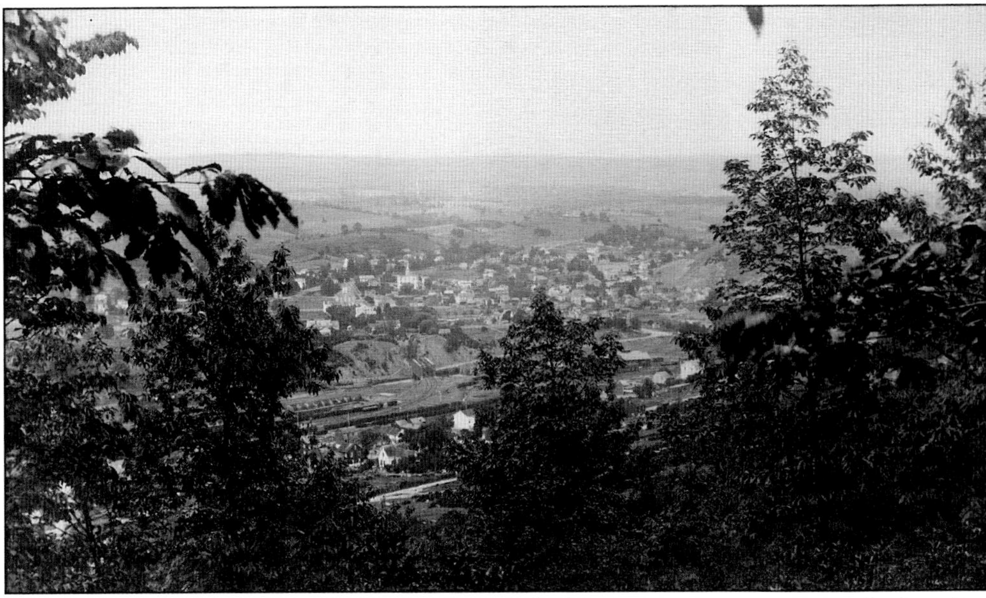

A rare view from atop Sharp Mountain above Palo Alto gives us an interesting look at Port Carbon and a portion of the Palo Alto Railroad Yards. The railroad cut in Salem Hill and the old public schoolhouse in Port Carbon are clearly visible. The Broad Mountain rises in the distance to the north of this pre-1895 picture.

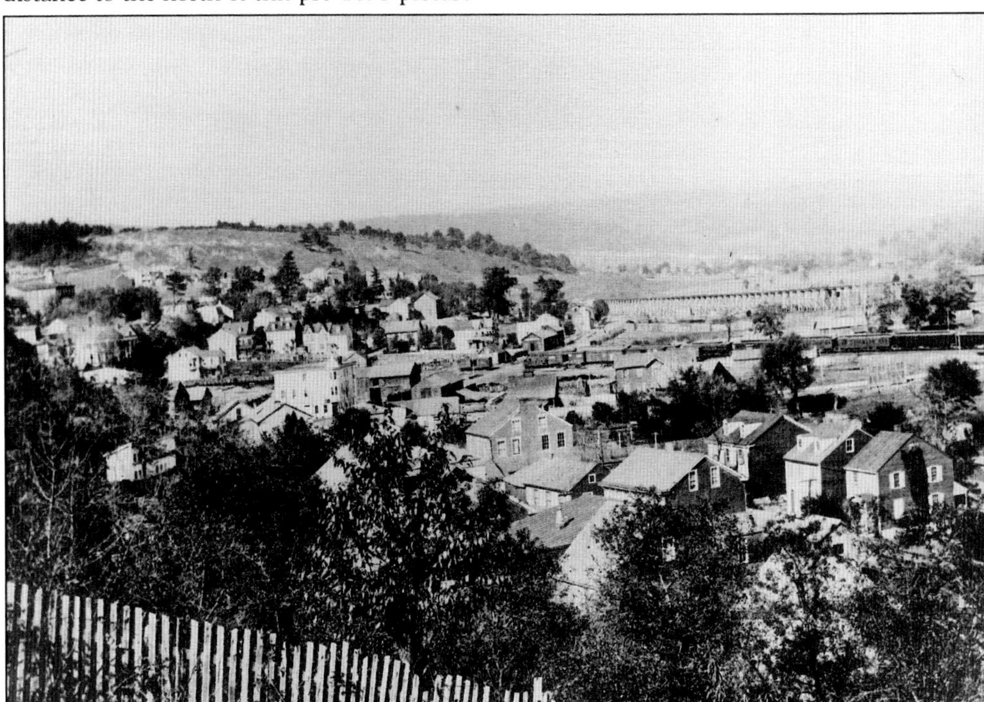

Minersville, Pennsylvania is featured in this *c.* 1880 photograph taken from Spruce Street in the borough looking north toward Duncott and Mine Hill Gap. The train tracks in the foreground are located along North Street. The Second Street Elementary building is seen in the upper left corner of this image.

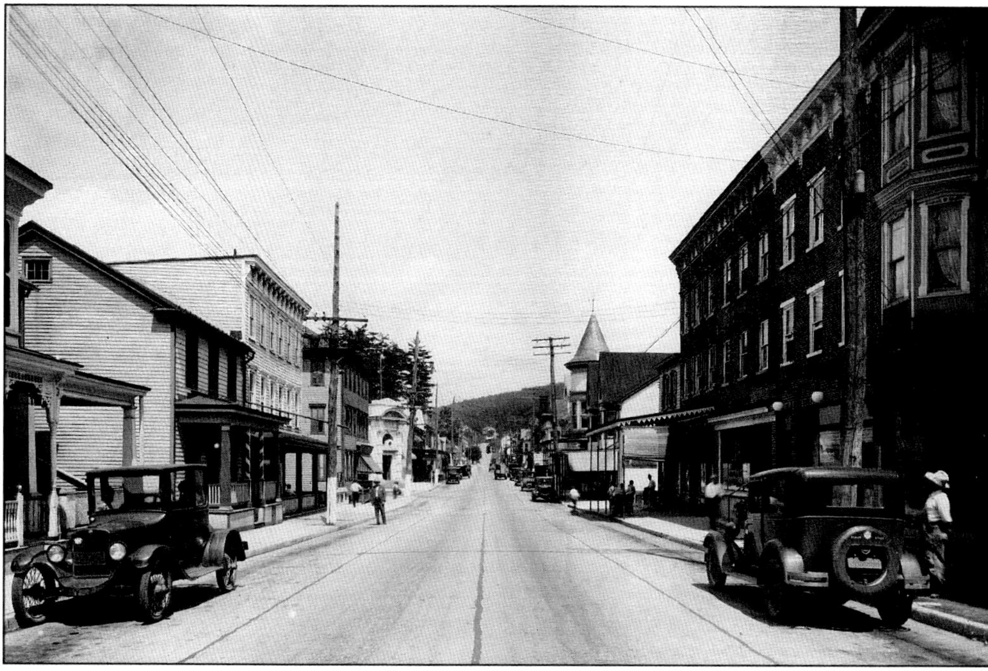

This wonderful view of downtown Tremont was taken in June of 1928 along Main Street (Route 209) looking to the east. Fortunately, many of these familiar structures have survived the century. A present-day drive through Tremont would attest to that fact.

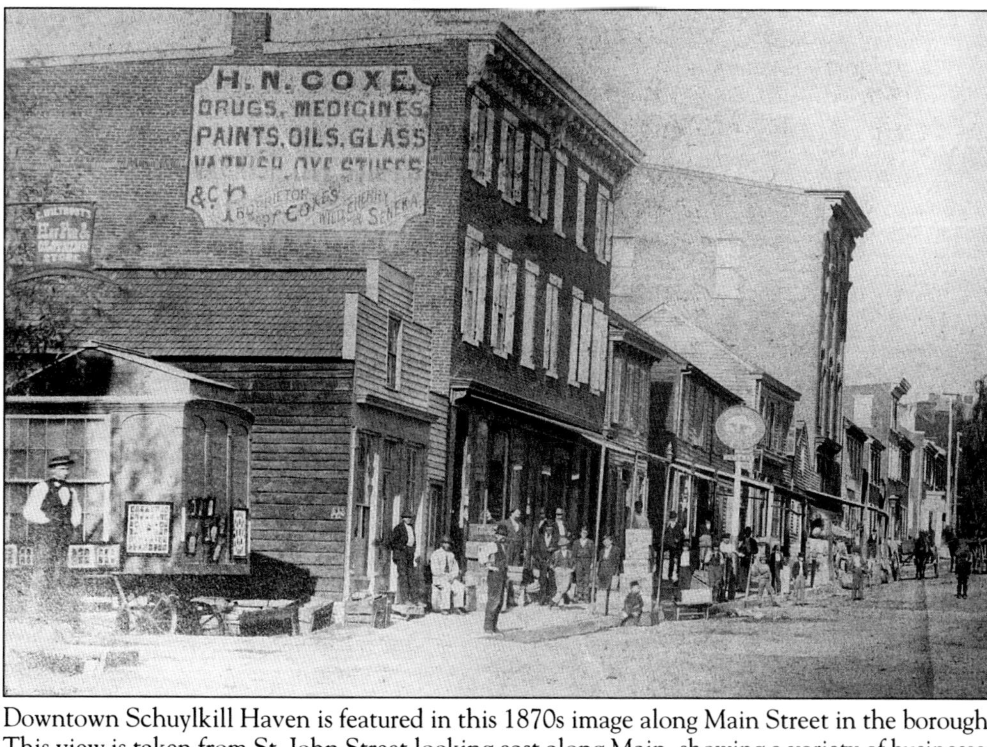

Downtown Schuylkill Haven is featured in this 1870s image along Main Street in the borough. This view is taken from St. John Street looking east along Main, showing a variety of businesses and a score of local men and children posing for an afternoon picture.

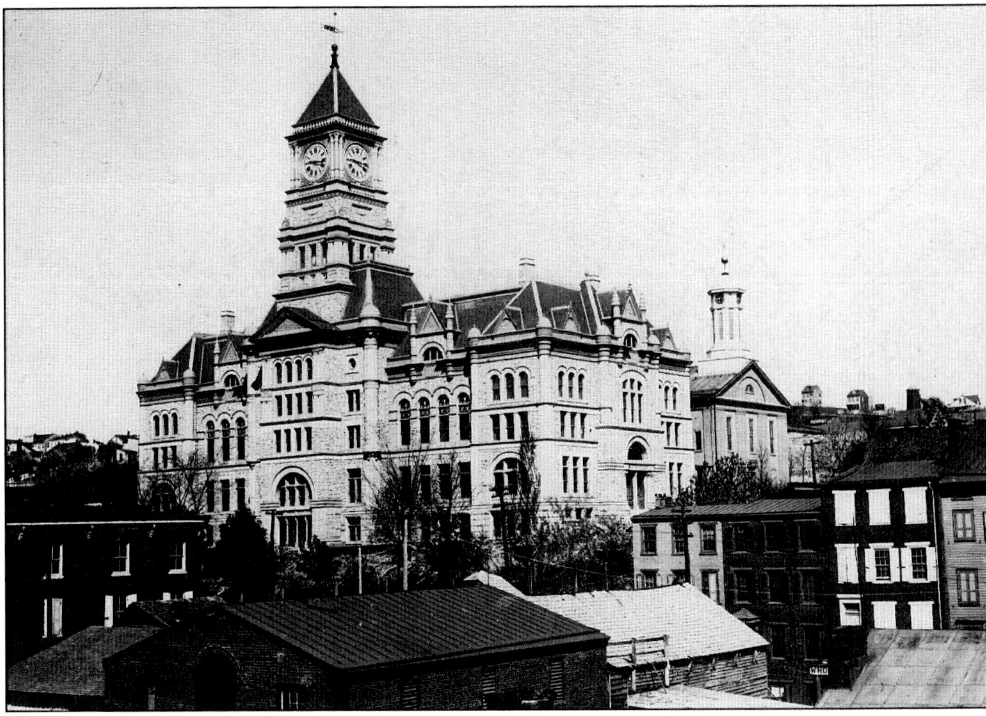

A two-for-the-price-of-one rare photograph shows both the present-day and the former Schuylkill County Courthouse in 1890. The "new" courthouse was constructed in 1889 and dedicated that same year. The old courthouse stood on this hill since 1850 after the move of the county seat to Pottsville from Orwigsburg.

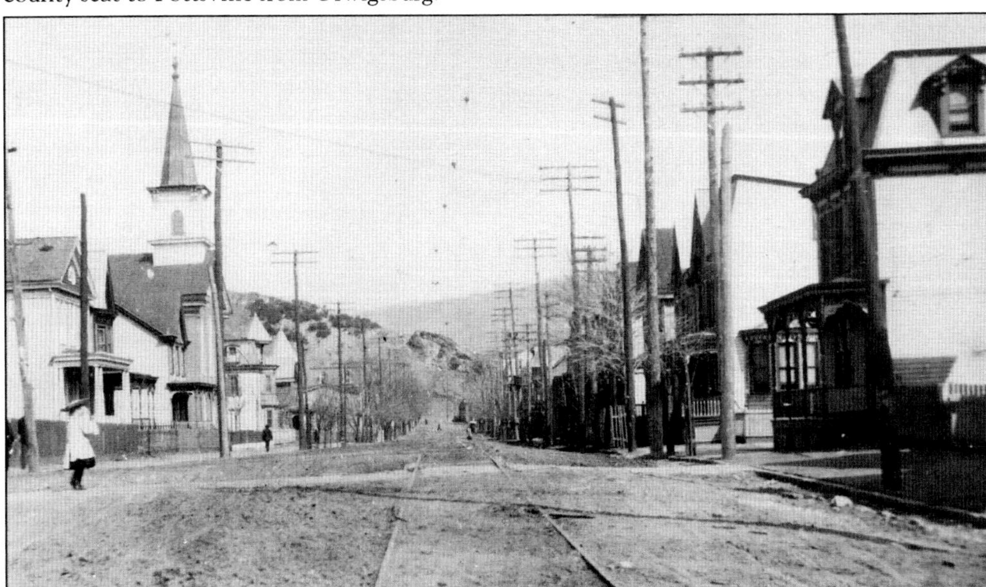

Downtown Port Carbon is featured in this c. 1895 view looking east along Pike Street. The United Methodist Church is seen on the left of this image while the goat rock section of present-day Monument Hill is seen at the far end. The trolley tracks shown here still remain, but are buried by several layers of macadam.

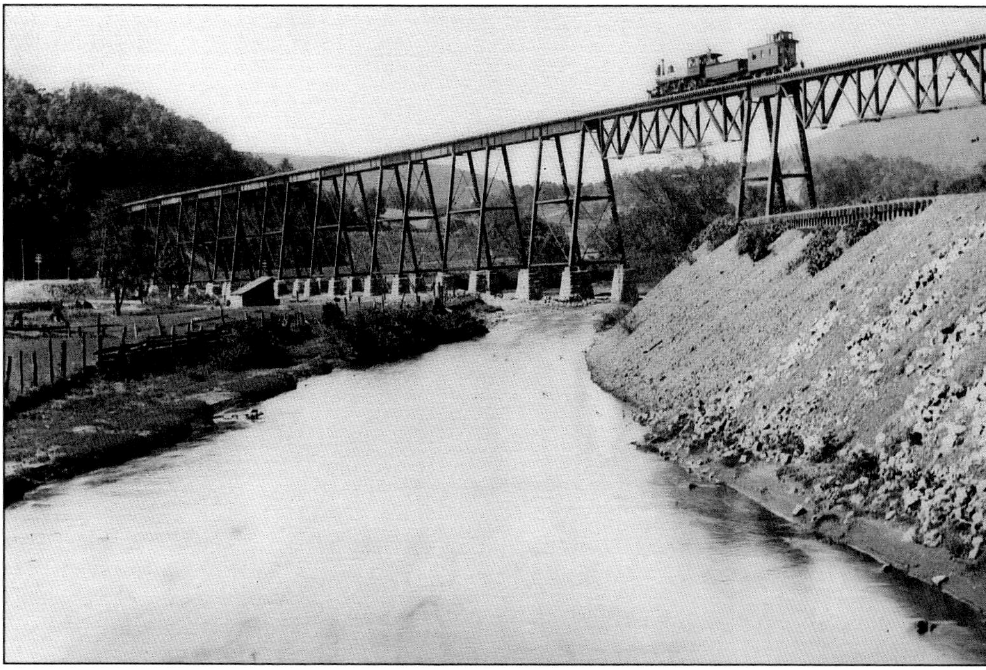

The Lehigh Valley Railroad trestle is shown in this *c.* 1885 image near Connor's Crossing, which is near Cressona. Today this is the site of the Cressona Mall and surrounding businesses. That is the Schuylkill River flowing toward the photographer in this view looking to the northwest from today's intersection of Route 183 and Route 61.

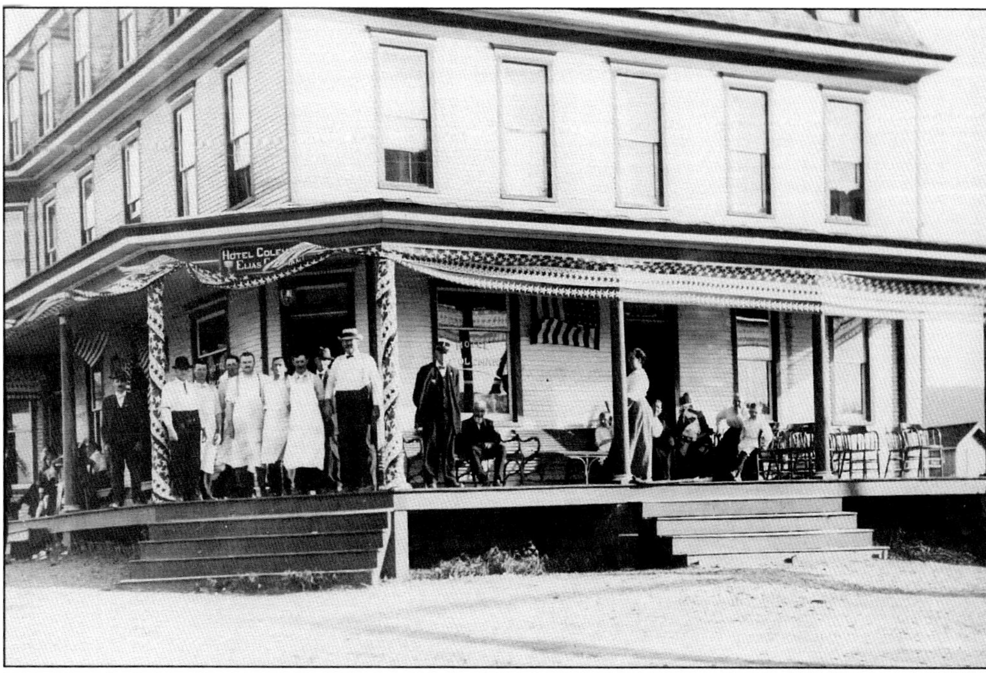

The Hotel Coleman located in downtown Valley View is featured in this early 20th-century image. This photograph, provided by Jay Meyer, shows the hotel on the southwest corner of Gap and Main Streets, during the Fourth of July parade festivities in 1911.

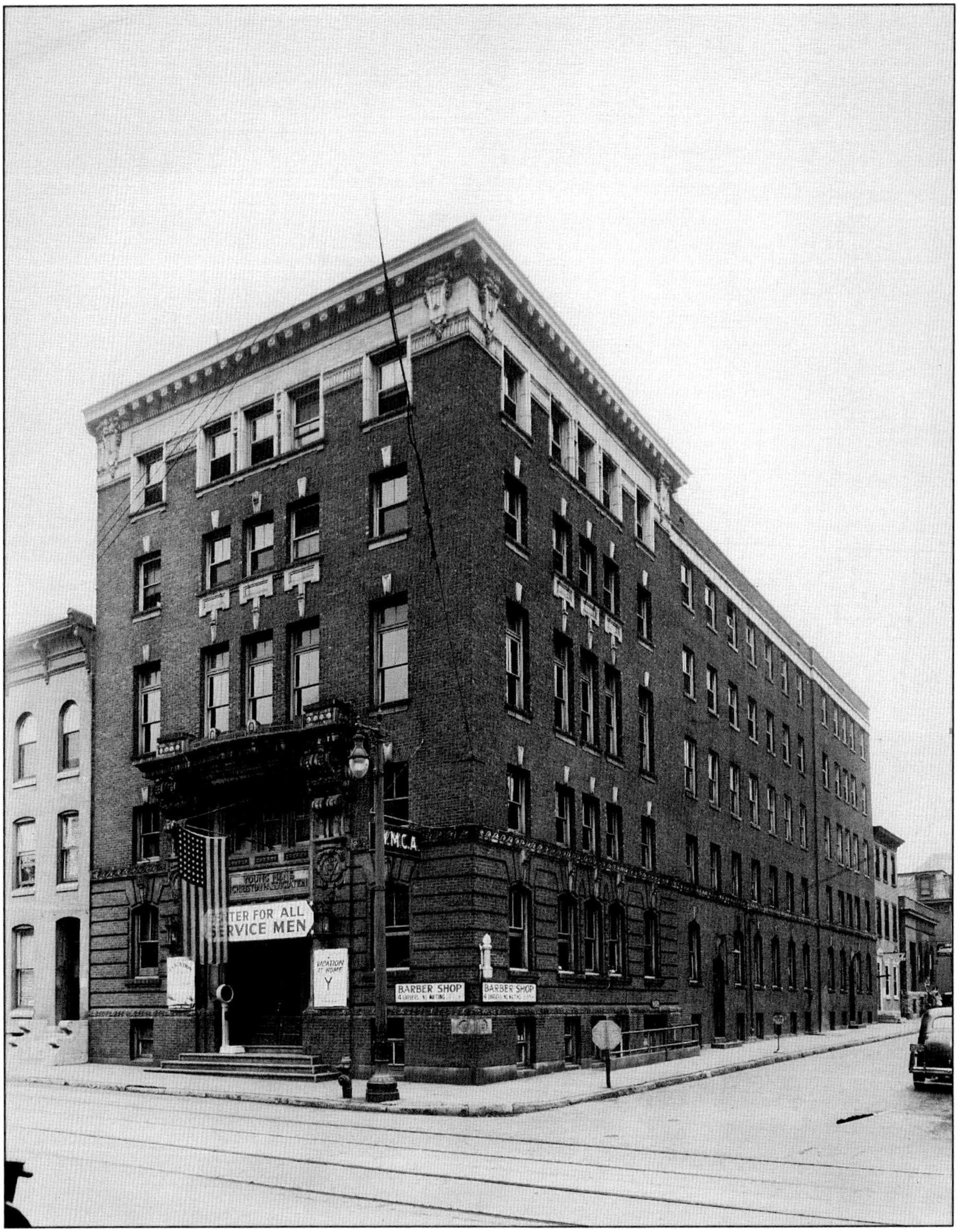

The Young Men's Christian Association (YMCA) building located at Second and Market in Pottsville is pictured here during WW II. This structure, built in 1907, served three generations of Pottsville's youth and featured a swimming pool, basketball court, running track, and bowling alleys. The building was demolished in the mid-1970s to make room for a parking lot.

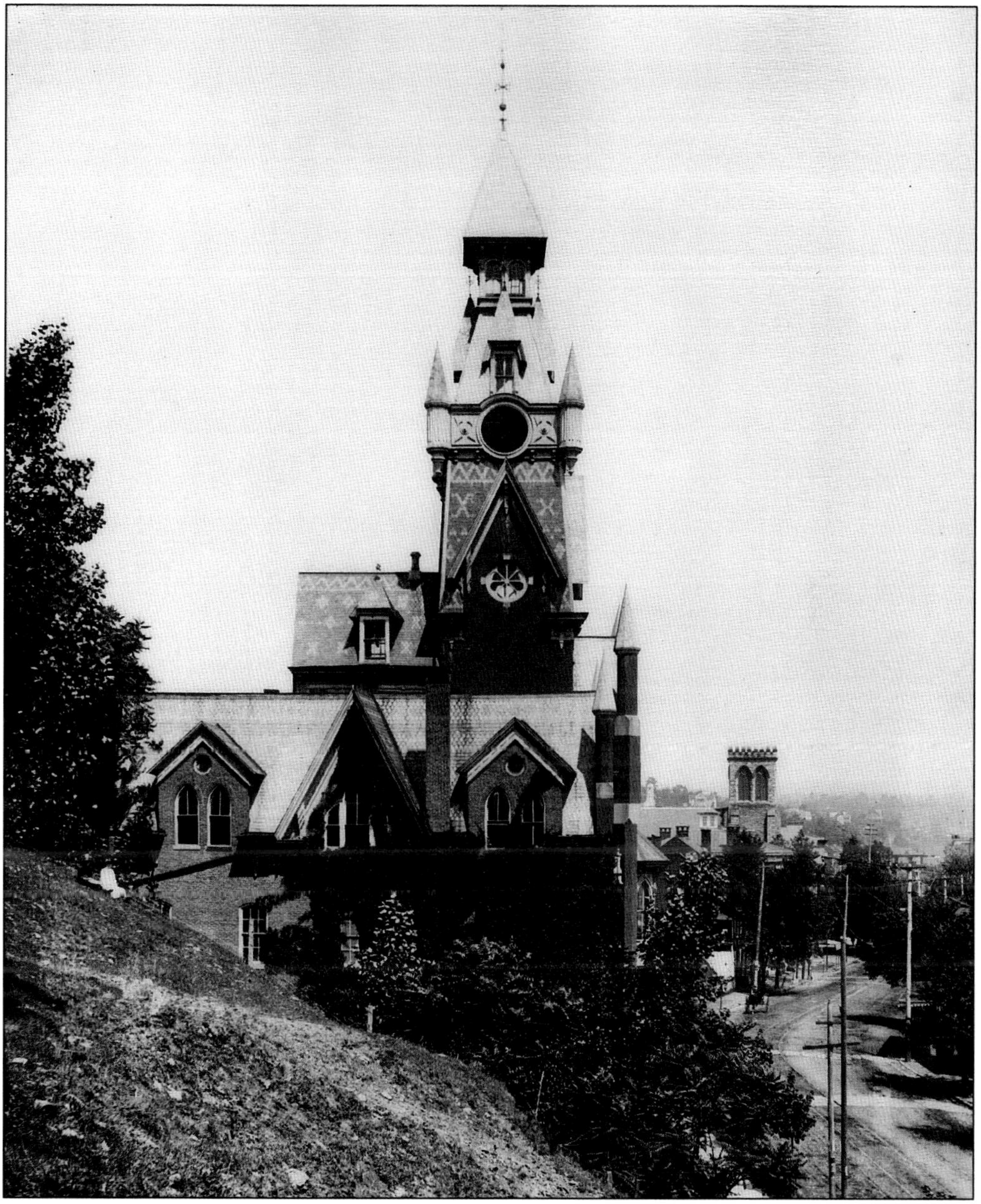

The *Miner's Journal* building was constructed along Pottsville's South Centre Street in 1876, but lasted less than two decades as it was destroyed by fire in 1892. The Young Women's Christian Association (YWCA) building currently occupies this property. This 1880s view is of the front of the Henry Clay Monument, looking north along Centre.

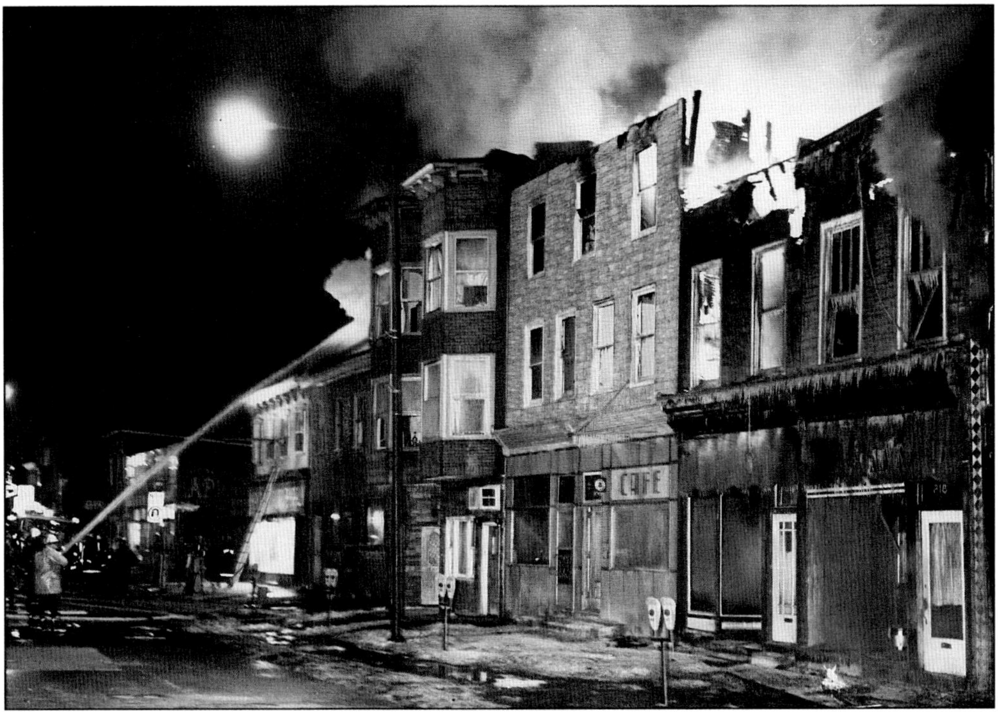

This Mahanoy city fire is in the process of destroying the two hundred block of West Centre Street in February of 1975. The A&P grocery store is visible as firefighters struggle to prevent the fire from spreading to McLaren's Auto Supply store at the corner of Linden and Centre. The Citizen's Fire Company eventually built their firehouse on this site two decades later.

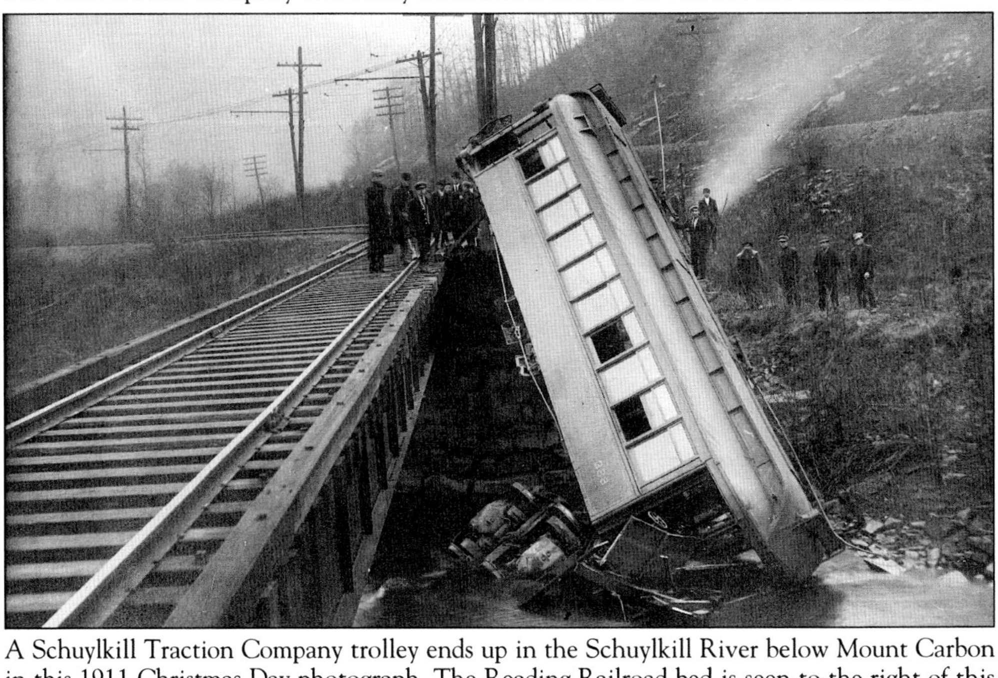

A Schuylkill Traction Company trolley ends up in the Schuylkill River below Mount Carbon in this 1911 Christmas Day photograph. The Reading Railroad bed is seen to the right of this image taken at Cape Horn, a notorious bend in the Schuylkill River.

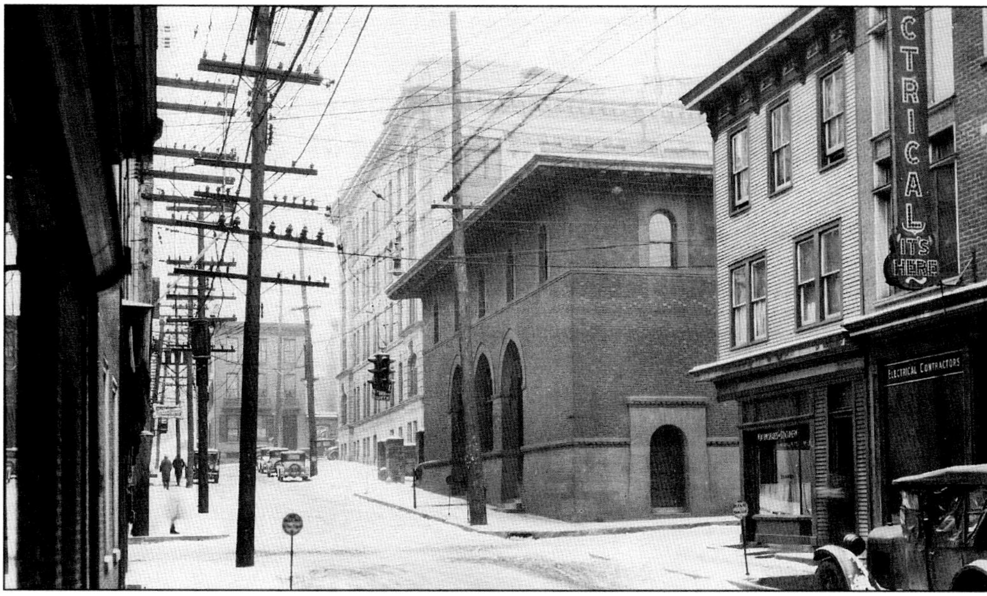

This 1920s winter scene in downtown Pottsville is at the corner of Second and Norwegian Streets. The building at the center of this image is the 1896 Pottsville Post Office. The Philadelphia and Reading Coal and Iron Company building looms large in the background, while a stationary store (now Kep's Corner) stands on the corner to the right.

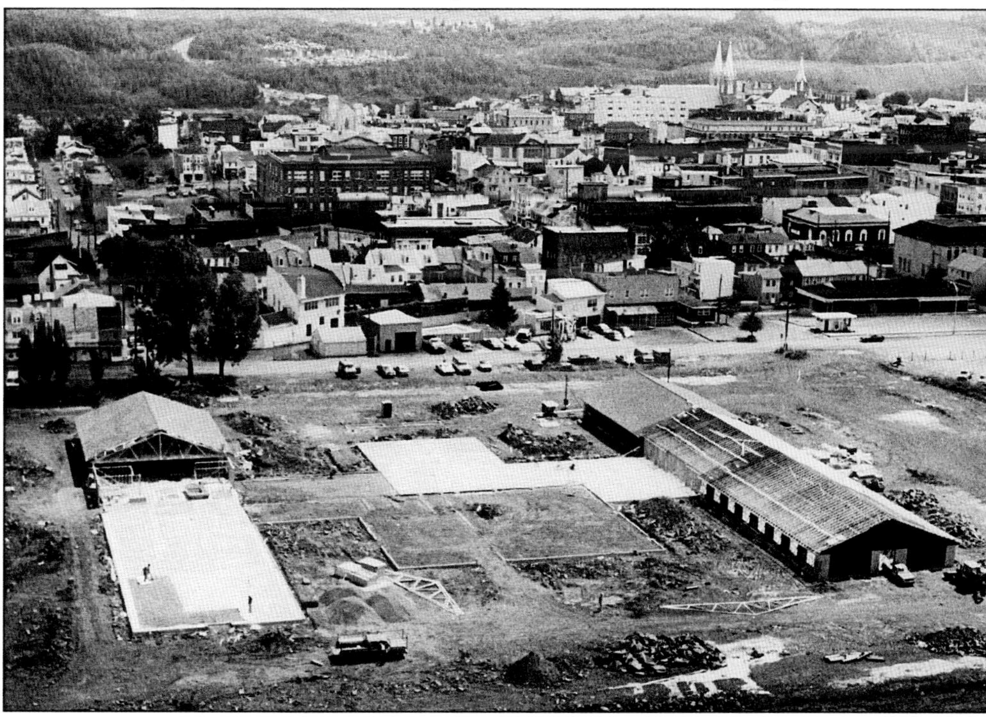

Shenandoah Manor Nursing Home along East Washington Street undergoes construction in this 1982 shot of Shenandoah from atop "The Heights." Also visible in this picture is the J.W. Cooper High School in the top-left center portion of the image. The twin spires of Saint George's Roman Catholic Church are seen in the distance to the right.

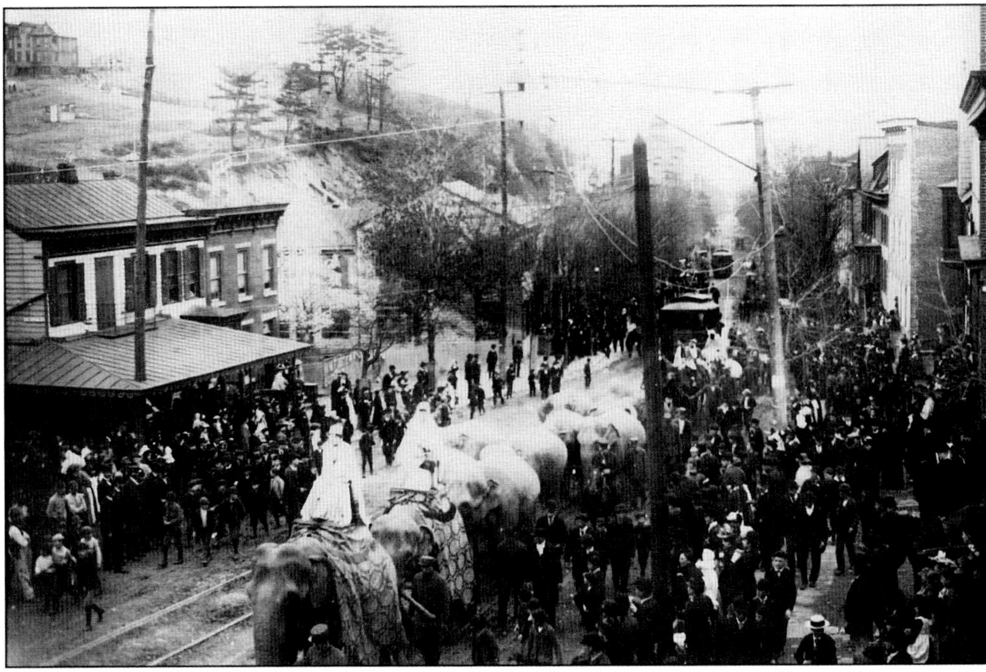

Those are elephants on Market Street! This image, taken from the corner of Twelfth and Market in Pottsville, shows the elephants of the Daley Brothers Circus moving westward toward the circus grounds at Dolan's Park in Yorkville. This 1880s image shows a curious crowd of men, women, and, especially, children along the parade route.

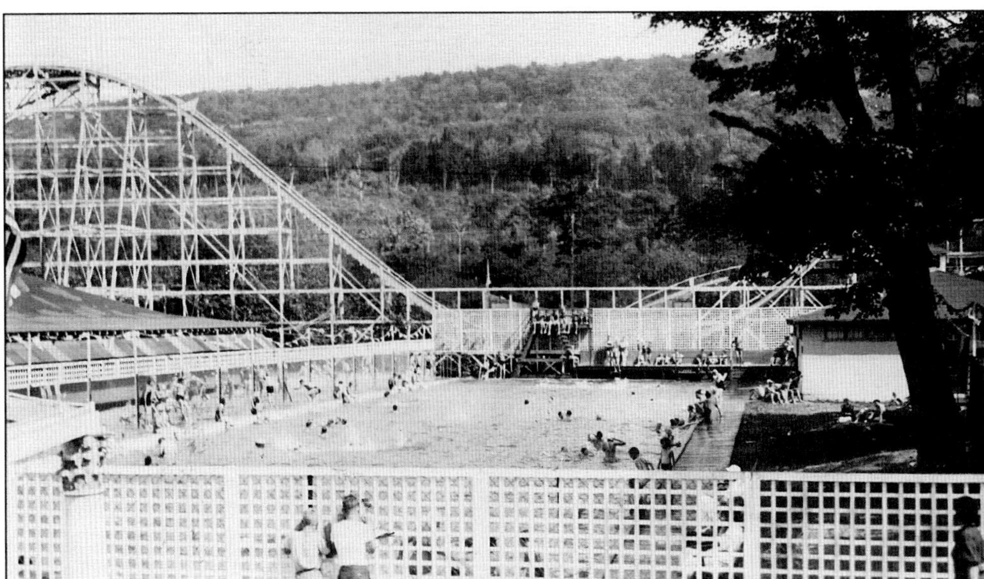

Dream City Park is featured in this 1930s image. Also known as Schuylkill Park, it was situated along Route 209 between Cumbola and Port Carbon in East Norwegian Township. The park was popular for its entertainment, roller coaster, roller-skating, and swimming.

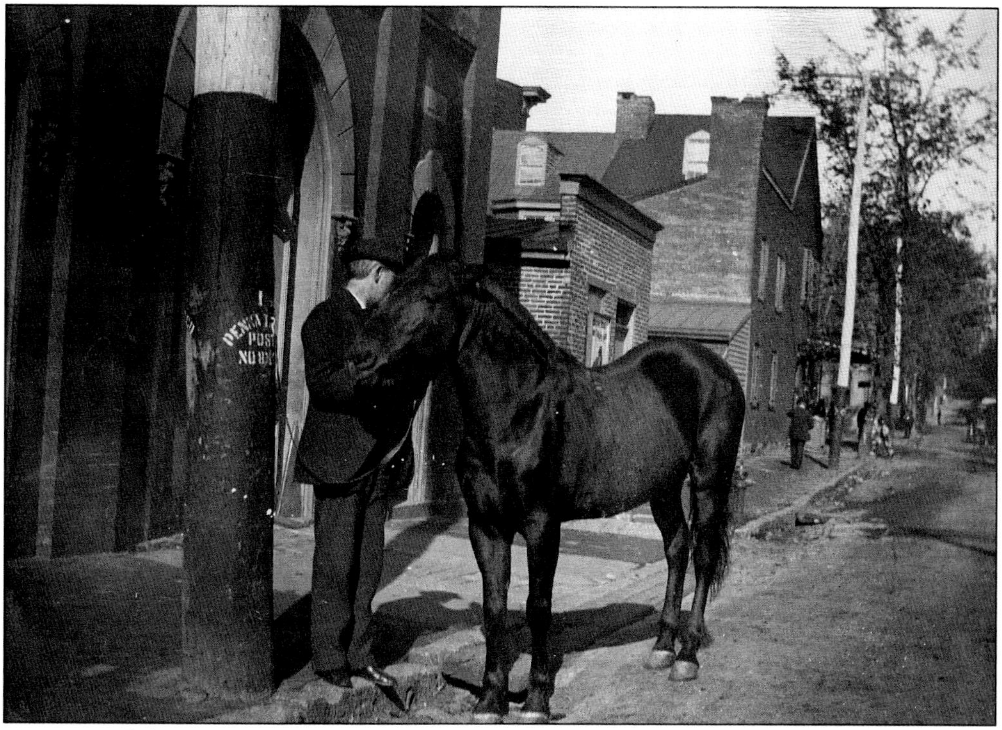

No automobile-engine powered fire trucks are in this picture. All the (1890s) modern-day horsepower is found in this unique four-legged contraption as pictured in front of the Good Intent Fire Company at Second Street in Pottsville. The view is a mid-day scene looking north along second toward Market Street.

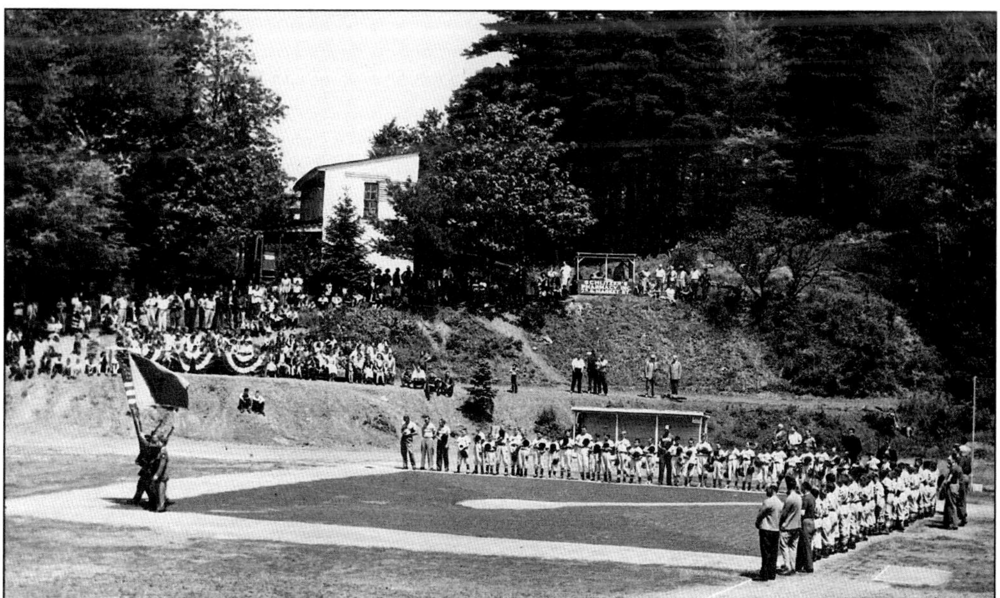

Those are the little leaguers as seen during opening day exercises in the 1950s at Railway Park in Pottsville. Even in the early years of Little League, business sponsors were important, as is noticed in the Schlitzer's Pharmacy banner at the center of the photograph.

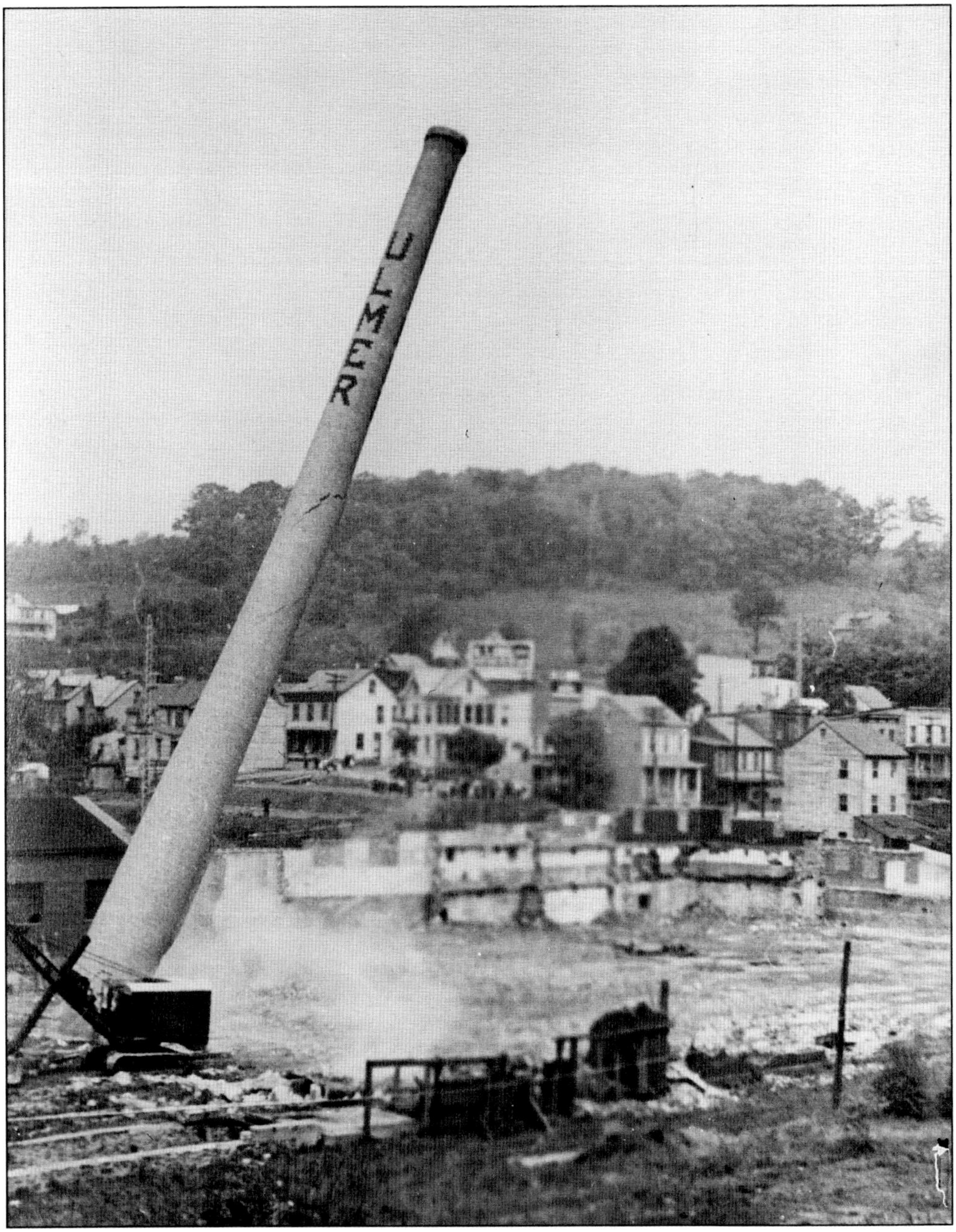

The Ulmer Meat Packing smokestack in Pottsville comes crashing to the earth in this rare image. The packinghouse was situated in the West Branch Norwegian Creek Valley (Fishbach) section of Pottsville. This image is one of a series of photographs depicting the stack's demise on May 7, 1944, at 12:15 in the afternoon.

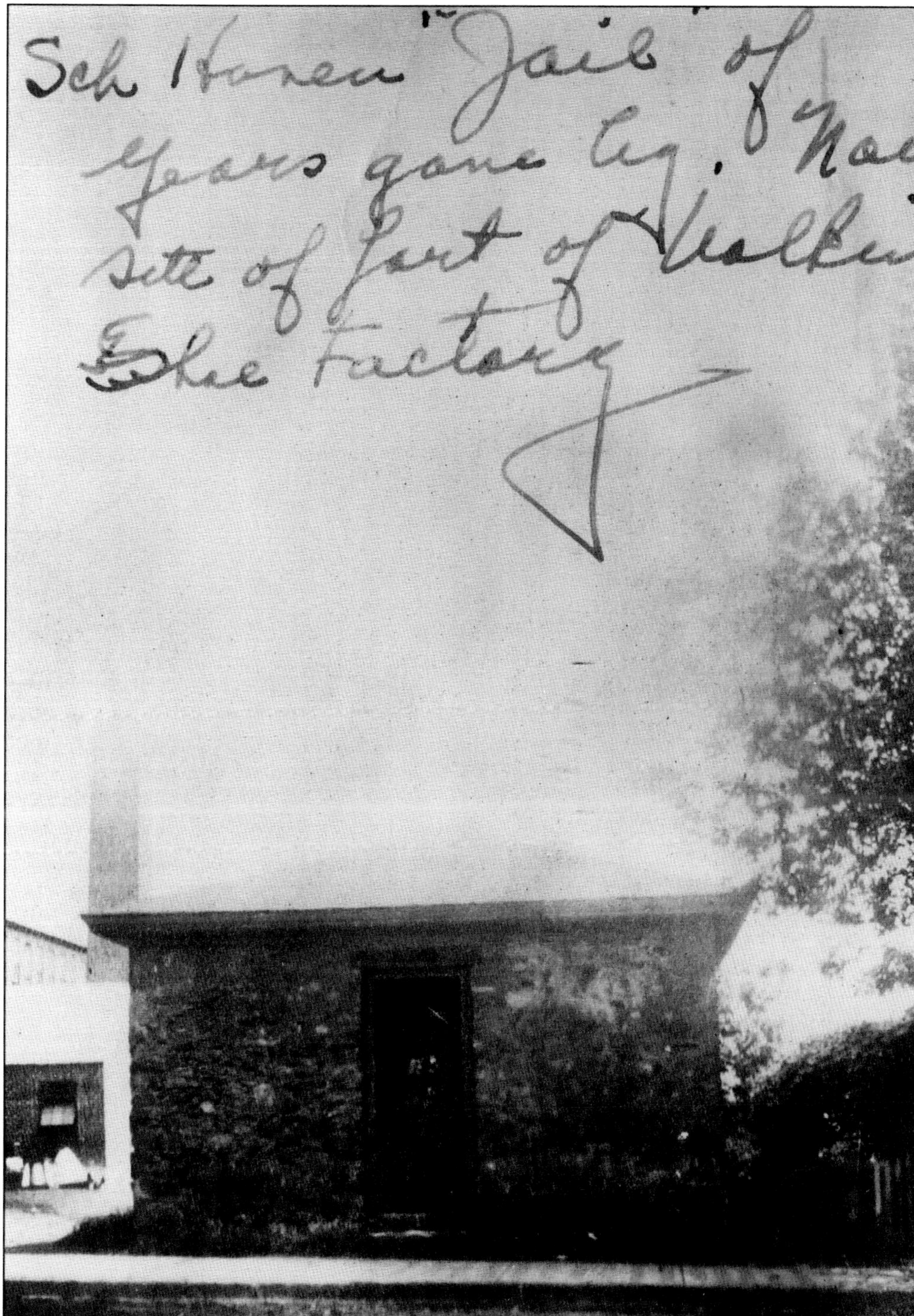

The old Schuylkill Haven Jail is seen in this ancient image. The old lock-up was on the south side of Columbia Street, about 60 feet west of Canal Street. This structure was torn down about 1915 and stood where the Walkin Shoe Factory was established in later years.

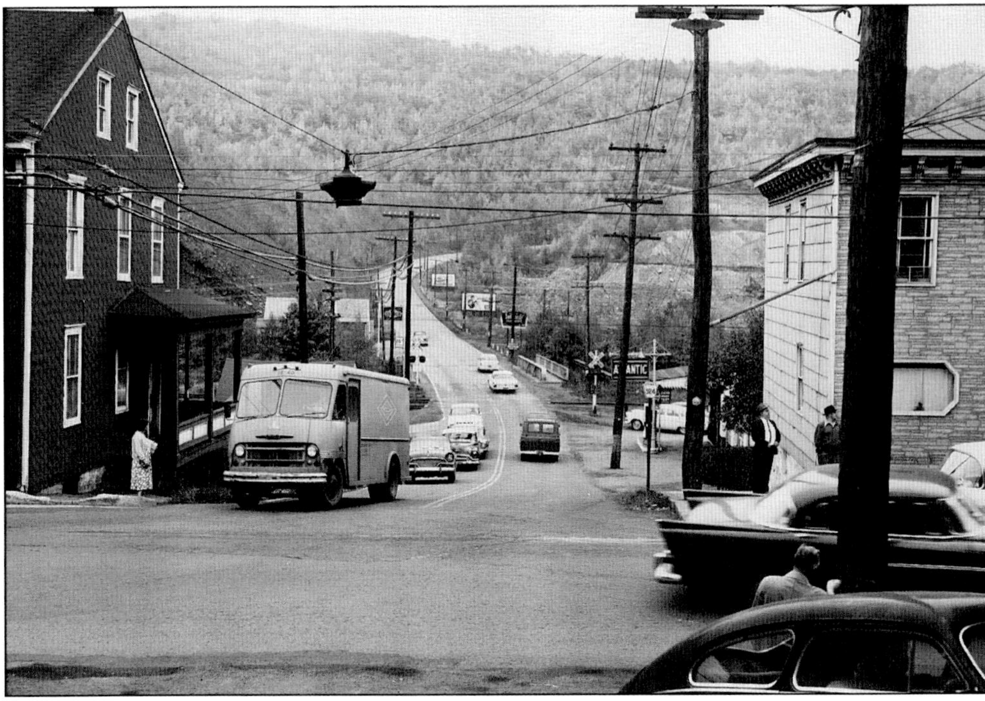

Maizeville is seen in this 1963 image taken prior to the construction of the Frackville to Shenandoah Highway. This image was taken along the main street looking south along Route 924 toward Broad Mountain.

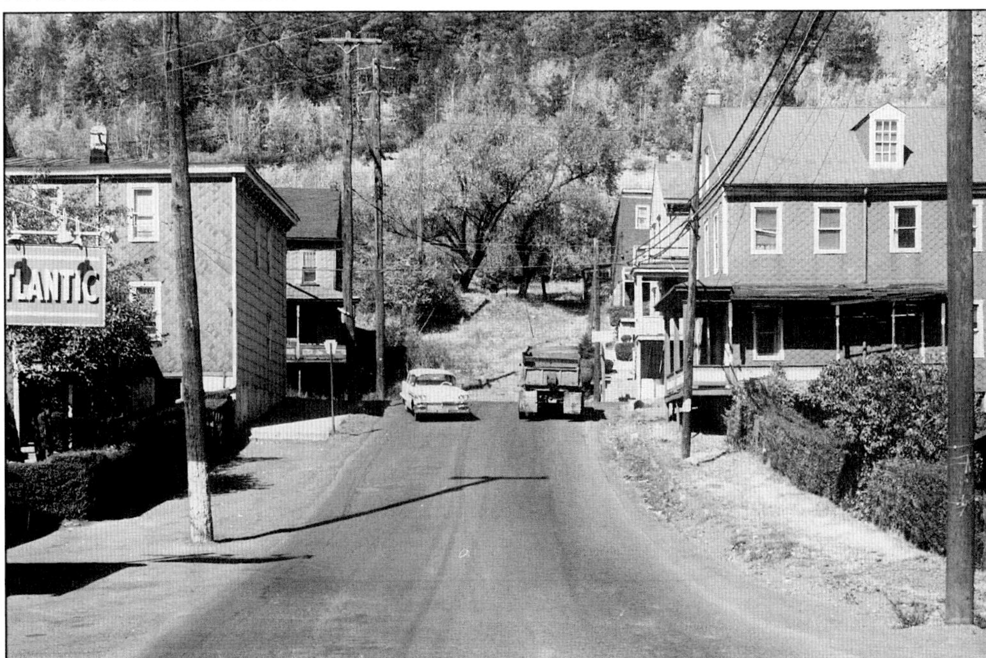

The reverse image of the photograph above shows Route 924 as it enters Maizeville, which is today part of Gilberton Borough. The village of Maizeville, historically a coal-mining community, was by-passed with the construction of the new highway in the mid-1960s.

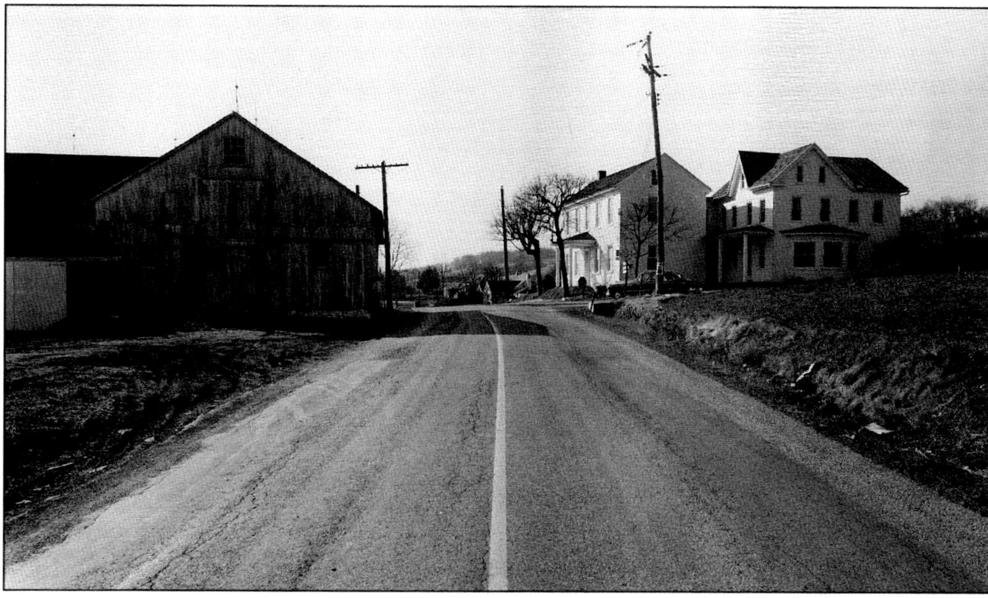

Looking west along present-day Route 443 at Long Run, this image shows this pre-Route 83 (renumbered 183) village in the late 1950s. Notice the car approaching the intersection from the right of the image. Cressona is located 2 miles to the north of this intersection.

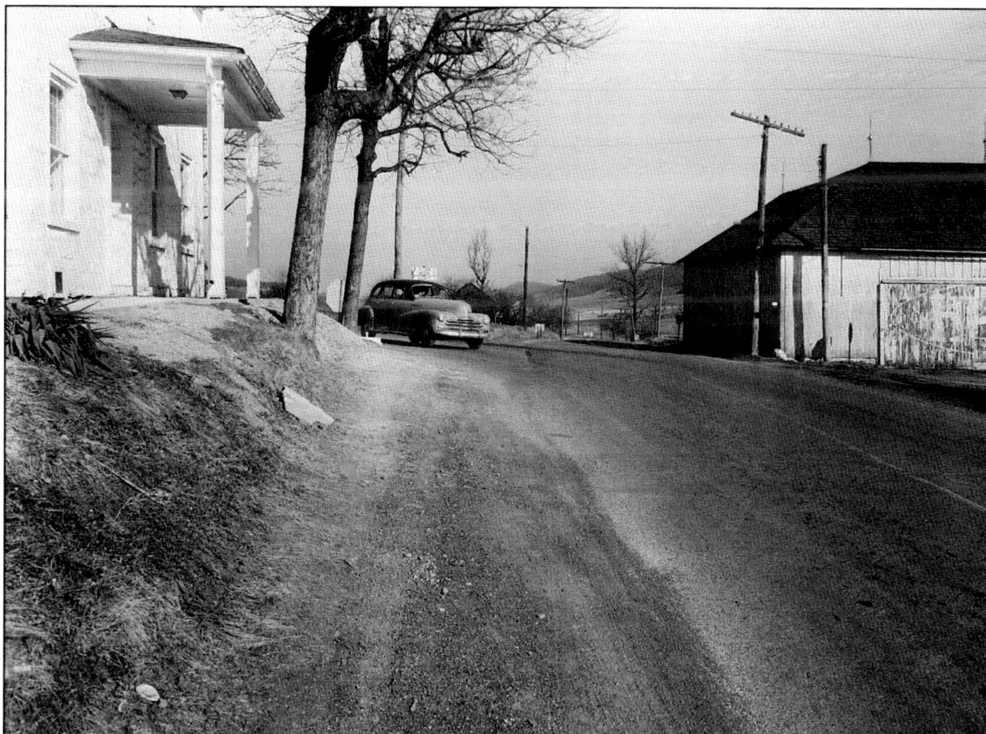

This image is looking east toward Schuylkill Haven (3 miles) at Long Run; we see traffic turning west onto Route 443 near Friedensburg. Today the intersection at Routes 443 and 183 near Friedensburg is busy with commercial and residential development.

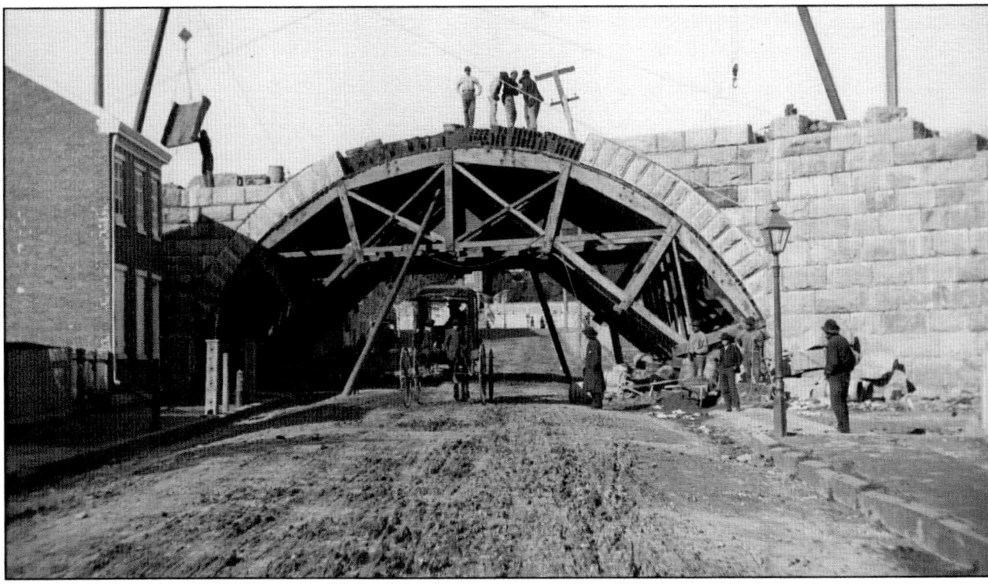

The Pennsylvania Railroad Bridge is being constructed over Dock Street in the vicinity of the present-day Rainbow Hose Fire Company in Schuylkill Haven. Looking north toward Centre Avenue, this image was taken in approximately 1885.

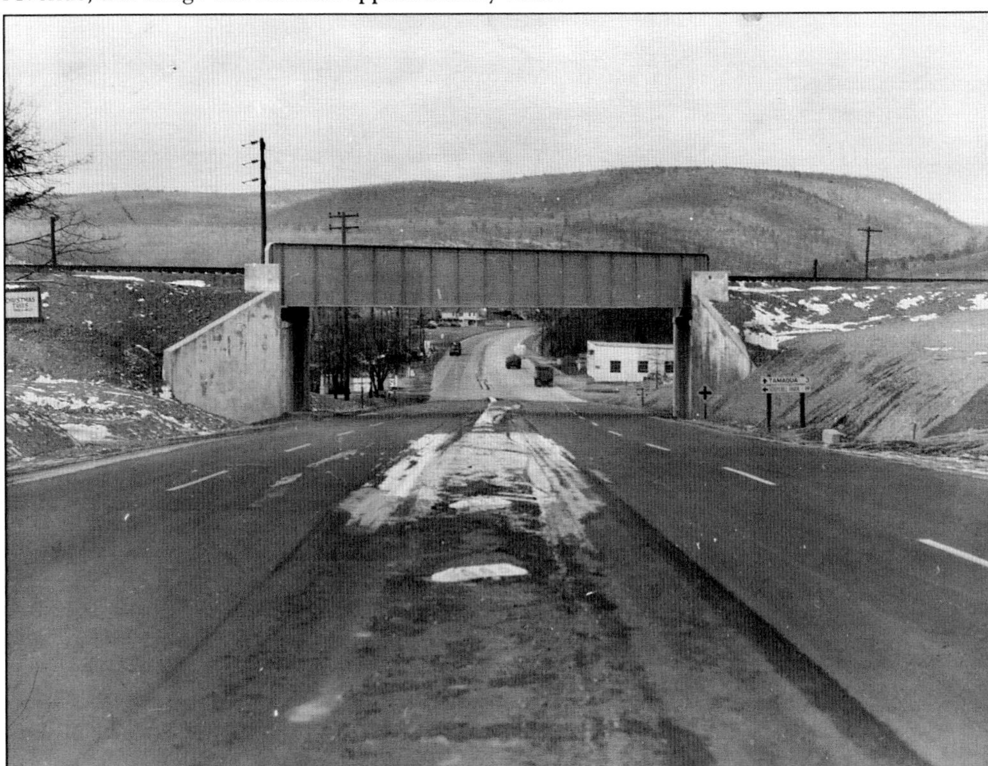

The Lehigh Valley Railroad Bridge at South Tamaqua is seen in this 1950s image. Tamaqua is 3 miles to the north, and Schuylkill Haven 19 miles to the west, from this intersection of Routes 443 and 309 in West Penn Township.

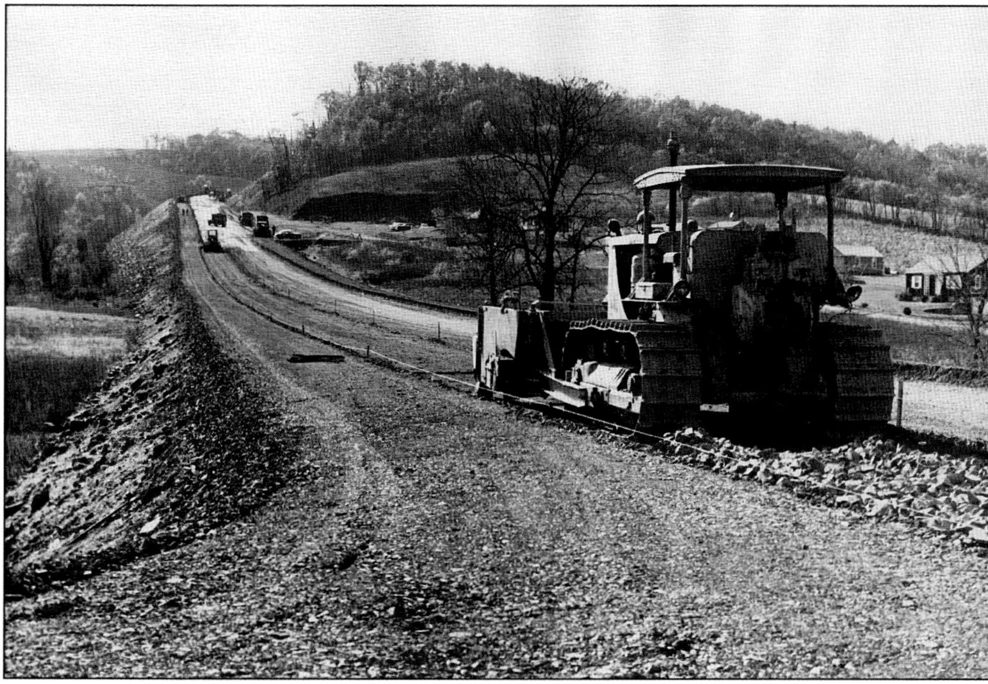

Construction of Route 83 (now 183) begins at Long Run in this 1960 image. This early-morning view is taken from Route 443 looking south along the highway bed in Wayne Township.

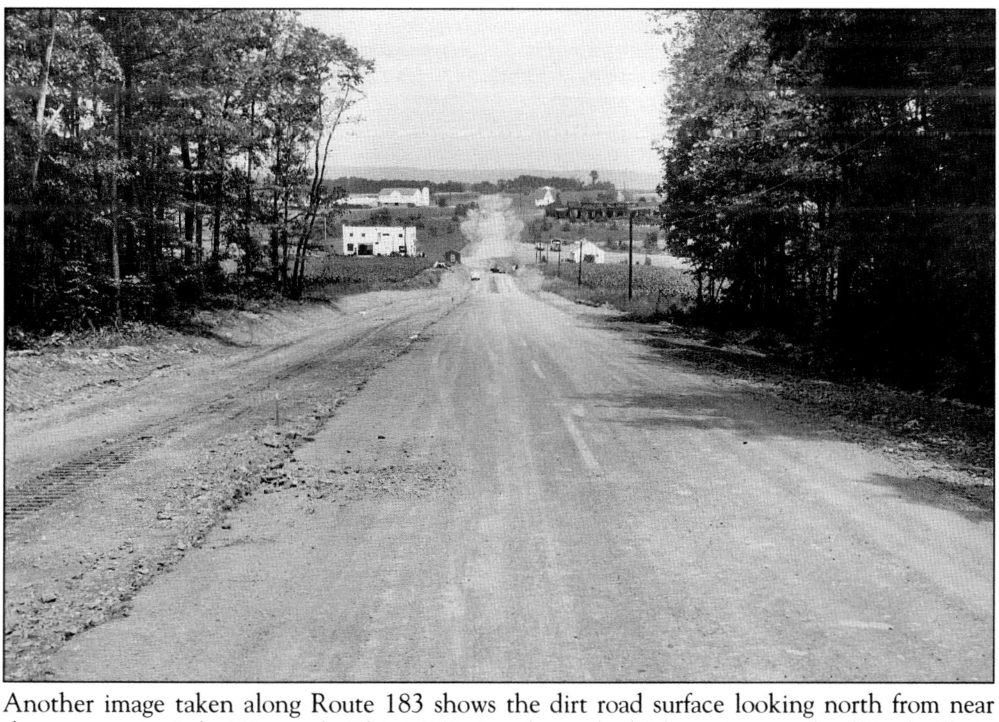

Another image taken along Route 183 shows the dirt road surface looking north from near the entrance to Lake Wynonah. This 1960 view shows the highway just south of Reedsville in Wayne Township. Second Mountain is seen looming in the distance.

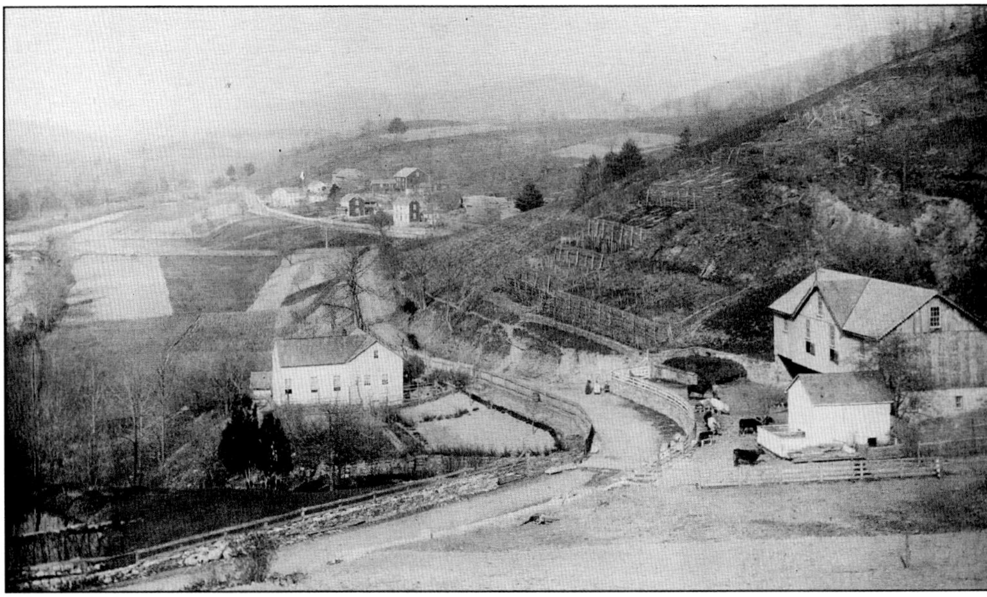

Here is an 1880s view of the Gordon Nagle Trail as seen from Hillside Road in North Manheim Township. The Schnerring farm is featured to the right of the dirt road leading from Cressona to Minersville beyond the mountains in the distance. Seider's Hill is seen in the center of this image.

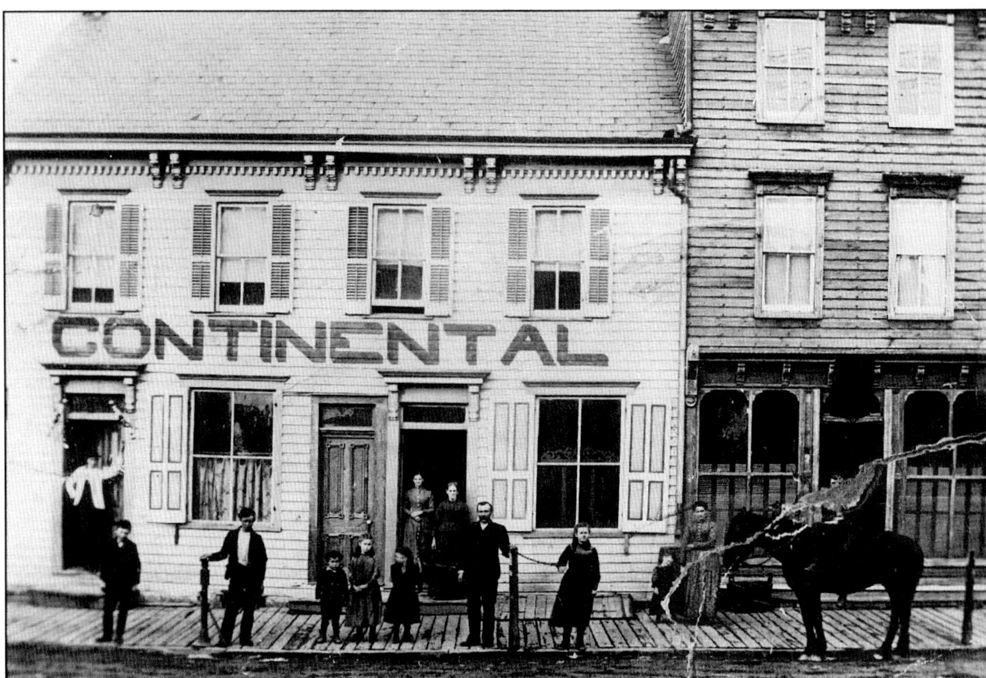

The Continental Hotel situated on Lehigh Avenue in Frackville is seen in this *c.* 1875 view. The Shadel family along with Philip and Barbara Prynn are featured in this photograph. Oh, and that is Dolly the horse on the right.

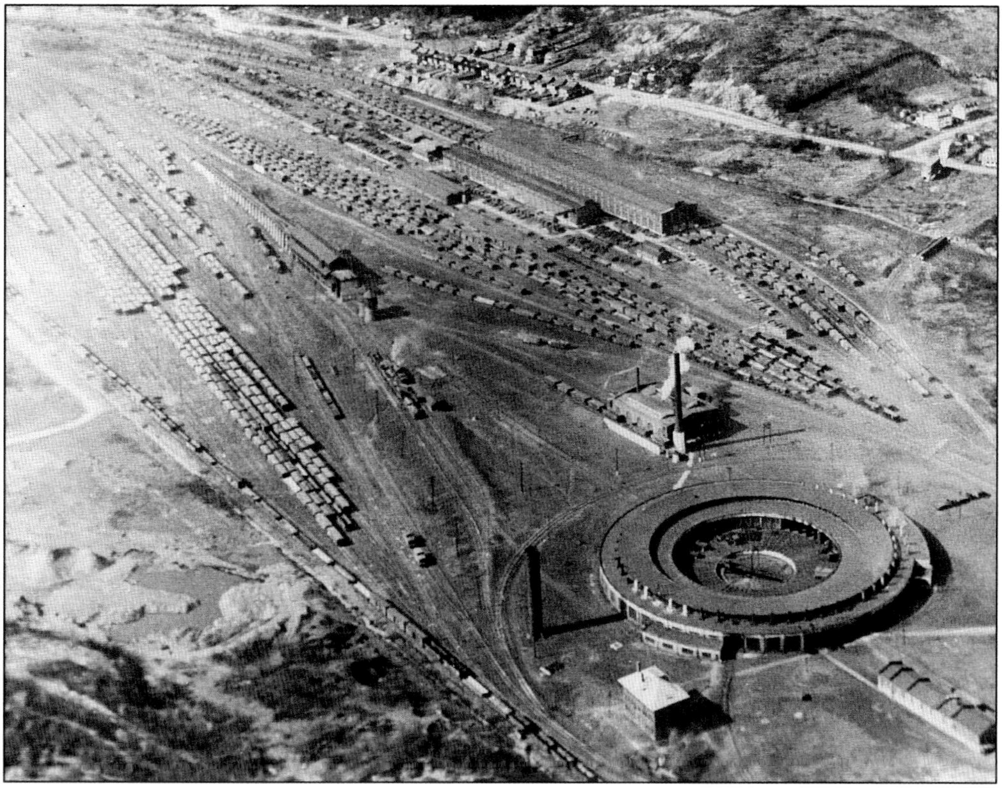

The Saint Clair Railyard as seen in this WW II-era aerial photograph shows the roundhouse, car shops, and a yard full of cars. The yard was laid out just prior to WW I and played a critical role in the shipment of coal. Mill Creek Manor is the village at the top of the photograph. Today this is the Saint Clair Industrial Park.

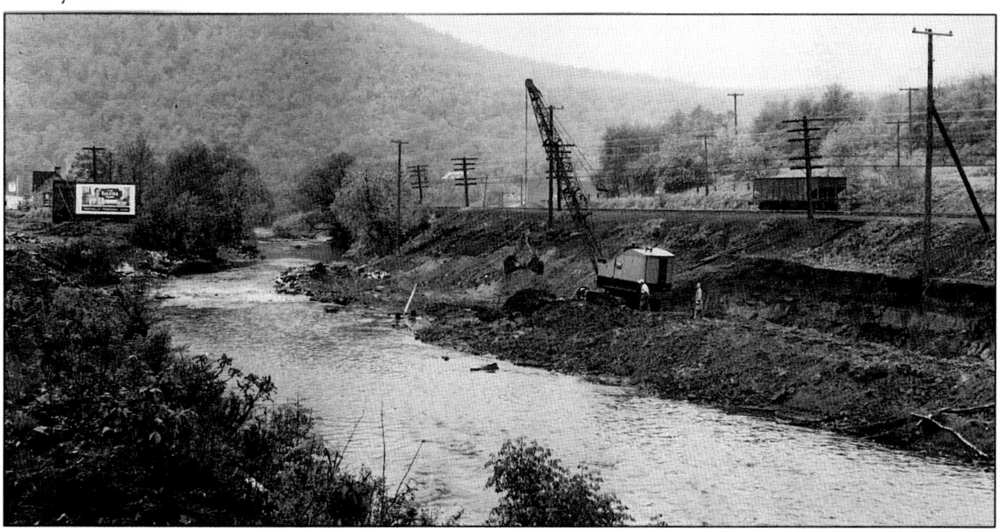

This 1950s image was taken looking southwest from Route 61 below Mount Carbon. This construction is aimed at moving the Schuylkill River. A retaining wall will then be built in an effort to protect the Reading Railroad Line at this location. The billboard at the left is for Reading Beer, "Traditionally Pennsylvania Dutch."

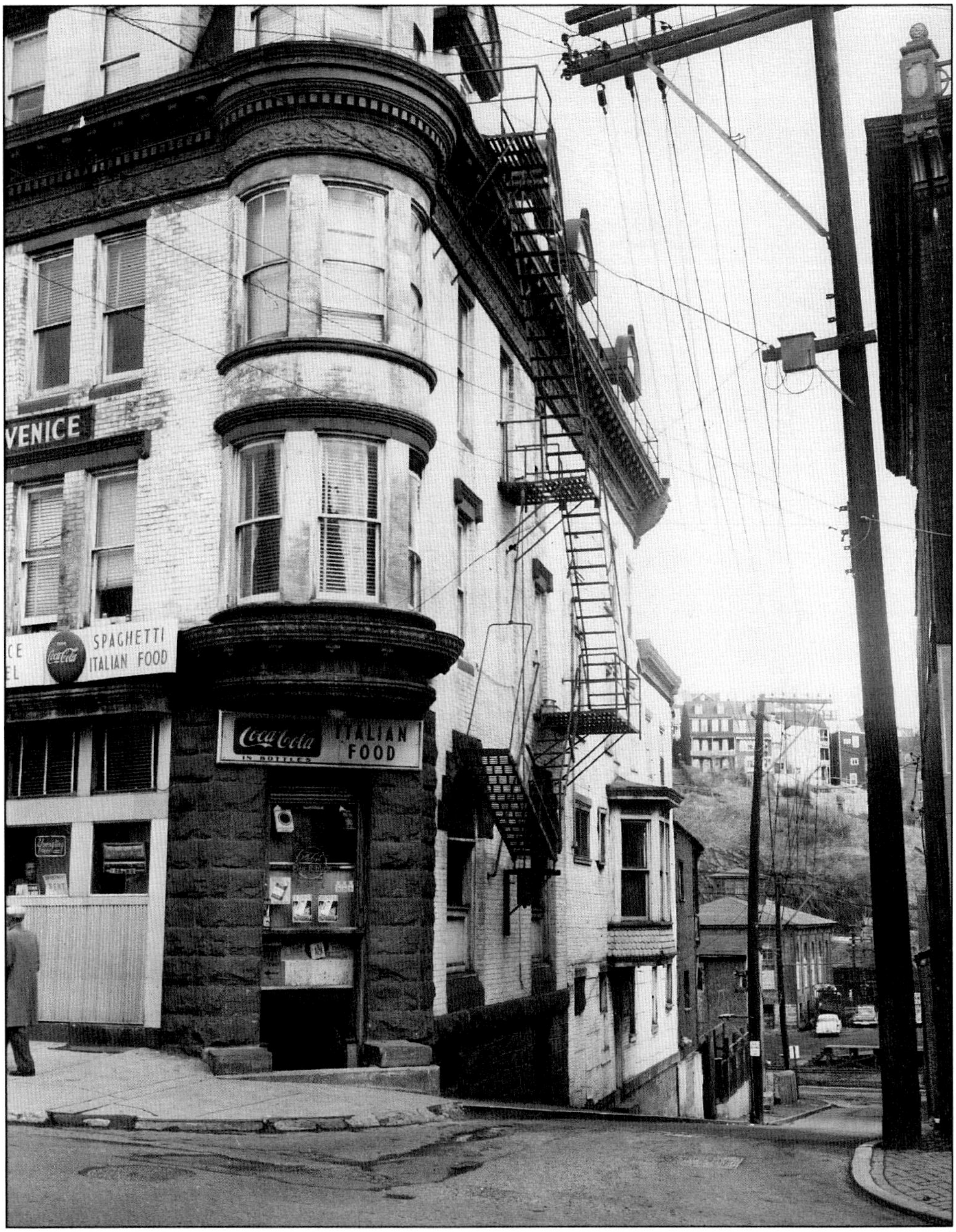

The Hotel Venice, where is that? This 1961 view is taken looking east from the corner of Laurel Boulevard and Centre Street in Pottsville. The Hotel Venice and the entire block was demolished during the 1960s Urban Renewal efforts. The street was widened and the Social Security and Human Services building constructed shortly thereafter.

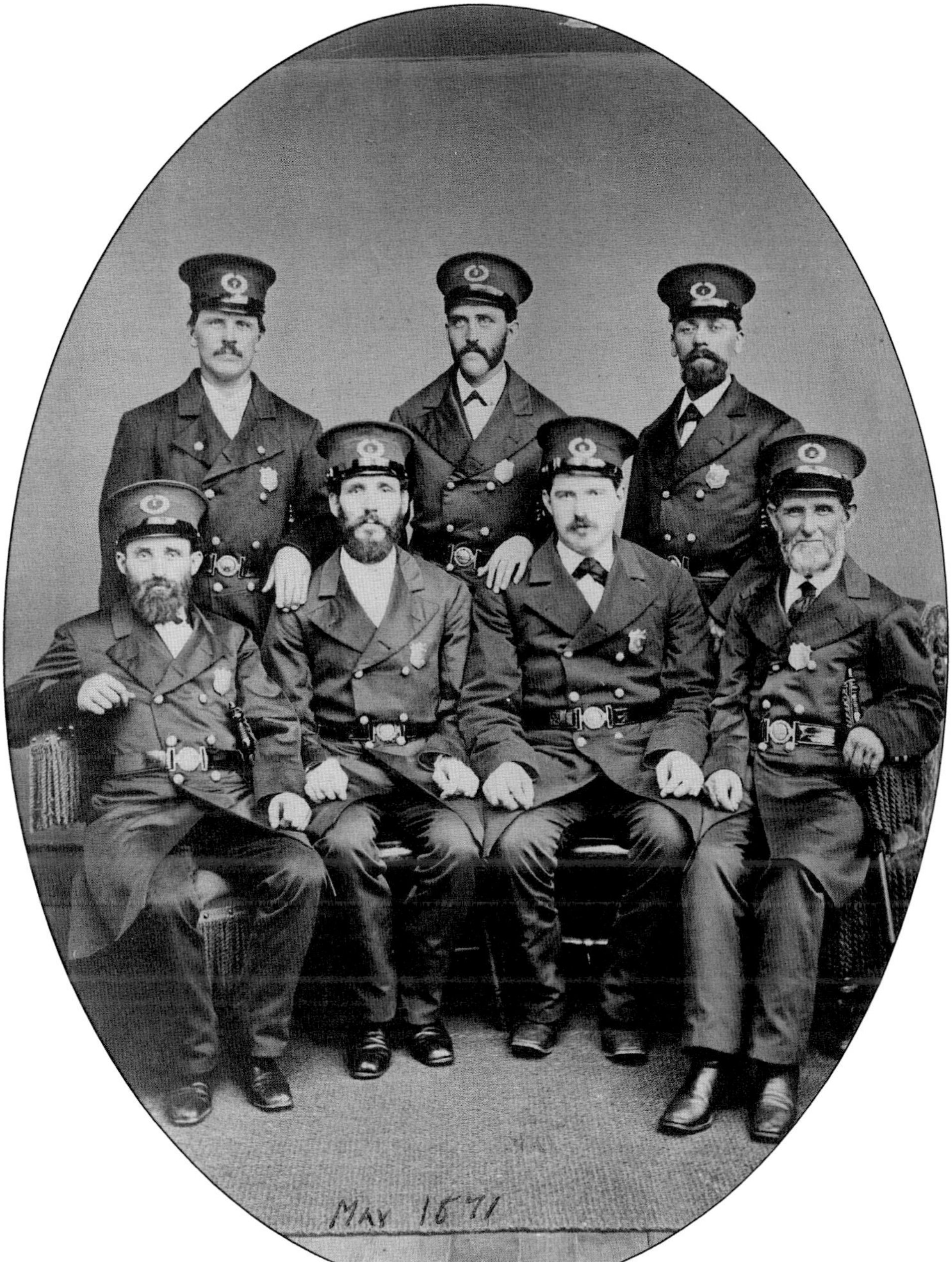

The Pottsville Police force is seen in this May 1871 image. Pictured from left to right they are as follows: (front row) Jacob Schumacher, James Shaw, Charles Lindenmuth, and Henry Byerle; (back row) Henry Heckler, Anthony Herbert, and Frederick Day.

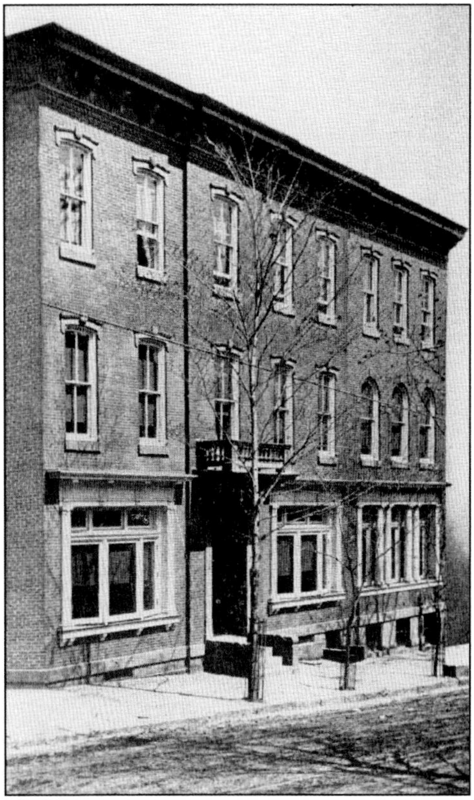

This is a view of the Pottsville Club, *c.* 1910, along Mahantongo Street. A gathering place for Pottsville and Schuylkill County's elite, this building was destroyed by fire in the 1970s. A parking lot for St. Patrick's Roman Catholic Church, today the "Gibbsville" Club, provided a setting for John O'Hara's *Appointment in Samarra.*

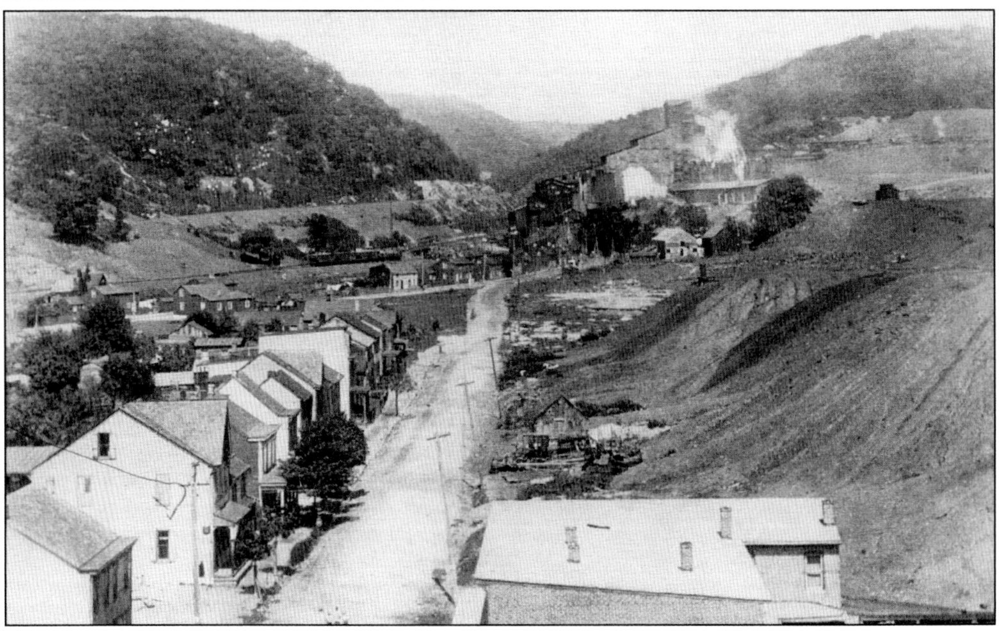

Looking north from Saint Clair, this photograph of Darkwater Gap in Broad Mountain provides a view of John's Patch, from Nichols Street in the Borough. The Herbine Colliery is seen in the distance in this turn-of-the-century image. Saint Clair's Veteran's Memorial Stadium is today situated where mounds of coal waste stand to the right.

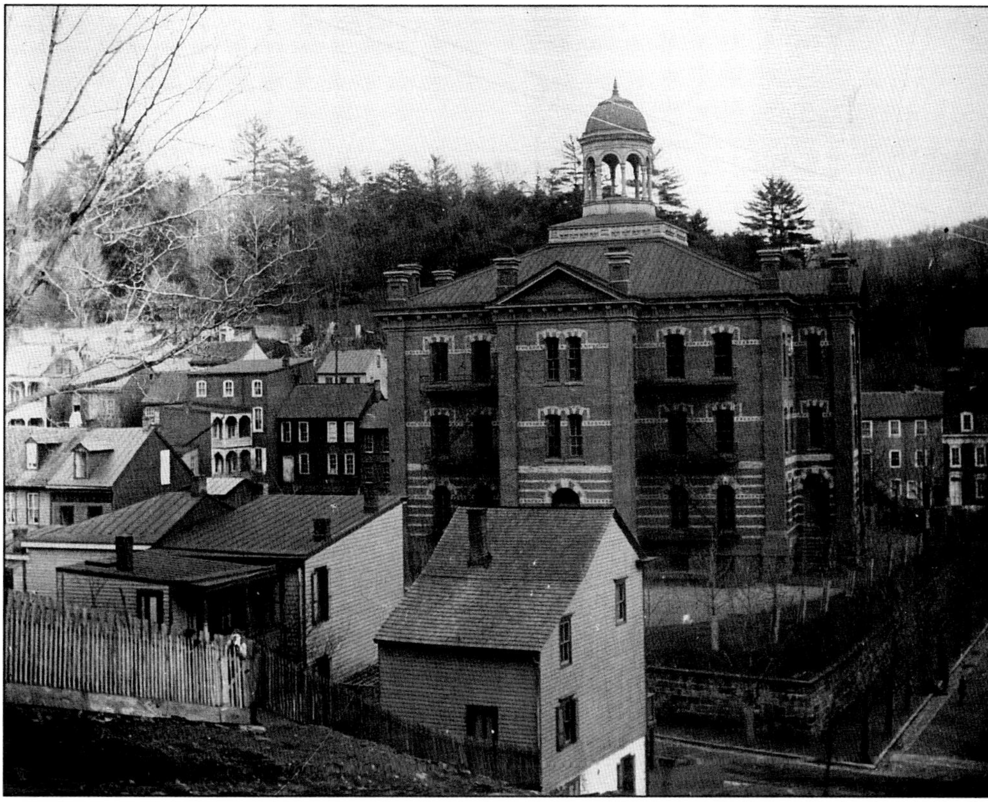

Pottsville's Jackson Street School is seen in this 1890s image taken from atop Arch Street at Jackson on the east side of town. Notice the cupola atop the school, a feature that is obviously missing from the structure today.

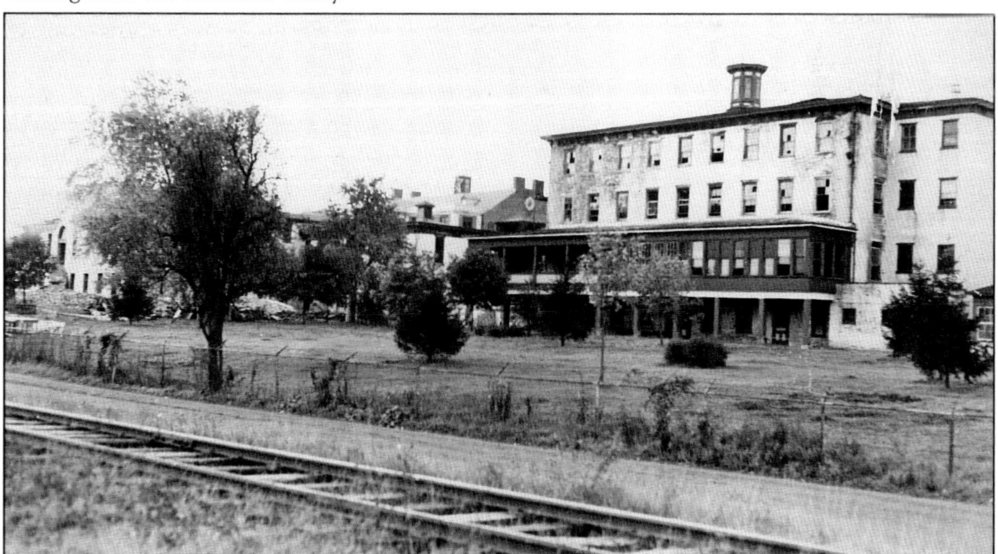

This 1940s image of the old buildings of the Schuylkill County Alms House is taken from where Route 61 passes the Penn State Schuylkill Campus tennis courts today. The Schuylkill County Alms House property was later converted into "Rest Haven" by the county commissioners.

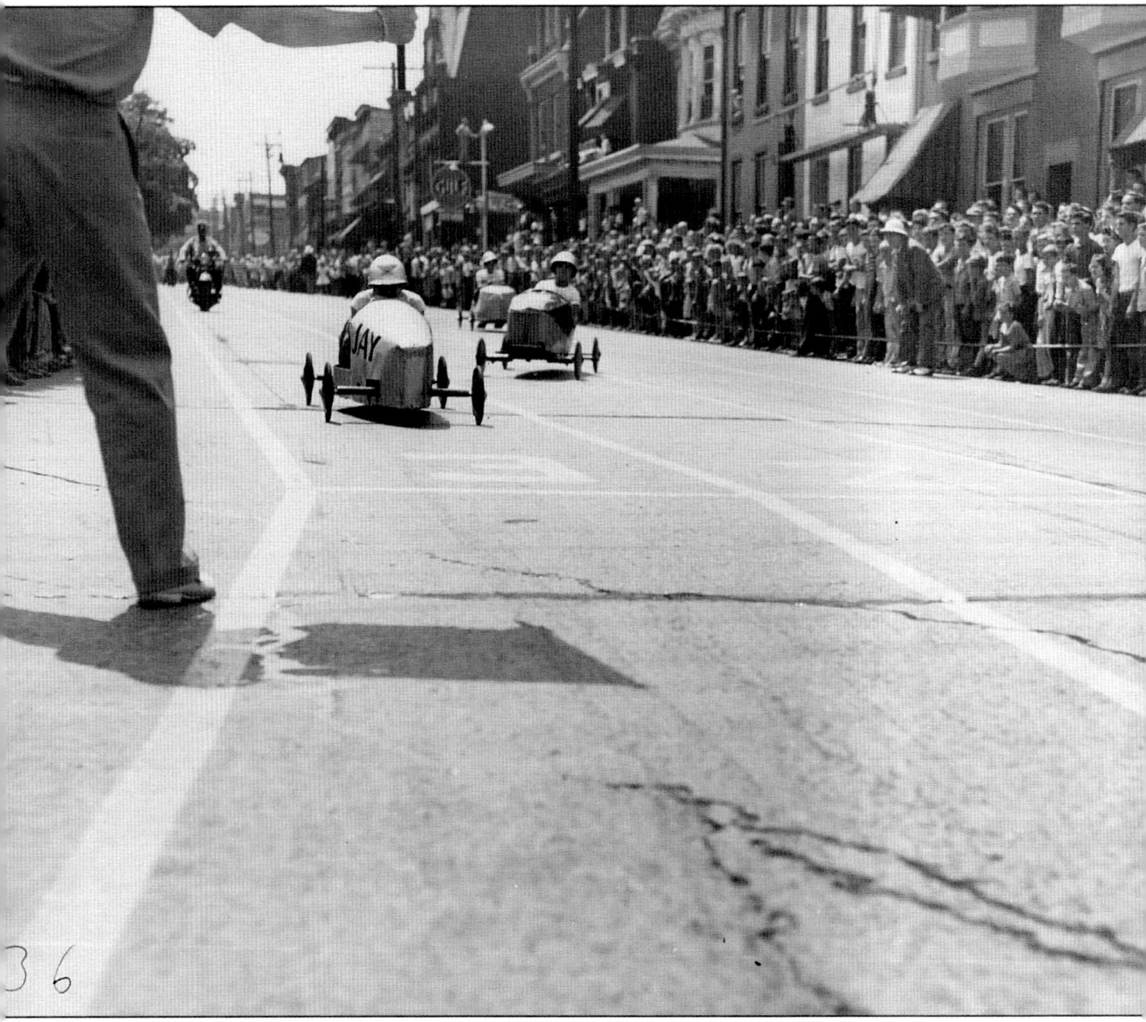

On a warm summer day during the 1950s, Pottsville's Soap Box Derby Champion is determined on this Market Street race course. Viewed from the intersection at Sixth and Market Streets looking west, this heat winner, sponsored by Jay Jeweler's, brings us to the finish line.

The Historical Society of Schuylkill County maintains a vast (over ten thousand) collection of local images. Unfortunately, many Schuylkill County communities are not well represented in our collection. The historical society invites you to contribute your photographs to our collection, as our mission is dedicated to preserving Schuylkill County's history through artifacts, manuscripts, and, especially, a photographic record of our communities.